Raising Racists

NEW DIRECTIONS IN SOUTHERN HISTORY

SERIES EDITORS
Peter S. Carmichael, Gettysburg College
Michele Gillespie, Wake Forest University
William A. Link, University of Florida

The Lost State of Franklin: America's First Secession
Kevin T. Barksdale

Bluecoats and Tar Heels: Soldiers and Civilians in Reconstruction North Carolina
Mark L. Bradley

Becoming Bourgeois: Merchant Culture in the South, 1820–1865
Frank J. Byrne

Cowboy Conservatism: Texas and the Rise of the Modern Right
Sean P. Cunningham

Lum and Abner: Rural America and the Golden Age of Radio
Randal L. Hall

Entangled by White Supremacy: Reform in World War I–era South Carolina
Janet G. Hudson

The View from the Ground: Experiences of Civil War Soldiers
edited by Aaron Sheehan-Dean

Reconstructing Appalachia: The Civil War's Aftermath
edited by Andrew L. Slap

Moonshiners and Prohibitionists: The Battle over Alcohol in Southern Appalachia
Bruce E. Stewart

Southern Farmers and Their Stories: Memory and Meaning in Oral History
Melissa Walker

Law and Society in the South: A History of North Carolina Court Cases
John W. Wertheimer

RAISING RACISTS

The Socialization of White Children in the Jim Crow South

KRISTINA DUROCHER

THE UNIVERSITY PRESS OF KENTUCKY

Scholarly publisher for the Commonwealth,
serving Bellarmine University, Berea College, Centre College of Kentucky, Eastern
Kentucky University, The Filson Historical Society, Georgetown College, Kentucky
Historical Society, Kentucky State University, Morehead State University, Murray
State University, Northern Kentucky University, Transylvania University, University of
Kentucky, University of Louisville, and Western Kentucky University.
All rights reserved.

Editorial and Sales Offices: The University Press of Kentucky
663 South Limestone Street, Lexington, Kentucky 40508-4008
www.kentuckypress.com

Library of Congress Cataloging-in-Publication Data

DuRocher, Kristina.
  Raising racists : the socialization of white children in the Jim Crow South / Kristina
DuRocher.
     p. cm. — (New directions in southern history)
  Includes bibliographical references and index.
  ISBN 978-0-8131-3001-9 (hardcover : alk. paper)
  ISBN 978-0-8131-3016-3 (ebook)
  1. Socialization—Southern States—History. 2. Children, White—Southern States—
History. 3. African Americans—Segregation—History. 4. Southern States—Race
relations—History. I. Title.
  HQ783.D87 2011
  305.23089'09075—dc22   2010052272

ISBN 978-0-8131-7578-2 (pbk. : alk. paper)

CONTENTS

List of Illustrations   vi
Acknowledgments   vii
Introduction   1

1. "My Mother Had Warned Me about This":
   Parental Socialization in the Jim Crow South   13

2. "We Learned Our Lessons Well":
   The Growth of White Privilege in Southern Schools   35

3. Consumerism Meets Jim Crow's Children:
   White Children and the Culture of Segregation   61

4. "The Course My Life Was to Take":
   The Violent Reality of White Youth's Socialization   93

5. Violent Masculinity:
   Ritual and Performance in Southern Lynchings   113

6. "Is This the Man?":
   White Girls' Participation in Southern Lynchings   131

Conclusion   153

Notes   159
Bibliography   205
Index   225

Illustrations

The lynching of Rubin Stacy, 1935   2

"Black Mumbo" character from Helen Bannerman's
The Story of Little Black Sambo, 1908   56

Cream of Wheat advertisement, 1914   64

Fairy Soap advertisement, 1898   68

Arm & Hammer baking soda advertisement   70

Gold Medal baking powder advertisement   72

Henry Sears & Son Cutlery advertisement   73

ACKNOWLEDGMENTS

This book would not have been possible without the help and support of many. The ideas and early research for this project began in graduate school, and I owe a debt to my dissertation advisor, Vernon Burton, for his guidance and support, as well as to the rest of my committee, Elizabeth Pleck, David Roediger, and Jean Allman.

I have enjoyed the complete support of my colleagues at Morehead State University, whose encouragement and assistance have meant so much to me. Tom Kiffmeyer, my mentor, talked me through ideas and read revisions, and I am indebted to him for his insight and time. I am lucky to be surrounded by excellent examples of historians, both as scholars and learners themselves. John Ernst, John Hennen, Tom Kiffmeyer, Alana Scott, and Adrian Mandzy have shaped my expectations and supported my research and writing. Thank you for all your encouragement. Morehead State University awarded me a Research Fellowship in 2007 to assist with research for this project. I was also supported by MSU's Undergraduate Research Fellows. Thank you to Matt Hurley, Chris Wiseman, and James Kyle Hager.

A particular note of thanks to Dr. Thomas Summerhill, who got the ball rolling for me when I was an undergraduate, and to Pete Daniel, for his mentorship and advice.

I would like to thank the University Press of Kentucky, especially Stephen Wrinn, Anne Dean Watkins, and series editor Bill Link, who encouraged this project through revisions and editing. I owe a debt to them for their assistance and patience. I would also like to thank the outside readers for their time and suggestions; your thoughts helped me clarify my ideas and improve the manuscript.

Portions of chapters 1 and 5 appeared in *Southern Masculinity: Perspectives on Manhood in the South since Reconstruction,* published in 2009 by the University of Georgia Press. I would like to thank them for permission to reprint that material here. A special thanks to Craig Thompson Friend and the readers for their feedback on those sections.

My parents have a love of history that has shaped my own life and career.

I would like to thank them for their support. I also would like to thank my husband, who spent the first years of our marriage sharing me with this book. Thanks for all your patience and understanding.

INTRODUCTION

In this South I lived as a child and I now live. And it is of it that my story is made.

—Lillian Smith, *Killers of the Dream*

In 1935, a white family traveled to a field in Fort Lauderdale, Florida, to pose for a commemorative photograph with the corpse of African American Rubin Stacy.[1] After Stacy's arrest for frightening a white woman, Mrs. Marion Jones, on Friday, July 19, a white mob removed Stacy from jail and lynched the homeless tenant farmer. Over the following weekend, whites traveled from nearby towns and counties to view the mob's handiwork. A photograph depicts Stacy's corpse hanging from a tree with a noose around his neck and his hands tied in front of him (see page 2).[2] Several white girls in their Sunday dresses stand around Stacy's body, their whiteness framing him. Perhaps the most shocking element of the photograph for the modern viewer is the expressions on the girls' faces. The children do not appear to be traumatized, upset, or even concerned; indeed, the girl on the right looks intently at the body with a smile on her face. Another girl peers around the tree for a better look at the corpse, while the youngest, who appears to be three or four years old, calmly gazes at the camera. A local Young Women's Christian Association reported to the National Association for the Advancement of Colored People (NAACP) the community's response to the mob violence. One white woman, who had brought her young niece and nephew to view the body, explained that the "opinion that it was a shocking sight for women and children was entirely erroneous." She continued: "It was not bad at all. He was just hanging there."[3]

Such images and reports attest to the normalcy of white children attending events of racial violence during Jim Crow segregation. Countless other images of lynchings included boys and girls, from a few years old to teenagers, enjoying these public spectacles both during and after the violence. White southern culture in this era accepted and encouraged the presence of white children at scenes of extralegal race-based violence. This became

The lynching of Rubin Stacy, 1935. Courtesy of Picture History.

obvious to Walter White, an antilynching advocate and the secretary for the NAACP, when he encountered three white children walking to school near the site where a white mob had recently lynched five African Americans. To the children, the African American White, with his blue eyes and light complexion, looked Caucasian. The girls eagerly told him about their attendance at the lynching. One, "the eldest[,] a ruddy-cheeked girl of nine or ten, asked if I was going to the place where 'the niggers' had been killed." When White replied that he might, the girl began to describe the scene "animatedly, almost as joyously as though the memory were of Christmas morning or the circus," with her younger companions interjecting about "the fun we had burning the niggers."[4]

The lynching ritual offers a microcosm for exploring white southerners' conceptions of race and gender, as all members of the white community participated. The role played by white youth in public racial violence has long remained unexplored, as no studies of the Jim Crow South consider this violence as a primary site of the construction of racial identity. Yet white southerners did employ the brutal lynching ritual to construct and maintain southern racial identity, and white children played an active role in the process. Examining white children's role within the white culture of the Jim Crow South, including its racial violence, reveals the shifting inter-sections of race, gender, sexuality, culture, and power in the New South. Lynching offered a central public ritual in which white youth encountered and helped to perpetuate the brutal practices that southern white males deemed necessary to maintain segregation and their position at the top of the southern social hierarchy.

The public mass mob lynching—from the leveling of the accusation against the lynch victim to the collection of souvenirs from the corpse—offers insight into the social understandings of white southerners during Jim Crow. The mass mob formed for only the most heinous of crimes: the sexual violation of white women and girls and violent acts against whites. As one of the most visible forms of violent socialization, the lynching ritual served the dual purpose of repressing African American resistance and reinforcing white adults' and children's own conceptions of racial and gender supremacy. Following the pattern of the ritual, after the female victim or the family of the injured party reported the allegation of wrongdoing, a mob led by the white male community secured the accused either through a manhunt or by storming a holding cell in the local jail. Joined by the larger community, including children as witnesses, the mob brought their victim to a presc-lected location, often near the site of the alleged crime. Mob leaders then publically accused their captive of his supposed crimes and attempted to gain a confession. The failure of the accused to admit to the alleged crime often led to torture, with male relatives of the accuser or purported victim, if available, serving as self-appointed avengers. The climax of the ritual arrived with the killing of the accused, who was usually shot, hung, or burned. Within the lynch ritual, this culminating act imposed justice, restored order, and allowed white men, women, adolescents, and children to realize their roles as protectors and dependents. The victim's death reinforced the understanding that a violation of the laws of segregation required deadly punishment. Afterward, the crowd took pictures while children and mob members scavenged for souvenirs from the victim's corpse as mementos of their experience. These acts of witnesses seeking remembrance of the event ended the ritual of the mob killing.

White southerners realized that the primary way to forge solidarity strong enough to maintain segregation was to indoctrinate white youth into the racial order, which included prescribed gender roles. Spectacle lynchings exhibited and demanded the acknowledgment of social roles for white men and women as well as boys and girls, and allowed the white community to model, produce, and reinforce a distinct racial and gendered identity. In the North during this period, white males could claim the title of superior manhood by meeting the requirements of race, gender, and class. In the Jim Crow South, however, only two things were demanded: he must be white, and he must be willing to uphold the culture of white masculinity in a public forum.[5] For white southerners of the Jim Crow era, masculine identity revolved around the readiness to protect southern white women and white supremacy. Class identity was less relevant to southern conceptions of masculinity as white leaders sought to maintain power by creating a collective racial consciousness that united all whites, regardless of economic status, in opposition to African Americans. Lynchings offered white men and adolescent boys a public venue in which to enact their ideal image of southern white manhood within a ritual where whiteness conquered blackness in a display of uncontested masculinity. This performance was intended both to remind white women and children to obey the boundaries set up by white males and to reinforce the cultural representation of white females as submissive and deferential to white men.[6]

The increase in the social importance of white females, who were highly visible in the lynching ritual, reflects one of the most decisive shifts in southern society after the Civil War. In the antebellum South, white women exerted little influence in the social sphere, and the community carefully scrutinized their allegations of sexual attack.[7] With the system of slavery firmly in place, white male southerners felt secure in their dominance, and at times, white slave owners protected black male slaves from accusations of sexual misconduct made by lower-class white women, frequently questioning the virtue of the accuser.[8] Maintaining white male patriarchy included controlling sexual access to white females, and during Jim Crow, the protection of white female sexuality became central to justifying segregation. The sexual assault of a white female by a black man came to represent the primary racial fear of white southerners, for to preserve racial purity, white women and black men had to remain separate. Whites perpetuated this attitude through a rape-lynch complex that was supported through the creation of a cultural image of African American men who had reverted to brutality without the chains of slavery to control them.[9] White southerners employed what became an established rhetoric to depict black males as having an uncontrolled sexual desire for white women, and they justified lynchings as necessary to protect white females from this threat. In doing so, they ensured the continuation of white supremacy since any white female, regardless of age, was now portrayed as symbolizing the future of the white race. As a result, in the early twentieth century, white southern men became increasingly concerned about the sexual activity of adolescent and young white girls, who might desire to enter intimate relations with black men and so threaten white males' control of their reproduction. Consequently, white men sought to maintain their sexual prerogative over white women, and as part of this effort, white southerners taught their daughters to fear their own sexuality and conduct themselves as the passive, protected assets of white males. While the racial rhetoric underpinning white supremacy was publically an attempt to control African Americans, it was also an effort to regulate white females' behavior, although white girls did not always adhere to these lessons of sexual chastity and submissiveness.

To investigate the racial brutality of the Jim Crow South and the role white youth played within it, however, is to begin at the end, for such actions were a culmination of the socialization of white youth. Recognizing the contribution of white southern children to racial violence first requires an exploration of the society that white southerners created for their children from birth, both in ideology and in practice. Such an investigation reveals how white youth functioned for white society in defining segregation and producing a distinct southern identity. During the height of Jim Crow, the continued survival of segregation and white supremacy required the participation of whites of all ages, but especially those of the rising generation, in upholding a strict social order. White adults utilized virtually every aspect of their daily life to socialize their children into their future roles. Among those children who experienced this indoctrination firsthand, those who understood it best grew up to reject the southern customs of racism. Southern social activists' autobiographies offer recollections of their early experiences with race and gender identity. By chronicling their youthful lessons, white activists sought to demonstrate their repudiation of segregation's mores, allowing them to correlate their childhood experiences with their adult efforts at social reform. Repeatedly, the autobiographical writings of white southern reformers acknowledge their own socialization into white supremacy and identify the sites of their indoctrination. The pattern that emerges is that early lessons occurred first in the home, followed by communal instruction and performances. These experiences often included knowledge or witnessing of the racial violence that enforced southern segregation.

Tracing out the methods and spaces in which white adults fashioned an identity for their children in the early twentieth century demonstrates larger shifts in segregation and illustrates the fluidity of race and racism. The concept of race is a variable construct reflecting a culture's viewpoint, and racism is thus a created belief that a society teaches its population. The concept of whiteness in the Jim Crow South, as a social creation, required that both whites and blacks conform to specific behaviors. Southern whites' claim to racial superiority, which justified their political and economic dominance, required them to control the black and white bodies of those below them on the hierarchy of white patriarchal southern society. Although early critical whiteness studies argue that whiteness is "invisible," the racial prejudice that children learned is the result of social interactions with whites and blacks, is performative.[10] This control, however, was gendered as young men and women each had a distinct identity shaped from witnessing, imitating, and participating in their defined cultural roles within a biracial society. Although gender roles were central to maintaining Jim Crow, gender was secondary to race as the fundamental delineator of social power in the New South. Thus, my primary focus in this study is white southerners as they actively attempted to retain authority through reshaping their cultural landscape. In looking only at whites in the Jim Crow South, I do not intend to minimize the role of African Americans, northerners, reformers, women, or others who opposed segregation. Indeed, they are the central impetus behind this examination, for it was opposition from these groups that prompted white southerners to recognize and clarify their own ideals.

As white southerners attempted to adapt their culture in order to preserve their vision of the New South, the format for teaching racial identity shifted. Broadly, white domination in the South, as reflected in the actions of white southerners and their children, underwent three stages between Reconstruction and the early civil rights movement. The first stage began with the end of Radical Reconstruction in 1877 and lasted until the 1890s, when the New South socially, culturally, and legally enshrined segregation.[11] The need to maintain a racial hierarchy became increasingly important after the Civil War as white men sought new ways to maintain their social position.[12] After Reconstruction, in seeking to "redeem" the South, white male southerners prevented others, for a time, from gaining any significant measure of cultural, political, and economic equality.[13] During these de-cades, white children did not figure prominently in the process of defining Jim Crow, likely due to the role of children in southern society as laborers. For much of the first half of the nineteenth century, parents considered their offspring as part of a family economy, with children working from an early age in the household's production. Until the Industrial Age, when other human resources became more readily available, there was less senti-mental attachment to children than in modern times.[14] By the close of the nineteenth century, however, the concept of children's innocence was born as parents begin to have fewer children and spend more resources protect-ing them from the harsh realities of life.[15] In the 1850s, children composed one-quarter of the entire U.S. population, but by 1940, this dropped by 8 percent to constitute only 17 percent of the total populace.[16]

The second shift in white cultural domination, and the focus of this book, spans Jim Crow at its zenith, from 1890 to 1939, as whites took active measures to preserve segregation as demonstrated by evolving methods such as standardized educational materials and new ritualized practices such as mass mob lynchings. With the rise of industrialization, urbanization, and mass culture, whites in the South faced an onslaught of potential threats to undermine their recently reclaimed social order. Without a clearly defined racial hierarchy, white males feared the disruption of the post-Reconstruction system of white privilege.[17] Although the antebellum social order could not be replicated since the law no longer considered African Americans as property, white southerners attempted to re-create the racial relations that had existed prior to the Civil War, drawing on a romanticized vision of former white rule as the model for stability and prosperity.[18] The genera-tions of white southerners that came of age during segregation had never known slavery, and older adults, fearing that these youth would fail to con-trol African Americans, took steps to disseminate their own racial beliefs. Thus, the newly popular concept of a sheltered childhood translated in the South during the early twentieth century as a desire to "protect" children, not from violence or terror, but from a racial breakdown, by encouraging white children to participate in the lynching of blacks in order to maintain white domination.

Since the 1940s, sociologists and anthropologists have studied children in the Jim Crow South, focusing primarily on African American youth and the effects of racism and poverty on their social development.[19] Examinations of white children predominantly center on their roles in economic matters, often concentrating on the issues surrounding child labor.[20] Until recently there has been little historical study of childhood identity formation, white or black, in the New South. Jennifer Ritterhouse's *Growing up Jim Crow: How Black and White Southern Children Learned Race* (2006) explores the socialization and cultural construction of race for southern youth.[21] Her examination focuses on literature and autobiographies, utilizing a framework of racial etiquette to recognize how southern adults scripted racial roles. Ritterhouse locates memoirs as the primary site of identity, relying on writings of both blacks and whites to determine the impact that racial protocols had in southerners' daily lives under segregation. Her exploration of the mores that shaped the day-to-day interactions between blacks and whites leads her to contend that racial customs functioned as a way for whites to control the levels of social intimacy.

Although we both seek to understand identity construction in the New South through examining the lives of children, my explorations diverge significantly from hers. Ritterhouse argues that white southerners viewed social etiquette as the best way to maintain social control, superior to methods of violence.[22] Yet, segregation ultimately was a system enforced by violence, both in small daily acts of injustice and in large public acts of brutality. A focus solely on societal racial etiquette does not account for white children's celebrated and desired presence at incidents of racial brutality. In this work, I explore how white southerners actively created and adapted the racial code of behaviors elaborated in Ritterhouse's study. Additionally, I examine how white southern adolescents adapted the racial instructions they received, modifying these idealized codes of behaviors to conceal their misbehaviors or disobedience. White youth's adaptation of these lessons for their own purposes demonstrates the contestation that occurred over the implementation of ideologies in the New South after their initial dissemination.[23]

As white southerners rebuilt the cultural ideal of race relations necessary to maintain white patriarchy during segregation, they recognized that unless they imparted these lessons to the next generation, all would be lost. White children had a critical role to play in the continuation of segregation for their actions would ultimately either maintain or destroy the system of white supremacy. White southern adults, in an effort to preserve their social and political authority, created a culture for their youth. The vocabulary, stories, texts, cultural images, and rituals with which white southerners surrounded their children normalized white supremacy and racial violence through perpetuating an idealized, patriarchal vision of their future roles as white southerners. White youth encountered these cultural images in the home, public schools, consumer culture, community performances, and public spaces. Of these places, the home was the only location in which white southerners emphasized economic status, as elite whites drew on their financial standing and rich historical background to teach the next generation about its social identity. These class elements largely disappeared as the children matured and their socialization began to take place in public spaces. The chapters in this study reflect the progression of white children's socialization from the relatively private and elite surroundings of the home to the equalizing space of the communal lynching ritual. In each stage, it is clear that race and gender remained central concerns, with class cohesion an evident benefit of white racial unity.

In order to delineate how white adults encouraged and transmitted their vision of white culture to their youth, in each chapter I explore a site of socialization, detailing its own sources and methodologies within each section. Chapter 1 focuses on the home and the parental teachings imparted to young children. As southern children increasingly attended public schools, white southerners exerted their influence in the curriculum through the bureaucratization of public education, as explored in chapter 2. In the third chapter, I investigate how mass culture became a stage upon which southern whites required African Americans to perform for their pleasure as a way to express white power over black bodies. While the first three chapters demonstrate how parents and communities sought to create and teach an ideal vision of whiteness and manhood or womanhood to their children, the remainder of the book explores the space in which white youth are most visibly participating in upholding white privilege: the violent, public lynching ritual. In the fourth chapter, I explore how public racial violence became the venue where white children encountered the reality of Jim Crow, which for some contrasted disturbingly with the benign, idealized image of white supremacy learned as a young child. In chapter 5, I examine the lynching ceremony as a public ritual of physical brutality that offered white southern males a forum in which to act out their idealized masculine role as protectors while exhibiting to the audience their ability to assert control over white women and African Americans. Finally, in chapter 6, I consider the roles of white girls as the primary accusers and identifiers of black offenders and the way in which white girls demonstrated their understanding of their prescribed gender roles within the lynching ritual. Some utilized their role in the lynching ritual to circumvent white patriarchal control of their sexuality or to otherwise divert attention from their activities.

As segregation evolved across time, it also changed in various locales. Since it is difficult to account for every regional variation, my approach subsumes local distinctions under the larger social and cultural trends and influences. The principles of white supremacy seeped into white culture, and even if not all whites in all places accepted it, they recognized these principles as part of a larger umbrella of social beliefs. Additionally, maintaining white male supremacy was the dominant cultural doctrine, suggesting that race, gender, and class all had a greater impact on segregation than did geographical environment. Local differences occurred, including urban versus rural, in the implementation of segregation, but they did not prevent its creation or perpetuation.

The story that unfolds is primarily one of a culture attempting to preserve itself by teaching its beliefs to the next generation, and white children's socialization in the segregated South offers an examination of white supremacy from the inside. White youth's indoctrination and acceptance of their cultural socialization can been seen in the faces of the white girls photographed standing around Rubin Stacy's corpse one Sunday afternoon, and are reflected in the numerous reports, images, and photographs that show that white children actively participated in upholding segregation. The threats from blacks, northerners, and women, combined with outside pressures and reform movements, led to an escalating anxiety about the continuation of white male patriarchy in southern society. Southern white adults, fearing that each generation that came of age during segregation would fail to control African Americans, responded by creating a society that disseminated racial knowledge to white youth in the home and community.

The socialization of white children was an essential aspect of the southern community's efforts to preserve the principles of white supremacy and perpetuate the institutions of Jim Crow. The struggle over economic, social, and political rights required the vigilance of all white southerners, regardless of age. The roles of white youth during the high-water mark of segregation reflect a change from previous attempts to uphold white supremacy and differ from those implemented after World War II. With the onset of the Second World War, southern whites' overt racial ideology altered, as both white and black southerners fought against global tyranny and confronted racial persecution. After 1945, Americans turned a critical eye to race relations in the United States, and maintaining and justifying segregation became politically and socially difficult for white southerners.

In exploring the sites of socialization, we see the places in which segregation was accepted, rejected, and reconstructed in daily life. These encounters broadly shaped the South's cultural, ideological, and political trends. In tracing out these historical antecedents of socialization in order to understand the shifts, maintenance, and perpetuation of power structures in the past, we might also reflect on our own culture today. The socialization of each generation is distinct and allows us, as historians and citizens, to consider these processes both past and present. Doing so will perhaps encourage us to recognize the power that the media, public schools, and social rituals still possess in shaping our cultural beliefs about race, gender, and equality.

1

"My Mother Had Warned Me About This"

Parental Socialization in the Jim Crow South

> If anything would make me kill my children . . . it would be the possibility
> that niggers might sometimes eat at the same table and associate with them
> as equals. That's the way we feel about it.
>
> —Unnamed southern white woman, 1904

Sarah-Patton Boyle, born in 1906 into a Virginian southern aristocratic family, described in her autobiography, *The Desegregated Heart: A Virginian's Stand in Time of Transition* (1962), an incident from her adolescence. She befriended her African American maid, Evelyn, and they chatted companionably for months, bonding over a shared interest in art. Despite their acquaintance, both always followed the prescribed measures of address until one fateful day when Evelyn referred to Boyle as "Patty" instead of "Miss Patton." The moment Evelyn said the words, emotion flooded Boyle, and her body stiffened in anger, for "A Negro had failed to call me miss!" After first blaming Evelyn for this violation, Boyle then faulted herself, for as a white she had failed in her duty to enforce the dictates of segregation. As guilt swept over her, Boyle imagined how she had invited familiarity with a black, and she recalled her childhood training about the importance of maintaining racial boundaries: "Oh, my mother had warned me about this!" Although Boyle had briefly relaxed her vigilance, she could not let the informality stand; she knew "It would be WRONG not to stop it—WRONG for her, as well as for me and the South," and so she took action, belatedly rebuking Evelyn and ending their friendship.[1] White southern families taught similar lessons across the South in an effort to prevent this type of breach.

White southern parents' instruction in regulating relations between the races was grounded in a highly idealized and nostalgic vision of a paternalistic white society. The ideological objective of this instruction, however unrealistic, was that the New South should replicate the romanticized social order of slavery. The lessons that shaped young children's identity were primarily racial, not surprising in a racially segregated society with idealized expectations of white masculinity and femininity tied to morality and contrasted with African American degradation. Instruction included lessons about the power of white skin, which created an anxiety about keeping whiteness separate from blackness. As young whites grew older, some recognized their socialization in racial issues as irreconcilable with their own experiences and observations, leading them to reject their childhood understandings. During their adult efforts as racial crusaders, they acknowledged that their youthful prejudices resulted from their early home life.

The social conception of childhood in the late nineteenth century recognized boys and girls as distinct from adults, and encouraged a newer, "sheltered-child" model of youth in conjunction with the trend toward smaller families and the growth of the middle class.[2] White southerners interpreted this call to safeguard their children differently than did those from other regions. In contrast to the efforts of Victorian-era northerners to offer their progeny a cosseted childhood, white southerners policed their children's early encounters with blacks as necessary for the preservation of white supremacy, ensuring their social and economic security. Parents' regulation of the social spaces for eating, sleeping, and playing demonstrated to southern white children both the process of and the necessity for controlling African Americans at any cost.

With the larger cultural shift in the understanding of childhood, the state began to take an active role in creating an environment that protected children. As reformers in the Progressive Era sought proactive legislation for social issues such as women's suffrage, temperance, immigration, and protection of the working class, they also focused on children. In 1912, Congress established the United States Children's Bureau as an advocate for the nation's youth.[3] In 1919, President Woodrow Wilson's "Year of the Child," the White House Conference on Standards of Child Welfare studied the nation's youth and demonstrated a public concern about providing children with a protected childhood.[4] In noting that "nothing illuminates more searchingly the character of a State than the methods it utilizes in the upbringing of its young," the report alluded to a state role in protecting the future of society.[5] The study advocated implementing standards to safeguard America's youth, suggesting that having a childhood was now a collective right and that the government bore the responsibly to shelter youth through labor reform, health care, and school laws.[6]

To assist parents in their social responsibility of shaping future citizens, a literature on child rearing burst forth with various suggestions for raising youth in a modern culture. Of course, not all mothers and fathers consulted such guides, but many increasingly relied on outside sources of advice since children during the early twentieth century confronted more external influences than had any generation before. Public schools, mass media advertising, toys, movies, and other side-effects of industrialization and urbanization meant that parents faced unprecedented competition in their children's socialization. Authorities counseled parents to consider the home as the most important institution in America.[7] A 1919 child-rearing guidebook published in Tennessee cautioned against the effects of modernization and emphasized the importance of a stable home life. The author warned of children who "are allowed to go from their homes when they should not, to attend theatoriums, theaters, shows, sightseeings of all kinds, and all kinds of amusements" with the result that "their whole being is unsettled."[8]

Regionally published parental guides and advice manuals offer a glimpse of how southern presses presented childhood and parenting to their intended audiences. Overwhelmingly, southern parenting handbooks emphasized the necessity of teaching children from an early age their appropriate racial and gender roles and demonstrated the consequences of unsuccessful parenting with fear-inducing anecdotes reminiscent of biblical stories of punishment.[9] One publication played on white anxieties, noting, "Your boy is poisoned before you dream he is in danger," and continuing, "it is impossible to build a wall so high around our homes as to protect them from moral contagion." This was a worry felt to be especially "true in the Southern land, where the [presumably black] servants of the household have such low views of morality, and especially of purity."[10]

Parents, authors noted, had a sacred obligation to educate their children; however, this duty to teach morality was possible only with the white race, as characteristics such as integrity were applicable only to whites. The sermon *Parental Responsibility,* published by the Presbyterian Committee of Publication of Virginia, noted that "whether they know it or not," parents provide their children with "an inheritance that is *within them,* in brain, and blood, and bone" (emphasis in original). The biological inheritance of white children reflects their "mental, moral, and physical tendencies."[11] The lecture warned parents not to believe it best to leave their children's minds "free, independent, and unbiased" as this evades parents' "God-imposed duty." To accentuate this point, the tract concluded that failing to teach children proper social roles was "*criminal*" and a violation of the "divine command to train them in the way they should go" (emphasis in original).[12] Parental responsibility required building children's character, as "character is not born" but learned.[13]

Southern advice guides underscored that parents' foremost duty was to teach their children their social roles, including appropriate gender roles. The 1935 manual *Preparing for Parenthood,* published in Florida, required that a proper home include "both Father as Protector, and Mother, as care-taker and trainer," defining tasks for parents based on sex.[14] For children as well, the expectations for males and females diverge. *Personal Help for Parents* noted that "the mental make-up of a boy, his superior strength, his natural aspirations and his duties in life" require his training to differ from that of girls, for boys are, "by nature[,] rough, rude, coarse and untidy." To summarize the point, the authors noted that "a girl's ambition is to be beautiful; a boy's ambition is to be strong."[15] *Preparing for Parenthood* also maintained the importance of gender divisions in children but included an additional discussion of age delineations. Parents could allow their child of between three and six years of age to play with either sex. Children from six to twelve years old, however, should play only with their own gender, and boys should participate in "different games from girls." For boys, parental manuals stressed their need to learn "to take orders, to give orders, to stand up for his own rights . . . to be sociable, to do [their] part."[16] *Personal Help for Parents* contained more explicit encouragement for fostering the notion of protective paternalism in boys, noting that they "should be instructed that it is natural for girls to not be as strong as boys, and that for this reason they should protect girls and never be rude with them."[17]

Such gendered socialization often included instructions for placing white women upon a pedestal, describing white woman's morality as a blessing to her husband and an inspiration for children and the larger white race to follow. One publication focused on teaching girls to devote their "charms," voice, and self to "redeeming the [white] race."[18] Another echoed a compa-rable sentiment, noting that women are "made in a finer mold than men," who "want to see our women better than we are, or at least on a higher plane of modesty and conduct."[19] In discussing gender roles and claiming that "the men of our South have always been noted for their chivalry, and their respect for women," such literature created a masculine code that rested on women playing their part. The minister William Cooke Boone concluded his teachings with the warning that men would not respect white women who failed to remain morally pure.[20] The implication is that women risk even more than a loss of admiration; if white women engage in sexual intercourse with African Americans, they endanger all of white society's racial privilege. Due to this threat, authors of advice books emphasized the parents' duty to teach morality, especially to white girls, upon whose shoulders the future of white domination rested.

Although discussions of virtue often targeted girls, some handbooks extended to boys the goal of maintaining innocence. In all youth, a wholesome mind leads to moral behavior for, "as a child's mind is kept pure[,] his outer life can be kept chaste." For girls, who (ideally) remain innocent until marriage, this was less of an issue. The inflamed passions of adolescent boys, however, received notice. *Personal Help for Parents* repeatedly identified masturbation in males as a subject of concern and discussed the detailed precautions necessary to suppress the sexual drive in boys. Suggestions for parents of boys included not letting boys sleep on their backs in order to discourage their "self-abuse" and forcing them to get plenty of physical exercise, thus making them too tired to engage in "exciting the passion of sex."[21] While female sexuality was presented in these guidebooks as having the potential to taint whiteness and threaten white supremacy, discussions of male sexuality focused more on self-control and determination, traits desired in adult white males.

Parental guides reflected how southerners approached their charge of safeguarding children by teaching them the South's unique vision of society. Ultimately, parents, whether they consulted advice manuals or not, shaped their children's lives by teaching them their expected social roles. In doing so, white parents employed the private sphere of the home to educate their children in the racial and gender roles required to maintain their world. These lessons often included teaching their children a racialized vocabulary, telling stories that reinforced their own racial opinions, and encouraging white-supremacist behaviors. For parents, the goal of this instruction was to lay the foundation that would prepare their children to combat African American opposition to segregation. Consequently, they taught their children that they, as whites, bore the burden of their race in keeping African

Americans subordinate to whites. The evidence of the day-to-day efforts of southern white parents to socialize their children can be found in the autobiographies and other writings by southerners who experienced this indoctrination in their race and gender roles during their childhoods.

Remembering Familial Teachings

Even though children appear to exert less direct influence upon the narrative of history than adults do, children have their own history that is ongoing and influential in the world.[22] Their youthful experiences shape their adult lives and society, and therefore constitute a crucial, but frequently neglected, avenue of insight for the historian.[23] Although examining childhood is a useful tool for understanding how early experiences shape adult lives, children rarely leave writings from their youth, have no political voice and little economic power, and live under adult authority. As historical evidence from childhood sources is limited, scholars must rely upon the highly motivated and constructed adult recollections of childhood and upon the observed behavior of adults and the community toward children.

Autobiographies are complex acts of self-making and essentially a self-reconstructing process.[24] As such, they are fluid sources, as people often forget, reshape, and even create memories from a larger social consciousness. While such subjectivity may seem to limit the usefulness of autobiographies, the process of shaping memories is a historical event in itself. As John Edgerton notes, "there are essentially three kinds of history: what actually happened, what we are told happened, and what we finally come to believe happened."[25] Despite their constructed and subjective nature, personal writings are valuable sources for reflecting the broad patterns of parental instruction that occur in the private space of the home, for certain aspects of life can be captured only in autobiographies.[26] That is not to say that scholars should accept autobiographies uncritically, as each author, consciously or not, writes to gain readers' sympathy and understanding.[27] Therefore, it is vital to contextualize the work, for reformers often "re-remember" their childhood based on their adult perspectives and politics.[28] The autobiographies of African Americans often "testify" not just to their own experiences but to those of an entire group.[29] Richard Wright's *Black Boy*, Anne Moody's *Coming of Age in Mississippi*, and Benjamin Mays's *Born to Rebel: An Autobiography* employ literary devices similar to those used in the autobiographies of white reformers, for in the act of writing, both black and white writers share how their culture shaped their conceptions of self.[30] A genre of memoirs by self-proclaimed southern white social reformers who grew up experiencing segregation emerged in the mid-twentieth century.[31] As these white writers detail their own experiences, their writings, like African American autobiographies, bear witness to those of the larger young white population of their time.

Due to the internalization of the rituals of the Jim Crow South by white youth, autobiographies allow rare glimpses into the lessons learned in the home during their young lives. Often the authors fixate on the process of their youthful socialization in an effort to trace out the development of their social consciousness. By writing about their childhood experiences with whiteness and their body, southern reformers portray their denunciation of white supremacy as something that set them apart from the bigoted, segregationist world in which they passed from childhood into adulthood. They depict themselves as the heroes of their narratives and use their autobiographies to establish their own identity and find their own voice.[32] White southern autobiographical narratives share the common theme of the writers recognizing their socialization, experiencing a racial awakening, and renouncing white supremacy.

While some scholars view southern autobiographical writings as efforts at personal redemption, most overlook the fact that these narratives present childhood as the site where the authors received their first lessons about racial purity, separation, and supremacy.[33] As these southern writers construct connections between their everyday early experiences and larger social practices, they demonstrate how the New South's children perceived their role in the adult narrative of white supremacy learned by so many.[34] Although these autobiographies reflect their authors' geographical and class differences, the socialization in gender and age distinctions that the authors describe having received appears to be consistent with the recommendations of contemporary parenting guidebooks. Women reformers recall their socialization happening in the private sphere, while men remember receiving boyhood instruction both from family members in the home and from other white men in the community.

White southern writers often describe their early grasp of the power of words. Katharine Du Pre Lumpkin's autobiography, *The Making of a Southerner* (1947), recounts her childhood in Georgia and South Carolina. Born in 1897 to a father who fought for the Confederate army, Lumpkin felt she inherited his "Lost Cause." Throughout her early years, she heard the "words and phrases at all times intimately familiar to Southern ears and in those years of harsh excitement carrying a special urgency: white supremacy, Negro domination, intermarriage, social equality, impudence, inferiority, uppitiness, good darkey, bad darkey, keep them in their place." She absorbed the notions of racial difference completely, speaking racially derogatory words "with special emphasis," although she claimed not to understand the meanings of these words beyond their demarcation of her superiority.[35]

Anne McCarty Braden acquired a similar terminology in her childhood. Born in 1924 in Louisville, Kentucky, Braden spent most of her youth in Anniston, Alabama. In her autobiography, *The Wall Between* (1958), Braden recalls understanding that "one of the things a child learns by osmosis without anyone ever putting it into words—that I was one of the 'better' human beings, more privileged because my people came of a 'superior stock.'"[36] By placing such knowledge in terms of racial and class supremacy, Braden demonstrates the ease with which white parents integrated ideas about white domination into home life. Sarah-Patton Boyle also achieved a "sense of social superiority. . . . I was taught to think of myself as a part of the very backbone of Virginia." Her family emphasized that due to her social background—her paternal grandfather had fought under Stonewall Jackson, a source of familial pride—she held the responsibility of maintaining a high social standard.[37] As a child, Boyle's understanding of the "'typical Nigra' grew as a result of a type of indoctrination which was, I think, eighty per cent pure implication, un-vocalized and unconscious, on the part of my elders."[38] Part of these inferences about race came from her mother, who "loved Negroes, but with the same deep tenderness she lavished on her riding horses, her dogs, and other pets." The connection Boyle makes between African Americans and animals is intentional, for her mother, Boyle notes, loved African Americans "without the slightest feeling that they were much like herself." This resulted, Boyle concludes, in her own thoughts becoming "saturated with the assumption that Negros belonged to a lower order of man than we."[39]

As three white women learned the language of white supremacy as young girls, they also achieved a sense of their social position based foremost on their white skin. Anne Braden's mother took pains to teach her daughter the appropriate behavior for an aristocratic young woman. The day Braden mentioned a "colored lady" prompted an essential lesson. "You never call colored people 'ladies,'" her mother lectured. "You say colored women and

white lady—never colored lady."[40] Her instruction in racial etiquette reinforced her own racial identity, for as a white, Braden would grow up to be
a "lady," a status of privilege and respectability reserved for whites. Even
a lower-class white woman could be a "lady," but an African American
woman could never be one, regardless of her social position. Sarah-Patton
Boyle learned a similar lesson from her mother. One day, as young Sarah
addressed a business letter to an African American, she asked her mother
if she should write "Mister" in front of his name. "'Oh, no, darling,' she
said. 'You don't use Mister to a Negro even on an envelope.'" Her reasoning
differed from that of Anne Braden's mother, although the issue remained
one of propriety, as young Sarah learned that calling a black man "Mister"
would "embarrass him to death." Boyle remembers being told "over and
over" that if she "didn't adhere to racial conventions[,] Negros themselves"
would be horrified, shocked, or embarrassed, and that she should accept
that blacks knew their places and that any attempt to treat them as equals
was futile.[41]

Such lessons in the appropriate use of language in the era of Jim Crow
demonstrated to the girls the power of address. Mothers taught their daughters the appropriate etiquette and social behaviors. Just as Boyle felt she had
failed to enforce the proper racial boundaries, Katharine Du Pre Lumpkin
remembered learning that her failure to act appropriately would lead to the
unthinkable: "To be ruled by Negroes! The slave ruling over the master!"
Only white supremacy could counter this "disaster, injustice, and outrage."[42]
As the daughter of an upper-class planter family, Lumpkin learned to fear
losing not only her racial advantage, but her economic one as well.[43] Her
elite white position gave her a personal stake in this privilege, and it would
continue only as long as she enforced the rules of segregation. Parental rep-
rimands instructed girls that their own power as white females rested upon
African Americans' remaining in their subordinate status.

As their mothers trained them in the dialogue of Jim Crow, fathers
demonstrated to their daughters, through stories and parables, the behaviors expected of both whites and blacks. Paternal teachings revealed that
males actively policed segregation, and stressed the subordination of white
females as both a historical truth and a future obligation. The fathers' stories
often revolved around a racial violation and the ensuing punishment of an
African American, which taught white children that it was acceptable to
discipline African Americans and to imagine themselves as separate and
superior, similar to a caste system.[44] Lumpkin and her siblings loved to hear

their father's accounts of his adventures as a member of the Ku Klux Klan, and she relates what was once her favorite story, which describes her father's visit as a Klansman to an "insufferably impudent" and unintelligent African American whom the Klan tricks into thinking he is encountering the ghost of a Confederate soldier. Lumpkin remembers how this story delighted her and her siblings: "we thought it funny to an extreme; our shrill young laughter would ring out whenever it was told. 'And did it scare them?' we would ask."[45] It did, she learned, for following that demonstration, her father told of how the Klan provided its African American victim a lesson in the rules of "good behavior." Her father's story not only affirmed her education in the inferiority of African Americans but also instructed her in white males' obligations in upholding Jim Crow and their prerogative to punish blacks who trespassed against whites. The presence of brutality within an entertaining story illustrates the close relationship to racial violence that existed in many of these lessons, which were related to children as a part of daily life to create white solidarity. Reformers, however, often discuss their experiences with white racial aggression as distinct from childhood memories of familial socialization.[46]

Lumpkin's father's stories of black "insolence" or "uppitiness" ensured that she knew both her own and African Americans' social roles. "Lest we forget," he would say to his children, "on the streets of Union Point, a darkey pushed me off the sidewalk and spit on me." Moreover, Lumpkin's mother was once "jostled by a negress, who then sassed her, nor [sic] would the woman give an inch of sidewalk" to let her pass. Lumpkin felt that her father hated such memories, but "he must tell the story, lest we have no concrete images such as haunted him."[47] The tales of her father served Lumpkin well when, at eight years old, she was walking down the sidewalk with a friend, and they came upon an African American girl their own age: "We did not give ground—we were whites!" Likewise, the black girl did not step aside, and a white arm brushed against a black arm. Lumpkin's friend turned and screamed, "Move over there, you dirty black nigger!" What made this encounter memorable for Lumpkin was that the black girl, like the African Americans in her father's stories, "did not shrink or run but flared back at us with a stinging retort, remaining dead in her tracks, defying us."[48] Lumpkin recalls this moment as one where her father's warnings came true, solidifying her understanding that without constant vigilance, African Americans would violently challenge and perhaps even overthrow Jim Crow segregation.

Regulating Spaces

These stories encouraged racial separation as southerners created a society that perpetuated the idea of social difference, with an inferior group and a superior group. For whites, this was deemed necessary to create solidarity; and indoctrination in this caste system, which required defined behaviors by each race, occurred early in life.[49] For the white children of the New South, these lessons were at times contradictory and confusing, for unlike in a permanent caste system, Jim Crow could not enforce a complete separation of the two races. African Americans worked in white homes and interacted with white adults and children on a daily basis. This contact made it vital that parents control their children's social relations with African Americans and teach them to keep white private space and the white body away from blackness.

White autobiographical accounts often document the writer's abrupt realization of racial difference through an encounter with a childhood black playmate. Such memories are common to almost every author, making them a subgenre that demonstrates the explicit adult regulation that occurred in the segregated South. Lillian Smith, born in 1897, grew up in northern Florida and spent her adult life in Georgia. One day her town's clubwomen found a little girl who looked white, named Janie, in the black part of town. They immediately removed the girl from the "dirty and sick-looking colored folks" and placed her with Smith's family. Smith and Janie became playmates and fast friends. Inseparable, the girls shared toys, clothes, and a bed. Everything changed, however, when a black orphanage called for Janie, who actually was a light-skinned black girl, and as such could not remain with a white family. Lillian's mother explained to Smith that Janie must leave because "you have always known that white and colored people do not live together." From this experience, Smith learned that she must keep blackness, even when it looked like whiteness, separate. After Janie left, guilt overcame Smith, for she had eaten and slept with an African American, intimate acts forbidden between whites and blacks.[50]

Like Smith, many reformers found that their early experiences with black children crystallized understandings of their own whiteness. The white labor reformer H. L. Mitchell recalled his childhood "sudden-realization-of-race-through-a-playmate" story. As a young boy, Mitchell played with his black companion named Johnny. One day, he wanted to continue their fun and asked if Johnny could sleep overnight at his house. "Since we played together all day long, neither of us could understand the reason why we could not spend the night together if we wanted to." Mitchell's mother explained there was no room for his friend to sleep, a rationalization that provoked Mitchell's protest, "I got lots of room in my bed." His mother clarified the matter: "It was alright for children to play together, but a black boy could not stay overnight, much less sleep in the same bed, with a white boy."[51] His mother's response forced Mitchell to confront his own race as well as understand the necessity of keeping his white body away from blackness. Sharing personal space, even in boyhood, violated the separation of the races required by white supremacy. Marion Wright, born in 1894 in Trenton, South Carolina, also played with African American boys, as having a black playmate "was more or less the custom in the South at that time."[52] His family's tolerance of interracial play, however, shifted as he entered adolescence; Wright's family informed him that must begin fulfilling his role as a white man, which demanded that he control those below him in the social hierarchy, especially African American males. Wright notes that once he entered his teenage years, his relationship with African Americans became "much less informal than it had been up to that time. And you lapsed more or less compulsively into a masterful and subservient relationship."[53]

White adults did not tolerate familiarity in play beyond a young age for girls, either. On her twelfth birthday, Sarah-Patton Boyle's parents informed her that now that she was a "BIG GIRL," her relationship with African Americans needed to change and "be formal." She recalls: "I was told sternly, it was no longer 'proper' for me to be 'familiar' with Negroes. I was a big girl now. Certain rules of adult conduct must now be observed. It was WRONG to violate these rules." From then on, she remembers: "I couldn't play with, or even talk to, colored children any more except graciously to greet them or inquire about their welfare. I was to make polite excuses when they asked me to play." Shortly after receiving this edict, Boyle encountered a former favorite playmate of hers, and writes that when she stiffly declined his request for a game "with proper Southern-lady courtesy" and inquired, "How are you today?" "the joy left his face. He lowered his head and walked away."[54] White children's first experience of being required to enforce segregation often operates in autobiographies as the moment when white reformers' idyllic youth is shattered by their newfound racial understandings.

For some white boys, the racial code was also implicitly absorbed from the public sphere, through watching how others regulated the African Americans around them. Julius Irving Scales internalized the language and gestures of Jim Crow from a playmate. As a five-year-old, Scales shouted at Aunt Lou, his black nanny, "Take your old black, nigger hand off me!" and struck her when she tried to brush his hair.[55] Scales modeled his actions toward his caregiver on an older white boy's treatment of an African American. While Scales had learned a disparaging term for his nanny from a peer, his slapping of her hand also showed a recognition of his own power, even as a white boy, over an adult black female. In the 1930s in rural Amite County, Mississippi, Will D. Campbell observed firsthand white men's authority over African American bodies. In the midst of playing, Will and his brother noticed a group of African American women running toward the schoolhouse. They followed and saw that the dead body of a young black man lay on the ground. Campbell and his brother Joe, excited to see a crime scene, stayed to watch the sheriff collect evidence. "By circulating through the group which had gathered at the old schoolhouse, Joe and I had learned the story. . . . We were little boys and the black men who had been present did not hesitate to talk to one another in our presence. The crime had actually been an execution." Noon Well, the dead man, had apparently enjoyed the favors of two women until John White, a jealous white man, shot him through the heart. The black men discussed how "White had steadied his pistol against a tree, and with careful aim, shot him through the heart. He [Noon] fell backward into the door opening and his own knife had been taken from his pocket and placed beside him."

The version of events reported at the preliminary hearing the next day, however, differed from the story circulating in the African American community: "The sheriff testified that Noon Wells obviously approached John White with a knife in a gambling dispute and that John White had no recourse but to kill him." After observing this drama—which Campbell associated with the disappointment he had felt when his uncle had canceled a planned fishing trip in order to attend the inquiry—he understood "crimes of black against black were not as serious as white against white. And certainly not as serious as black against white."[56] What looms largest in this narrative is Campbell's omission of white crimes against blacks. He, as a white child, did not consider white men's attacks upon African Americans an offense. By watching the actions of the whites around him, Campbell had internalized the racial code of Jim Crow, recognizing that white men could kill African Americans and the white community would protect them. Campbell's inclusion of this incident in his biography enables the reader to understand how his adult activism as a Baptist preacher and civil rights reformer reflected the opposite of the lessons he had absorbed as a child.

The White Body

In order to protect their whiteness, adults taught children to keep themselves physically separate from blackness at all cost, for sharing any intimate space resulted in an intolerable familiarity between the races. Melton McLaurin's autobiography, *Separate Pasts: Growing up White in the Segregated South,* recounts his youth in rural Wade, North Carolina. When he was thirteen, McLaurin's childhood lessons culminated as he and his black friend, Bobo, prepared to play a game of basketball. Finding the ball flat, Bobo began to reinflate it. After a while, McLaurin took his turn, placing the inflation needle, to which Bobo had applied a "lavish amount of saliva," into his mouth. Horrified, McLaurin imagined Bobo's spit as black germs infiltrating his body, defiling him and jeopardizing his racial purity. McLaurin felt this contamination threatened his existence "as a superior being, the true soul of all Southern whites." His revulsion resulted from the knowledge that blackness would degrade him and make him, like Bobo, "less than human." McLaurin responded by angrily throwing the ball at Bobo, and then tried to reclaim his purity by repeatedly rinsing out his mouth. After this event, McLaurin realized that he and Bobo "belonged to two fundamentally different worlds," as distinct "as life and death."[57]

Although white adults taught both boys and girls to keep whiteness pure of blackness, they focused primarily on females due to the consequences for white supremacy if young women engaged in sex with black men, for the ensuing children would destroy the racial binaries underpinning the system of white supremacy. In an effort to prevent interracial liaisons, white southerners taught young girls to fear their bodies and carnal desires, which often resulted, in adulthood, in anxiety about their sexuality. Although Lillian Smith writes that she knew that to treat an African American as her equal would result in a "terrifying disaster" for the South, in the same sentence she also acknowledges the danger her sexuality posed, noting that misfortune would befall her family if she were to have a "baby outside of marriage."[58] Her sexuality was to remain the property of white males, for she could only marry a white man, and it was only within the confines of marriage that society considered sex acceptable for a southern white woman. This concern extended only to white female sexuality and resulted in a racial double standard, for white male sex with black women did not threaten future white generations, as southern society regarded any child born to an African American woman as black.

Southern women who became crusaders for racial equality found that the childhood lessons about their white bodies colored the rest of their lives. Few publically discussed their struggles, relegating their sexuality to the private sphere, but some encountered difficulty maintaining healthy sexual relationships with men or distanced themselves from their southern upbringing with their alternative lifestyles. For white southern women, their bodies were the site where the beliefs underpinning the segregated South played out. Although the nebulous quality of ideologies can make them difficult to locate, in the Jim Crow South the central contested space of white supremacy was white female sexuality. White southerners believed that the continuation of segregation required keeping all whiteness separate from blackness in order to enforce power based on a racial binary, and the primary focus of this partitioning was separating white female and black male bodies. The lessons white southerners taught their girls created apprehension about bodily purity designed to reinforce fears of sin, blackness, and black bodies. The body, however, is not simply a passive receptacle but one with the power to perpetuate or undermine the power relationships embedded in social ideologies.[59]

Despite being a southerner, as an adult Lillian Smith felt like an outsider due to her radical writings on racial equity and her unconventional lifestyle. In a 1961 *Datebook* article, Smith describes how, when she was a child, her family taught her not just to segregate white and "colored," but also to divide the female body into "good" and "bad."[60] In her autobiography, *Killers of the Dream,* Smith recalls her mother explaining to her that her "body was a 'Thing of Shame,'" and that she should never show her naked body to anyone except the doctor and "never desecrate it by pleasures."[61] These lessons about her body made segregation seem natural to Smith as a child, for the "signs put over doors in the world outside" reflected the signs "already been put over forbidden areas of our body." Despite learning to be ashamed of and secretive about her body, Smith also recognized that her white skin offered a "source of strength and pride which proved one better than all other people on Earth."[62] Thus, Smith discovered during her childhood, as many southern white girls likely did, the contradictory nature of social perceptions of the white female body.

One consequence of this strict regulation was that as white girls matured, they struggled with complicated feelings about their fathers, who taught them that white men protected and policed women's bodies, resulting in resentment and fear toward the male head of the household, and in some cases, all white males.[63] Alice Spearman Wright, born in Marion, South Carolina, in 1902, recalled that as a child she felt both admiration and bitterness toward her father. As a girl, she eavesdropped on a conversation between her mother and older sisters about sex, which led her to believe it natural for males to control white female sexuality.[64] In an interview, she connected her difficulties with sexual intimacy to her anxiety about her father and the larger white male community. She felt that a man imposed sex on a woman, and that, by withholding her body, she could punish men for the way she felt about her father and protect herself from male domination. Spearman Wright recognized a correlation between white male control of white females' bodies and white male dominance over African Americans: "It was some kind of worship that I guess men have of women when they kick them upstairs while they are kicking the blacks downstairs, and keep them both under control."[65] White men exploited intimacy as a form of social control for white women in order to maintain patriarchy and their economic and political power. Spearman Wright countered this male authority through her position as the first female administrator in a county relief program, as an activist working to educate and rehabilitate rural workers, and as a member of the South Carolina Council of the Commission of Interracial Cooperation.

Literary writing was one of the sites that allowed white women to communicate their own apprehension about gender relationships. In her collection of more than twenty novels, including the Pulitzer Prize–winning *In This Our Life,* Ellen Glasgow created heroines who defied feminine conventions. Glasgow herself drew on close friendship with other females to defy patriarchy and circumvent the traditional roles of women such as marriage and motherhood.[66] In the late-nineteenth-century South, Augusta Jane Evans wrote southern fiction that expressed a hostility toward men. Her male characters often became wounded, maimed, or emasculated, while the novels' women delayed marriage and avoided domestic duties.[67] Literature allowed ideals to flourish, but successful real-life challenges to the cultural conventions of southern femininity were rare. The ideology of southern womanhood stood at the core of the rhetoric of the Jim Crow South, and the image of the pious, deferential woman was where the white-supremacist vision began and ended. White southern men needed to remain in control of white female sexuality to protect their social positions.[68]

The bodies of white women, conceived as the vessels of future racial purity, became the contested terrain of segregation. Many reformers omit discussions of sexuality from their narratives; while these writers publically discuss race as part of a political structure, the body remains personal.[69] Smith and Lumpkin openly wrote about issues of race and their struggle with it, but they never discuss their sexual orientation; both lived their adult lives with other women. Once these reformers recognized that their white bodies were being used as a tool to maintain patriarchal control, they sought to resist this domination through various means. Lillian Smith found companionship with Paula Snelling for over thirty years.[70] Alice Spearman Wright did enter into marriage, although she did so in 1970, at the age of sixty-eight and after a lengthy career as an activist. Others such as Ellen Glasgow never married. By withholding their physical selves from the narrative of racism and redemption, white female reformers asserted control over their sexuality and privately disregarded the white male rule of the Jim Crow South.

Rejection

It is in the conclusion of their autobiographies that white southern reformers renounce their childhood socialization into Jim Crow society and present themselves as having conquered their upbringings. The sites in which white southerners examine and subjugate their racial assumptions are often the same ones parents had placed off-limits. As white youths matured, public encounters with African Americans challenged the ideas of separate spaces as some whites confronted the humanity of African Americans, exposing the inconsistencies within the system of segregation. Violating the regulations of Jim Crow, they claimed, liberated them from their racist socialization.

Katharine Du Pre Lumpkin questioned her racial prerogative after she encountered an African American as an equal for the first time. Nineteen years old and a recent graduate of Brenau College in Gainesville, Georgia, Lumpkin remained on campus as a tutor. She participated in a leadership conference held by the Young Women's Christian Association, where the director proposed that an educated African American woman "speak to us on Christianity and the race problem." Lumpkin remembers that if their leader had "just called the person '*Jane* Arthur,'" her sense of foreboding would not have been so great. "But he had called her *Miss* Arthur." Lumpkin found this form of address, reserved in the South only for whites, unacceptable when referencing an African American. In her narrative, she recalls: "We had known and forgotten tens of thousands of Negro Marys and Janes. But never a *Miss* Arthur?" The question arose, "must we too say: '*Miss?*' Would we be introduced and have to shake her hand and say; '*Miss* Arthur'?" Although it was allowable to shake hands with an African American—Lumpkin notes that whites often shook "the hands of a 'darkey' in a genuinely kindly way"—this handshake would imply equality.

At the talk, the organizer introduced the speaker as "Miss Jane Arthur." During the speech, Lumpkin panicked when she closed her eyes and could not tell Miss Arthur's race. Yet, after the talk was over, Lumpkin realized: "the heavens had not fallen, nor the earth parted asunder to swallow up this un-heard of transgression. Indeed, I found I could breathe freely again, eat heartily, even laugh again." She felt that this experience symbolized her growth as a reformer, for once she "had done it, and nothing, not the slightest thing had happened," she realized the extent to which her youthful lessons had controlled her life.[71] Lumpkin, after her experience with Miss Arthur, felt unable to continue with her old beliefs and noticed that her "old mental habits began to slip away." As those practices faded, Lumpkin began to question the "indefinable assumption that we whites were to be served, not as a job performed for which we paid certain specific individuals, but as a duty owed to us by Negroes as a race."[72] From a privileged background, Lumpkin also established her awakening as not just race-related; she also began to question assumptions of gender and class, identifying this event as the turning point of her self-realization and the impetus for her emerging liberal beliefs.

Reformers often equated eating with an African American as a disruption of the natural order. Boyle recounts her earliest lessons as a white: "You never, never, never sat at a table with a Negro in your own dining room." As a child, Lumpkin also learned of "the sin it would be to eat with a Negro."[73] This separation of physical space along racial lines was never relaxed, regardless of gender or class. Boyle notes that if a black, immaculately dressed, college president showed up, he would be served on back porch, whereas an "ignorant poor-white, unwashed and in rags," would eat in the dining room.[74] Larry King, born in 1929 in Texas, recalled a "horrifying moment" when his mother discovered his brother "in the act of taking alternate bites off an apple with a Negro boy."[75] For many white southerners, overcoming one of the first lessons learned of never sharing intimate space with an African American became a larger symbol of their antiracist transformations and a rejection of their families' ideals.

In her autobiography, Lumpkin shares an experience that demonstrates her full conversion to antiracism by taking part in the "sin" of sharing intimate space.[76] When Lumpkin traveled to New York to attend graduate school at Columbia University, she went to a tea party at a professor's house where African American guests were present. She found that she could eat with African Americans, and afterward she felt "relief to have had the chance to prove that this taboo no longer held domination" in her mind. Lumpkin concludes her narrative with this act of redemption and her recognition that segregated social space served the purpose of "keeping the Negro in his place." Having consciously removed racialized thoughts from her life and, in doing so, no longer participating in the perpetuation of segregation, Lumpkin describes herself as having become an outsider to it.[77] Anne Braden's experience of eating with an African American also revealed to her the truth of social equality. In New York, Braden accepted an invitation to a dinner where a black woman would also be present, a situation that terrified Braden as it would require her to eat with an African American. As the meal progressed, however, Braden became so absorbed in the conversation that she forgot about race and discovered: "Why, there is no race problem at all! There are only the people who have not realized it yet."[78]

Parents taught both boys and girls from a young age that sharing a meal not only signified equality but would also physically contaminate whites. Alice Spearman Wright's experience during the mid-1920s made it clear that eating with blacks remained a forbidden practice in her parents' home. Spearman Wright postponed returning from her job for the Christmas holidays to attend a dinner with Alain Locke, an African American philosopher and author. At home, during supper, when her delayed return came up, "I said that I stayed over for this dinner party for Dr. Alain Locke. Well, my brother Joe, who was about sixteen years old, asked, 'Who is he?'" Spearman Wright responded by describing Locke's position at Howard University, his book, and his cultured manners. Joe responded, "'What? You ate with a Negro?' I said, 'Why certainly.'" Joe then looked to their father and said: "'Daddy, I don't want to eat with Alice if she has been eating with Negroes. May I be excused?' Daddy replied, 'We'll excuse you, Joe.'"[79] The fear that eating with blacks could lead to a corruption of whiteness apparently extended to whites who violated the sanctity of segregation's mores, and thus were seen as little better than African Americans themselves.

In surviving a breach of racial etiquette, white reformers discovered a new world. Their rejection of white supremacy and the roles it required of both whites and African Americans compelled them to abandon other southern mores they had learned in childhood. Before H. L. Mitchell fought racial inequality directly as an activist, he put his newfound beliefs to the test when he opened a laundry business in Tryonza, Arkansas: "At one point, some bigoted white women in Tryonza told me they were going to send their husbands' suits to Memphis, to prevent them from being cleaned together with clothing from those plantation 'nigras.'" Mitchell assured the women that, while "I had a few colored customers, their clothing was kept separate. I pretended that white people's clothing was always cleaned first, and that when the cleaning solution was ready to be dumped, the colored helper then did the colored folks' cleaning." Later Mitchell pointed out the two washing machines to anxious white customers and claimed that one washed whites' clothing and one washed blacks'. "There was no truth to any of this. All clothing was spotted, dumped in the machines, and cleaned. The only way anyone could identify clothing was by the tags affixed to each piece."[80] Such indirect activism often fed into larger efforts to secure racial equality both nationwide and in the South. Reformers describe the experience of their racial awakening as having left them no other choice but to abandon their former beliefs. For Katharine Du Pre Lumpkin, once she opened her eyes, there "was no turning back."[81]

Tracing out the lessons of childhood socialization illustrates how children acquired racial knowledge in a society dependent upon a racial and gendered power structure. In telling stories of their guilt and shame, white reformers draw on their youthful lessons to criticize society and offer an alternate vision to racial inequality. A few white children broke free from the societal norms imposed upon them and, shaken by the lessons of racism, attempted to right the injustices they had unknowingly absorbed and helped to perpetuate. Reformers' efforts to absolve themselves of the shame and guilt of their racist past by fighting segregation are also attempts to reshape their own identities. Some white women rejected the relationship between their body and their identity that had been part of their childhood socialization, denouncing southern patriarchal society and renouncing typical patterns of marriage and motherhood.

That so few southerners experienced moments that brought them to question their society's racial assumptions and allowed them to empathize with African Americans indicates how successfully southern society reinforced white supremacy. Those who examined their childhood socialization are exceptions, and their reactions set them apart from the many others who accepted African Americans as lesser humans. Southern white Rollin Chambliss knew by the age of ten that "the Negro had to be kept in his place," and he was "resigned to my part in that general responsibility." Chambliss took his duties as a white male so seriously that as an adolescent, he almost murdered an African American man. One afternoon, as he and some white friends lounged by a roadside, a black girl passed them. The group began to make suggestive remarks to her, and Chambliss felt "she might have been flattered" as "she was a bad sort." An African American man approached from the road and attempted to defend her. Since a black man had never defied any of the white boys, they ran to Chambliss's house to get a gun, but once armed, they could not find the man. Chambliss did not doubt, however, that he would have used the gun "if necessary, to keep a Negro in his place."[82] This example not only illustrates the effectiveness of these lessons on how to uphold the supremacy of whiteness, but also how white boys, by their teenaged years, understood the need to enforce African Americans' subordination with violence.

As a generation of white children came of age in the late nineteenth and early twentieth centuries, their parents sought to socialize them into what they considered an appropriate worldview. Parents embraced the emerging conception of a protected childhood in order to create and teach the ideal vision of "whiteness" by contrasting it with blackness in an effort to counter threats to white supremacy and maintain the racial system of segregation. As white children grew older, public schools, the community, and popular culture reinforced these ideals, allowing for white children's total immersion in the white-supremacist vision. This communal support led to a seamless transition from the home into white society, one that solidified children's early lessons. Sarah-Patton Boyle notes that, without her socialization in the home, "I certainly would not have learned the rules so well, and probably would have rejected them much sooner. As it was, I patiently learned and believed them all."[83]

2

"WE LEARNED OUR LESSONS WELL"

The Growth of White Privilege in Southern Schools

> The past is never dead. It's not even past.
> —William Faulkner, *Requiem for a Nun*

When Katharine Du Pre Lumpkin was a child, her father told her of his adventures as a participant in the Ku Klux Klan. One of his favorite anecdotes concerned a Klansman intimidating an African American man by pretending to be a slain Confederate soldier who was "thirsty in hell." The man commanded the group's victim to haul over buckets of water, which the Klansman pretended to drink, but in reality, the water streamed onto the ground. The story Lumpkin recounts also appears in the popular *History of the Ku-Klux Klan* (1915) by Mrs. S. E. F. Rose. In this "historical" accounting, Rose explained that the Ku Klux Klan adopted many ruses "to scare the negroes into submission." One of these stratagems called for a Klan member to ask for a drink of water while remarking that it "was the first drink he had had 'since the battle of Manassas' or Shiloh or some other famous battle." The water, instead of being swallowed by a thirsty ghost, "went into a rubber bag concealed beneath the costume."[1] The white public read and enthusiastically endorsed Rose's book for their youth. Former Confederate officer General Bennett H. Young decreed that "all the children and all the descendants of the men of the South" should read this tale of southern whites' triumph over "carpet-bagger and negro rule." The historian Mildred Lewis Rutherford concurred, noting: "This book should be placed in the hands of young people in the South in order to instruct them in the truth of its history. Parents should read the book to their children. Teachers should have it as a reference book in school libraries."[2]

The similarities between Lumpkin's story and the description in the book indicate the prevalence of these tales in southern white culture. Schools' use of the *History of the Ku-Klux Klan* perpetuated this story and the white-supremacist ideals it represented. C. F. Capps, the superintendent of city schools of West Point, Mississippi, considered the book "admirably fitted for use as a supplementary reading in schools," and adopted it for history courses. Mississippi's Southern Christian College also embraced the book for classroom use, making it a mainstream text for Mississippi youth.[3]

The scarcity of publishers in the colonial and antebellum South placed southern students at the mercy of northern textbook manufacturers.[4] These texts, in southerners' eyes, failed to include lessons applicable to their peculiar racial history, especially discussion of the positive relationships between whites and subservient blacks, such as that of the white child and his "Mammy."[5] Southerners' sensitivity to northerners' portrayals of their life was not entirely without cause. In the antebellum period, for example, one northern text noted that elite southerners, unlike temperate New Englanders, imbibed alcohol, played cards, and frequently gambled.[6] In order to avoid this skewed educational material, elite southerners often sent their youth overseas for education.[7] In the Old South, formal education was considered to be, for the most part, the province of men, and women, even the elite "Southron" belles, struggled to justify any desire for advanced study.[8] For women, the traditional antebellum education was not about reading, writing, or arithmetic, but receiving an education from their mothers on their future household duties.[9]

After the Civil War and Reconstruction, the New South emerged, and with it innovative ideas about education and schooling. Even though Massachusetts passed the first compulsory attendance law in 1852, requiring twelve weeks of school per year for all children between the ages of eight and fourteen, it was not until the early twentieth century that southern children began to attend school regularly.[10] By then, the 1896 Supreme Court ruling *Plessy v. Ferguson* had affirmed social, cultural, and economic inequality between blacks and whites by upholding the constitutionality of separate but equal facilities, which were, of course, rarely equal. During this time of segregation, white southerners refocused their education system, formalizing teacher training and creating an educational bureaucracy.[11] The formation of the Southern Education Board in 1901 reflected these ideological shifts in southern white education. Composed of fifteen southern members, it began a regionwide effort to reform public schools.[12] In this way, southerners monitored students' texts and created a curriculum that presented students with the instruction their own communities wished to see in the classroom. Although the systematic restructuring of the public-school system focused on both urban and rural schools, rural schools remained lower attended. In 1910, 41 percent of southern rural children attended school, although enrollment rates showed 65 percent.[13] Southerners also increased funding for public schools, for white children at least, and between 1900 and 1914, expenditures for education quadrupled.[14] This financial support extended only to white schools. In 1915, the average expenditure for a white child was $12.37, while the allotment for an African American child was one dollar.[15]

The emergence of educational reform in the South brought the standardization of texts and readings. Across the South, whites appointed members to boards of education and chose administrators responsible for selecting the educational material for their children. The South also began manufacturing school literature on a grand scale, creating seven new textbooks for every ten books produced between 1850 and 1930.[16] Thus, southern white citizens rose to meet the community's demand that their schools be provided with "history books true to the South!" This mobilization led to Confederate veterans' claims in 1905 that "the most pernicious histories have been banished from the school rooms."[17] Katharine Du Pre Lumpkin remembered how Confederates at their reunions sounded the slogan, "Educate the children!" Former southern soldiers argued that since they had made history, they must "see that it is written!"[18] The historian Mildred Lewis Rutherford applauded efforts to remove every northern book from southern schools. The author of a new southern history book herself, Rutherford composed one of the more radical texts, containing a list of the "Don'ts of History" that included the injunction: "Don't say you believe that the South was right; say *you know she was right!*"[19] She would have been proud of the South Carolina elementary school children who, in 1913, assembled to form a Confederate flag on the steps of the statehouse.[20]

Public schools by the twentieth century became sites of socialization that influenced students' social understanding of the world around them, as public schools do today. A 2001 study on social perceptions of equality found when teachers created a higher-status "blue" group of students and a lower-status "yellow" group, children in the blue group developed biased attitudes toward those in the yellow one.[21] Southerners' own educational literature reflected a similar dichotomy, portraying whites as the high-status social group relative to African Americans. By creating their own textbooks, southerners concerned that teachers might not "properly teach [their] children what they should know" about southern history ensured that their children were schooled in a version of the past that was consistent with contemporary white southern beliefs.[22]

In their perpetuation of the myth of African American inferiority, the textbooks and literature white southerners created for schoolchildren reveal how completely white supremacy was embedded in southern white culture.[23] Approved readings and school materials, both fictional and nonfictional, idealized the antebellum South, especially regarding race and gender roles. The Old South was portrayed as a time and place in which white men and women occupied hierarchical gender roles and the system of slavery rewarded both whites and blacks. Although the Thirteenth Amendment prevented the New South from replicating the relationships created under slavery, white southerners used nostalgia as powerful tool to justify and reinforce white supremacy. As the southern historian Francis B. Simkins notes, "what is often important to Southerners is not what actually happened but what is believed to have happened."[24]

Teaching the Text

Despite mass-produced southern textbooks and reading lists standardized by state boards of education, it is likely that some local school districts or teachers adopted counternarratives. Authors such as Mark Twain constructed stories that humanized African Americans and showed them resisting the social order. The more subtle aspects of these tales may have reached some southern children, perhaps leading them to question the social mores that accompanied segregation. Yet as a whole, the standardized curriculum reveals what southerners thought should be taught in their communities' ideal classroom. The treatment of African American men in textbooks and fictional readings used in southern classrooms is consistent, for these materials almost universally portray African American men as effeminate and, ultimately, powerless. These narratives taught white boys, especially, that as long as they kept African American males in their subordinate place, black men were incapable of offering a threat to the South. Thus, southern whites countered the physical threat of African American men by symbolically castrating them in educational materials for children. Along with reinforcing white supremacy and paternalism, this dehumanization of African Americans laid the groundwork for white violence against blacks who resisted white domination.

The newly printed textbooks for the South applauded the history of white men while simultaneously discussing blacks only in the context of their inferiority and ineptitude. Texan Larry King recalls in his autobiography that in school he never heard of African American leaders such as W. E. B. Du Bois or Marcus Garvey; instead, his American history class "marched to the Yucca Theater to be educated by *Gone with the Wind*."[25] Indeed, he notes that the lessons he learned at school failed to disturb his worldview; King was twenty-one when he realized that his history textbooks had neglected to mention the achievements of any African Americans. Nowhere "was it hinted," King writes, "that black people had played sustaining roles in our national history or made significant contributions to American culture."[26] King describes thinking, upon learning this new information, "Hell, if they lied to me about *that*, they've lied to me about everything." His recollections of his education are consistent with the themes presented in the majority of southern school textbooks, which were chosen for the messages they contained that perpetuated the social and cultural beliefs of white southerners. A 1937 study of the treatment of race in southern school textbooks found that in fifty history and civics textbooks, none contained examples of African American contributions to American culture, history, or service to their country.[27] A 1941 study of southern school textbooks examined nineteen elementary textbooks containing 589 references to African Americans, with similar results. Eighty-four percent of the books discussed African Americans' social and civic qualities in negative terms and neglected to mention African Americans' cultural contributions, history, achievements, or productive domestic and personal lifestyles.[28]

Southern school textbooks presented white children with information about and images of African Americans that identified blacks as unquestionably racially inferior. A 1941 study of eighty-six single-volume histories of the United States for elementary and secondary classrooms found that school textbooks consistently portrayed blacks as a primitive race requiring enslavement.[29] One of these books described African Americans as "docile, being able to work in the field better than the white man . . . faithful, black, humble, heathen, and practicing wild African customs."[30] Reference works joined school history texts in lending authority to a view of African Americans' inferiority, as these materials categorized the black race as similar in appearance and thought to animals. The *Encyclopedia Britannica* and the *Encyclopedia America* placed African Americans next to the ape in physiognomy due to the purported similarities in their "bodily build" and "capacity to think."[31] In contrast, positive lessons about the white race abounded, with particular attention given to white male southerners' achievements as the leaders responsible for the maintenance of the social order.

While these narratives portrayed blacks as separate and inferior, their representations of other whites, or at least of other southerners, remained positive, as their authors sought to deny class or ethnic differences among whites. The titles of textbooks, including the history book recommended for the fourth through sixth grades in Arkansas schools, *Mighty Men from Beowulf to William the Conqueror*, express admiration for the powerful white males of the past.[32] The textbook *Tennessee History*, recommended for public schools in that state, noted in its preface that students should "be electrified with the spirit of their ancestors," among whom were included the "pioneer heroes" whose "character and aspirations" had possessed a "simple noble type of manhood equal to any human emergency and developed into greatness by their romantic environment."[33] These lessons of "great" white men also reminded white girls of their dependence upon males for their past and future protection.[34]

In addition to chronicling the accomplishments of great white men throughout history, southern history books limited their treatment of African Americans to the times of slavery and Reconstruction. In discussing these periods, the textbooks created a historically based justification for white supremacy, demonstrating that slaves had appeared to be content with slavery, and when given their chance during Reconstruction to exercise their rights as American citizens, had nearly destroyed the South. Many indexes of textbooks listed African Americans in such entries as "Negroes—Problems of" or "Negroes—see slavery."[35] Southern public-school textbooks use this rendering of blacks as the central justification for slavery, which is portrayed as necessary to help civilize blacks and as a paternalistic obligation for whites.[36] The elementary school textbook *American History for Grammar Schools* described African Americans as "ignorant and unfit to govern themselves."[37] Charles A. Beard and William C. Bagley's *A History of the American People* (1939) mentioned that "many worthy people, particularly from the far south[,] thought it [slavery] not only necessary for the planters, but on the whole, good for the negroes."[38] Charles A. Beard and Mary R. Beard's *History of the United States* (1921) noted: "Slavery was no crime; it was an actual benefit to the slaves. The beneficial effects of slavery were proved, they [the slave owners] said, by the fact that the slaves were happier, more comfortable, and more intelligent than their ancestors in Africa, and it was believed that they were better off in bondage than they would be if they were free." Lawton B. Evans's *Essential Facts in American History* (1929) claimed: "The condition of the slaves generally was not a hard one. They were well cared for with good cabins to live in and plenty to eat. All day long they worked in the fields and at night sang their songs around the fires of the negro quarters."[39]

Various authors expounded repeatedly upon the idea that blacks enjoyed slavery, and included as an example of this satisfaction that slaves "sang songs around the fire" and had a "real affection" for their masters.[40] In the text *History of America* (1929), by Carl Russell Fish, readers learned that slaves were "a merry race, for they had no responsibility. They had a real gift for music and sang at their work."[41] Rolla M. Tryon and Charles R. Lingley's *The American People and Nation* (1927) is even more descriptive of slaves' alleged gratitude to white owners: "Although he was in a state of slavery, the Negro of plantation days was usually happy. He was fond of the company of others and liked to sing, dance, crack jokes, and laugh; he admired bright colors and was proud to wear a red or yellow bandana. He wanted to be praised, and he was loyal to a kind master or overseer."[42]

Illustrations in textbooks offered concrete representations of the black race serving and entertaining whites. A drawing in Charles Chadsey, Louis Weinberg, and Chester F. Miller's *America in the Making: From Wilderness to World Power* (1928) showed "A Southern Ball" where African American fiddlers played in a separate area. Earle Rugg's junior-high textbook *America's March toward Democracy* (1937) includes a representation of a "Negro in cotton field." An illustration in Mary G. Kelty's *Growth of the American People and Nation* (1931) depicts "slaves having a good time on the plantation," with several slaves in the foreground shown playing a banjo and dancing while two benevolent white men watch on horseback in the background.[43] Perhaps the ultimate representation of a history of subservience appeared in the picture of George Washington's home, in which an African American caretaker is shown supervising a white child on the lawn.[44]

In their treatment of Reconstruction, these textbooks continued the narrative of African Americans' inferiority, describing blacks as incapable of caring for themselves, let alone prepared to responsibly exercise political rights. African Americans' mismanagement of their authority during Reconstruction, these textbooks reasoned, led to white southerners taking necessary actions to control blacks. Well into the 1950s and 1960s, most southern textbooks accepted the Dunning school of thought on Reconstruction, which held that Radical Republicans had allowed carpetbaggers, scalawags, and former slaves to bring the South to the brink of destruction, a fate that was avoided only when heroic white southerners seized control from the corrupt Republican politicians. This narrative offered a linear story of redemption that, as Larry King notes, failed to disrupt his worldview and reflected the assumptions of schoolbook authors that "high school students should not be burdened with issues on which they might be called upon to do some independent research and thinking."[45]

With this narrative of Reconstruction, textbooks emphasized the similarities between the pre– and post–Civil War South. Lawton B. Evans's *Essential Facts in American History* noted that life "went on as before." Despite this assertion, Evans's next sentence demonstrated one major change: "The Negroes were no longer slaves who had to work; they were free to work or not as they chose." Evans, however, drew upon his previous arguments regarding white paternalism and slaves' contentedness with slavery to contrast that state of affairs with his portrayal of Reconstruction. Without whites, former slaves soon "had no money, no food, and nobody to care for them. Some of them became vicious and even thought they could take by force what they needed." Without slavery, Evans showed, blacks reverted to savagery, necessitating that the "white people of the South" form "a secret order known as the Ku Klux Klan."[46] The Klan's appearance is universally justified in southern textbooks as necessary for the greater good. Although some authors did not focus at length on the Klan, those who did rarely detailed the brutal methods the Klan employed, merely noting that the organization engaged in violence only when necessary. Waddy Thompson, in *History of the People of the United States* (1929), recorded details of the heroic white men who restored order, observing that the "Klan was famous."[47]

Lawrence D. Reddick's 1934 examination of American history textbooks of the South concludes: "Most of the books in these sixteen States are pro-Southern with a definite sectional bias. The picture presented of the Negro is altogether unfavorable."[48] The NAACP's 1939 study of southern schoolbooks further connects the informal lessons white youth received from white parents and family with the negative portrayals of African Americans in textbooks, noting that such images socialized white American youth into accepting segregation as desirable and natural. The NAACP believed that, unless corrected, this would lead to white children's "miseducation" and allow each generation of white children to grow into adulthood "with the fixed notion that Negro citizens are inferior to white citizens."[49] Indeed, white southerners, by using their own texts chosen by their own school boards, ensured that school materials contained exactly what they desired their children to learn. As Francis Simkins remarks, they used "formal schooling as a tool to teach what they think happened."[50]

Fictional Imaginings

Print has long been a tool of socialization in Western countries, and books are a primary method of teaching cultural values to the next generation.[51] White southerners chose a fictional literature for their children that reflected their sense of self and defined a specific southern identity.[52] The white adults who deemed these materials necessary for children's welfare demonstrated a purposeful choice and clear motive.[53] Like nineteenth- and early-twentieth-century fiction authors, white southern adults viewed literature for children as a way to shape morals and model social roles.[54] These roles remained highly gender-specific, with approved fiction writers portraying male characters as "athletic, courageous, enthusiastic, [and] respectful." Female characters, on the other hand, remained passive. They exhibited domestic skills, had an appreciation for female fashion, and always maintained good manners.[55] None of the readings approved for southern children portrayed girls or women in assertive roles, and women never dominated white men. African American characters, regardless of gender, appear in children's fiction only as slaves, in subservient roles, or as comic relief.

White culture constructed images of African Americans as a series of caricatures, and these representations became iconic in children's materials on both a regional and national scale, even in books offering counternarratives. They reinforced to a white audience the simple, even animal-like nature of African Americans. Illustrators and authors portrayed adult black women in the limited role of the "Mammy."[56] Represented as a black woman with large breasts (indicative of her ability to nurture) and dressed in bright-colored clothing usually including a kerchief tied around her head, the southern "Mammy" cared faithfully for her white family, and in doing so sacrificed her sexuality. A maternal figure, she was without a family of her own, as her world centered on the white children in her care.[57] Of the various caricatures of African Americans, the representation of the "Mammy" remained the most flexible and fluid, with white southerners continually remaking the image of "Mammy" in consumer culture through advertisements such as those depicting "Aunt Jemima." The "Mammy" caricature was the most soothing stereotype for white southerners to embrace as it represented what they considered as the most positive of interracial relationships and, beyond that, white economic and social privilege.[58]

The cultural depictions of adult black males varied depending on their age. The "Coon" and "Sambo" caricatures were often used to portray young or middle-aged black males, while a "Tom" or "Uncle Tom" was an aging, faithful servant.[59] All three stereotypes represent African American males as lazy, easily frightened, inarticulate, and unintelligent. Depicted as a perpetual child always happy in his service to whites, the "Sambo" contrasted with the "Coon," who often complained about his workload.[60] Illustrators portray black males as thin, and the "Tom" image often showed an elderly black man stooped from age. Clothing also designated inferiority, as "Sambos" and "Coons" often wore overalls and straw hats and went barefoot. Like the images of "Mammy" that reduced her to a nonthreatening, asexual being, images of male African Americans depicted them as physically and intellectually deficient. These men fail to offer a threat to white supremacy because they are too weak, too lazy, or too simple-minded to improve their circumstances. Black boys and girls, often referred to as "pickaninnies," appeared with large eyes, kinky, unkempt hair, and enormous red lips. This term from slave days references the age of black children; of those too young to pick cotton, it was said "they ain't pickaninny."[61] The children were often portrayed underdressed or naked, and their lack of clothing reinforced whites' stereotypes about inferior black parenting and blacks' lack of civilization. Black children were usually depicted interacting with animals in order to emphasize African Americans' purported primitive qualities.[62] Although other negative portrayals of African Americans abounded in mainstream beliefs, such as the violent Brute or the sexualized Jezebel, authors rarely included these images in children's materials or literature. Instead, whites produced images of African Americans whom they could control in order to represent the white southern ideal of race relations.[63] Although the stereotype of the African American male as a savage was not widely utilized in literature aimed at children, southern whites did employ this imagery as a justification for racial violence.

As in textbooks, fictional writings in the early twentieth century modeled paternalistic relationships between men and women as well as between blacks and whites, reinforcing the racially polarized patriarchy that represented white society's ideal race and gender behaviors.[64] Mass production led to a proliferation of children's literature, and its availability began to trouble librarians and teachers. They feared that "improper" literature that did not follow the approved guidelines for social interactions would find its way into children's hands. In the white South, the fear of children being exposed through fiction to minority voices or ideals led to the banning of books that were judged to be threatening to southern social mores. By 1912, state boards of education created a suggested purchase list for public schools, vetting materials for children.[65] Thus, schools became agents of socialization, and their choices reinforced the dominant cultural values of white society.[66] Recommended book lists by state boards of education existed for Alabama (1939), Arkansas (1934), Florida (1939), Georgia (1931), Kentucky (1937), Louisiana (1934), North Carolina (1941), South Carolina (1938), Tennessee (1914), Texas (1939), Virginia (1937), and West Virginia (1917, 1939). Although state-approved book lists reflected the books chosen for classrooms, it is difficult to know how many children read these materials. The process that white adults used to select reading material for their youth, however, demonstrates how white adults defined appropriate literature for children and the standards they desired to transmit to the next generation.

The detailed nature of each list varied by state. The lists of some states, such as Georgia and Alabama, numbered only a few pages, while those of others, including Florida, Louisiana, and Kentucky, were extensive and included annotated descriptions of each book. Kentucky's was the only list to contain recommendations for black schools, using "BLK" to identify the books recommended for African American schools. Even without a notation, books selected for black schools were identifiable by the language used to describe the African American characters; literature aimed at African American children described the black characters as "Negro" instead of "colored." E. K. Evan's *Araminta,* described as "Stories about a little Negro girl who lived in the city and who visited her gran'ma down in Alabama," was recommended for black schools, while A. V. Weaver's *Frawg* (1930), an "amusing dialect story of Frawg, a little Alabama colored boy," was suggested for a white audience.[67]

Many of the annotations in these lists demonstrate a close relationship between library books and classroom instruction, emphasizing that these texts served as a connection not only between the school and home, but also between the student and classroom lessons. Virginia's list of books to be purchased for elementary schools (1937) suggested that Ellis Credle's *Little*

Jeemes Henry (1936), a book about a black boy's attempts to go to the circus, be "read aloud by teacher" to the class.[68] This story, also recommended for elementary schools across the South, concerns the son of a sharecropper. Represented in the book's illustrations as the "pickaninny" stereotype, Jeemes lives with his mother, as his father has left home in order to find work. His mother is unable to afford a trip to the circus, so Jeemes tries to make extra money by helping the white people around him. His clumsiness and simple-mindedness always undermine his moneymaking attempts, but after a series of mishaps, Jeemes is finally able to raise the money to go to the circus. There he attends the freak show and sees the caged "Wild Man from Borneo." Jeemes watches the "Wild Man," who is wearing a grass skirt and necklace, jump around his enclosure and roar at the crowd. In the plot twist required to give the story its happy ending, the "Wild Man" turns out to be Jeemes's "pappy," who was "just actin' wild 'cause dat's de job Ah got wid de circus."[69] The image of a black man wearing a skirt and jewelry entertains the viewer and perpetuates the stereotype of feminized black males. The illustrations of African Americans in *Little Jeemes Henry* are caricatures; in contrast, all of the white characters are wealthy, clean, and realistically rendered.

This story presumably amused its young audience through Jeemes's hapless antics, for try as he might, he is unable to exert the self-control or demonstrate the intelligence to earn money, while his father can earn a living only by humiliating himself for whites. Although *Little Jeemes Henry* does not explicitly frame the context of the story as a sharecropper who has left home to seek better employment (only to find what is intended to be worse), the central theme of the narrative is money and labor. This story, read to children in classrooms in Virginia, South Carolina, and Florida, and by white children all across the South, reinforced the historical lessons from textbooks that, without direct white supervision, African Americans could not care for themselves. This story not only feminizes Jeemes's father but also reduces him to a childlike state, providing the reader with proof of the superiority of white patriarchy.

Two common types of fiction—southern historical nostalgia and the white-man's-burden stories set in faraway locations—employed African American characters as comedic objects by ridiculing blacks' speech, behavior, and appearance. Fictional children's works about plantation life illustrated the proper roles of whites, who should paternalistically care for indolent African Americans incapable of independence. Children's literature presented this fictional romantic view of the days of slavery as historical fact. The caricatures of blacks are used to justify their submission to whites, allowing the authors to depict African American servitude as part of the conventional social order. African American characters functioned within these stories primarily as comic relief, as their antics and silly mistakes were intended to amuse white children and mark blacks as inferior. Also used for racial marking is the speech of black characters, which is always in dialect, and often almost indecipherable English. The issue of dialect is puzzling considering that the plantation genre often stressed how a loving "Mammy" raised the white children, who rarely venture off the plantation. Yet, as one scholar notes, the white children spoke "as if they had Ph.D.'s from Oxford," while the African American children were nearly unintelligible.[70] Illustrations in children's books also offered comic relief as drawings of African Americans exaggerated their facial features, making them appear animal-like. Other images included African Americans engaged in animalistic activities such as climbing trees like monkeys or performing stereotypical behaviors like eating watermelons.

Most texts directly connected slavery and the ideal social order through creating a racial nostalgia, in which hierarchical plantation life was made to appear natural.[71] Although fictional, this romanticized context reflected the larger effort of history textbooks to underscore the inferiority of blacks and present antebellum slavery as the zenith of race relations. In fictional writings, authors blurred the historical narrative to create a past characterized by happy slaves to emphasize the organic nature of white domination and suggest parallels between slavery and sharecropping.[72] The premier writers of plantation and Civil War stories who idealized antebellum southern life include Louise-Clarke Prynelle, Thomas Nelson Page, Dorothy Leetch, Maud Lindsay, and Rose B. Knox.[73] Their works repeatedly appeared on the lists of approved literature for elementary schools across the South, for they promoted an idealized vision of southern racial and gender roles for boys and girls.

In her autobiography, Katharine Du Pre Lumpkin fondly remembers reading Louise-Clarke Prynelle's *Diddie, Dumps, and Tot* (1882) as a child.[74] Prynelle professed the authenticity of her book's depiction of plantation and slave life, writing in the preface, "I KNOW whereof I do speak; and it is to tell of the pleasant and happy relations that existed between master and slave."[75] *Diddie, Dumps, and Tot* centers on three sisters on a Mississippi cotton plantation with a "large number of slaves," including three slaves, each of whom belongs to one of the girls, referred to as the "little nigs." On the plantation, slaves are content and not as "mizer'bul as er free nigger[s]."[76] South Carolina's catalog of books recommended by the state Board of Education (1938) recommended the book for the second through sixth grades, offering this plot summary: "The true story of children on a plantation in the South. It preserves many old stories, traditions, games, hymns, and legends of a generation that is passing with the death of the older negroes."[77] Virginia's (1937) annotation confirmed the book's veracity, suggesting this "charming and informational" book for fourth-graders.[78]

Thomas Nelson Page's *Two Little Confederates* (1888) began as a monthly children's publication about two young boys and their adventures during the Civil War, and its popularity led to its reproduction as a book.[79] Page wastes little time before beginning to reinforce the nostalgia of slavery and its essential point—slaves' devotion to their white masters. The first page introduces Old Balla, the oldest slave on the plantation, and his counterpoint, Mammy. When Union soldiers approach the plantation and their white mistress allows them to leave, Old Balla replies: "Whar is I got to go? I wuz born on dis place an' I 'spec' to die here."[80] The rest of the slaves echo his response and express their desire to remain loyal to their white owners. During this time, Old Balla locks a drunken Union soldier in the henhouse, only later to find he escaped through the roof, supplying the comic relief. The two title characters ridicule Old Balla for his failed attempt at outsmarting a white man—even a drunk, northern one.[81] At the end of the Civil War, the owners must send their steadfast slaves away because there is no work for them on the plantation. When the white family's fortune returns, however, so do their former slaves, who are happy to resume their work, thus ending the story with an image of sharecropping that mirrored slavery.[82]

In addition to remaining loyal to masters, slaves in children's literature expressed contentment with their care and surroundings. In fictional writings, the slave characters themselves acknowledged their own happiness. Dorothy Leetch's publisher recommended *Tommy Tucker on a Plantation* (1925) for teachers "perplexed with the problem of showing the children plantation life."[83] Louisiana (1934) promoted the book for the third and fourth grades because it presented "in simple story form the pleasant and busy plantation life in Virginia."[84] At one point in the book, Tommy visits the living quarters of his "Mammy." Although he notices her house and other slaves' houses are decrepit with broken dishes and furniture, he remains unaffected. His lack of concern is justified as the slaves claim their surroundings "good enough foh us" and praise the master for giving them such nice lodgings.[85] The preface of Maud Lindsay's *Little Missy* (1922) also assures the reader of the book's historical accuracy. It will be familiar, Lindsay writes, to "those who grew up on the plantations, in the midst of the kindly black folk." Lindsay continues, "Southern slaves were a child-like people, full of songs and stories and superstitions." The servants in the book, she claims, "are typical of the hundreds of loyal servants in the old South."[86] One example is the description of a visiting female slave who has "the humble pleading look face often found among slaves." Without being asked, she extols her mistress's beauty to Missy, noting "Mis' Sally's powerful good ter all her niggers."[87]

Through the voices of black enslaved characters, authors perpetuated the myth of black gratitude toward whites. In *Diddie, Dumps, and Tot,* the oldest male slave on the plantation, Daddy Jake, explains to the three little white girls the origins of the black race.[88] He notes, "Ef'n de nigger hadn't ben so sleepy-headed, he'd er ben white, an' his hyar'd er ben straight des like yourn." Daddy Jake explains that after the Lord made African Americans, he wanted the sun to dry them. They fell asleep, and when an angel came to fetch them, they slept so soundly that the angel could not wake them. Because blacks were burned by the sun, the Lord wanted to throw the race out, and "wuz des 'bout'n ter thow 'im 'way, wen de white man axt fur 'im."[89] After the black man's laziness caused God to mark him as inferior, the white man saved the black race from extinction. Because God never finished him, the black man could never aspire to be equal to the whites; he could only strive to serve the white race loyally.[90]

To ensure that the white children reading these novels understood the proper place of African Americans in both the past and present South, some plantation stories moved beyond comic images of blacks to include passages that encouraged violence to keep African Americans subservient. Rose B. Knox's *Gray Caps* (1932) begins with numerous complaints about the laziness of slaves and their penchant for shirking work.[91] This remains a theme throughout the book, as one white character notes that blacks are "lazy, good-for-nothing, wasteful creatures! You couldn't get three fair days' work out of 'em in a whole week. They wouldn't even work their own patches. Oh, no, they'd rather loaf and then steal from their master."[92] During one scene, a white man falls in the water, causing a nearby black slave and his owner to laugh. Enraged, the man yells, "You black scoundrel, I'll teach you to laugh

. . . !" He then climbs out of the water and threatens to beat the slave, who, the text notes, begins to whimper. This attempt to circumvent punishment further enrages the soaking-wet man, who gives the slave what appears to be a spanking, taking a nearby rod and smacking the slave's behind. This abuse to his slave causes the owner to defend his property, responding, "He's my nigger, and I'll whip him if I want to." The scene ends with the two white slave owners arguing about the proper way to beat the African American.[93] This lesson in the need to violently subordinate black bodies doubles as an exhibit in proper masculine behavior. A southern white man would never allow himself to be humiliated by an African American. If such an incident were to occur, it would require the southern male in question to retaliate violently, reinforcing his supremacy.

Thomas Nelson Page, in *Two Little Confederates,* portrays the title characters of Frank and Willy as role models for the male reader, and encourages an idealization of adult males who heroically fought the North during the Civil War. The book was recommended by Louisiana for the sixth and seventh grades, and the description of the novel noted that the main characters were "loyal sons of the Old South, watching the war surge by their plantation gates. Their fervent patriotism, laughable mistakes, and manliness in bearing of the hardships of war have endeared them to countless readers."[94] This "manliness" resulted from the boys' attempts to hunt Confederate army deserters and protect their families. The *List of Books Suggested for First Purchase for Virginia Elementary Schools* observed that the boys "caught the same spirit that made their father and their father's comrades heroes in the Great War."[95]

Although the plantation genre offered few roles for girls, female characters modeled implicit gender lessons, offering examples of acceptable behaviors for white girls. In *Little Missy,* the title character, although only eight years old, is preoccupied with her manners and behavior. When Missy mimics the slave children's game of spinning around to raise dust, she immediately becomes concerned about her unladylike behavior. The thought of a white woman, such as her neighbor, seeing her and perhaps reporting her "bad" behavior frightens Missy.[96] Consumed with her future role as a plantation wife and mistress, Missy often asks her Mammy about her marital future. Mammy tells her she will marry "de handsomest man in de Country," but only if Missy is "a pretty little gal an' mines yo' manners."[97] These instructions in etiquette, aimed at a mistress in training, are uniquely feminine. Later in the story, Missy encounters a slave looking for some of his master's money he lost, and he mentions fearing his master's violent punishment. Outraged, Missy urges her father to buy him in order to save him from being beaten. Her father does so, and he gives Missy the slave, "Uncle" Solomon, telling her "to take might good care of him."[98] The story ends with Missy taking on the role of plantation mistress, adopting the benevolent role of an idealized white southern lady.

Counternarratives

Plantation novels viewed the antebellum South through a nostalgic lens that emphasized the naturalness of Jim Crow race relations. A few novels of this genre, however, offered counternarratives within these plantation stories. The themes in this literature often humanized African Americans, pointed out the ironies of Jim Crow race relations, and illustrated to both white and African American children how, by subtle ruses, the underling could gain a measure of power. Two authors whose narratives contained these elements are Samuel Clemens, who wrote under the pen name Mark Twain, and Joel Chandler Harris. Although their novels might appear to the average reader to be similar to other books of the plantation genre, these works could draw the careful viewer into the moral quandary of race and racism in the South.

On the surface, the novels of Twain and Harris appear to reinforce white supremacy. Indeed, school boards of education selected their works as appropriate for children's consumption, as at least one of Mark Twain's novels of boyhood adventure and at least one of Joel Chandler Harris's plantation stories appear on every recommended reading list for public schools in all of the states surveyed. Mark Twain wrote with a "Socratic irony," and many students even today struggle to read against the tone of the novel and to separate the words of the characters from Twain's themes.[99] This subtle racial dynamic, which is possible to miss in a superficial reading, might explain the popularity of *The Adventures of Tom Sawyer* (1876) and *The Adventures of Huckleberry Finn* (1885) in the Jim Crow South.[100] *The Adventures of Tom Sawyer* follows the escapades of Tom, a southern boy of twelve or thirteen, in a Missouri town. South Carolina's public schools described the book as "intended mainly for the entertainment of boys and girls" and portrayed the text as based on actual events, giving it historical authority, noting, "most of the adventures really occurred and some of them are actual experiences of the author."[101] Twain, who grew up in an environment similar to that of the novel, did draw on some experiences from his childhood but altered them for his works. Despite this, Louisiana's library list also described the novel as the "story of boy life in Missouri based on the memories of the author's own boyhood. Flow of incident, and absurd and odd superstitions then prevalent among children and slaves, combine to make this a classic of fun which reveals rare understanding of boys."[102]

At first, Twain's *The Adventures of Huckleberry Finn* may appear to epitomize mainstream white southern beliefs about the roles of whites and African Americans. Huck accepts African Americans' subservience, noting, "Each person had their own nigger to wait on them."[103] An illustration of Jim personified the stereotypical images of "Sambo," with Jim wearing a straw hat and overalls and yawning, reinforcing the image of African Americans as lazy.[104] Unlike other authors of plantation stories, Twain avoids romanticizing the antebellum South.[105] The story of *Huck Finn* centers on the relationship between Huck, a white boy, and Jim, a runaway slave. This already defies one convention of the plantation genre—that blacks enjoyed their enslavement. Interestingly, South Carolina's description of the novel omitted any mention of race, instead focusing on the adventure part of the title. The annotation observed that *Huck Finn* "is a story of the life of a boy on the Mississippi, full of humor, glamour, and a thorough understanding of boy nature."[106] Louisiana, however, recognized the racial tension, characterizing the story as being about "how Huck helps Jim, a negro slave, to escape by floating down the Mississippi River on a raft."[107] Although Jim appears to be a caricature, as the story progresses his multi-faceted character is revealed.[108]

Through Huck's adventures down the Mississippi River, readers could find an alternative discourse in which Twain attacks the system of slavery, points out the hypocrisy of white southerners, and satirizes their treatment of African Americans. While Jim begins the novel as a "Sambo" character, Twain's writing humanizes him.[109] Jim's longing for his family and his feelings of loss allow Huck (and the reader) to see Jim as a person, not just property. Huck observes, "He was thinking about his wife and his children, away up yonder, and he was low and homesick; because he hadn't ever been away from home before in his life; and I do believe he cared just as much for his people as white folks does for their'n."[110] This humanizing of Jim does not prevent Huck from playing pranks on Jim for his own amusement. One time, Huck hides a snakeskin, which Jim feared as bad luck, in Jim's blankets, and the snake's mate bites Jim and sickens him for days.[111] White readers may have responded to this passage in several ways; some may have found humor in an African American's pain, while for others, Jim may have become a sympathetic character, stepping outside of his caricatured role.[112] Jim's pains, both emotional and physical, make him human. Huck's evolving relationship with Jim allows him to state at the end of the novel, "I knowed he was white inside."[113] In doing so, Twain exposes the careful reader to the contradictions and inconsistencies within the discourses surrounding race in the South. If an African American man could be a real person, with genuine feelings, then he was no different from a white man and arguably deserved the same social, political, and economic freedoms as whites. Twain's own beliefs on race relations resulted from his changing consciousness, and readers must be careful to separate Huck's voice from Twain's.[114]

Another writer who used the South's own rules and beliefs against it is Joel Chandler Harris, whose Uncle Remus stories also contain messages that subvert the lessons evident in other contemporary children's literature. Harris's novels, like Twain's, occur in the antebellum South but focus less on boyhood adventures and more on slave plantation folklore. As North Carolina's description for one of the most popular books, *Uncle Remus: His Songs and Sayings* (1886), observed: the "stories of Br'er Rabbit, the Fox and others, told in the quaint negro dialect, will be interesting to every grade. The stories should be read to children of the Primary Grades."[115] The Uncle Remus stories follow the pattern of an elderly slave, a "Tom" stereotype, telling stories to the master's grandson, a young white boy. These tales focus on Brer Rabbit, the clever central character who regularly escapes the clutches of his nemesis, Brer Fox. As Lawrence W. Levine notes, these stories are thinly disguised anecdotes about how African Americans (Brer Rabbit) could use cunning to fool white southerners (Brer Fox). These stories model how African Americans, like the rabbit, could often gain what they desired by acting stereotypically foolish.[116] *Nights with Uncle Remus: Myths and Legends of the Old Plantation* (1881), the first Uncle Remus book, offers an example of this. Recommended for schoolchildren in Florida, Louisiana, South Carolina, Texas, and West Virginia, this book contains the story "How Mr. Rabbit Was Too Sharp for Mr. Fox." This tale chronicles how Brer Fox catches Brer Rabbit and gloats, "Well, I speck I got you dis time, Brer Rabbit," to which Brer Rabbit responds with "talk mighty 'umble.'" Brer Rabbit suggests several ways for Brer Fox to kill him, always begging that no matter what, Brer Fox not throw him into the briar patch. "'Drown me des ez deep es you please, Brer Fox,' sez Brer Rabbit, sezee, 'but do don't fling me in dat brier-patch.'" Of course,

Brer Fox throws Brer Rabbit into the briar patch, from which he is able to quickly make his escape, "skip[ing] out des ez lively as a cricket in de embers."[117] Thus, the rabbit manipulates the fox into doing exactly what he desires by taking advantage of the fox's belief in his own superiority.

Many white children likely understood the superficial level of the story, enjoying the adventures of animals and the satisfaction of an underdog outmaneuvering the "bad guy."[118] For those children, this literature affirmed what society taught them about African Americans, invoking nostalgia for elderly slaves who would fondly remember the plantation days.[119] It is only through analysis that the struggle between the rabbit and the fox becomes a message about how the defenseless could manipulate those in power. It is unclear whether many children in the Jim Crow South received these messages instead of accepting the superficial narratives that reinforced African American inferiority. Most white southerners note that their youthful readings romanticized their views of their world as opposed to challenging or altering them. Both Joel Chandler Harris and Mark Twain, however, shared a sense of despair for their world and countered this sense of hopelessness through trickster figures who defied the conventions as they could not.[120] Their novels of the antebellum South offer an alternative discourse that could open the eyes of both white and African American children to dissenting narratives about race within the plantation genre. As any text is open to multiple readings, it is difficult to know if Twain's and Harris's writings directly elicited subversive ideas about race, yet such an interpretation is possible and valid.

Outside of the South

The plantation genre was just one type of children's book utilized by public schools to teach children the proper roles for blacks and white boys and girls. Other children's literature transposed the lessons of the plantation genre into a context outside of the geographical South, while maintaining the core racial ideology of white supremacy. For young children, the popular *Little Black Sambo* series, originally set in India, moved to the white South when American illustrators created images of the black characters that reflected the stereotypes white children encountered every day.[121] Other stories occurring outside of the South also portrayed dark-skinned peoples as inferior and in need of whites to help "civilize" them. Children's authors often applied a "white man's burden" approach to literature to sug-

gest that there existed a universal connection between race and civilization, for in these novels the white characters remain the providers, the
problem solvers, and the caretakers of their inferior black dependents.[122]
The Story of Little Black Sambo, aimed at elementary school children, and
the adventures of Dr. Dolittle, recommended for high school students,
both suggest that no matter where one goes, dark-skinned peoples are
inferior, incapable of white behaviors, and require white paternalism.

The Story of Little Black Sambo (1899), written by the Englishwoman
Helen Bannerman, describes a dark-skinned child's adventures in India with
four tigers as he takes a walk in his new, bright-colored clothing. Sambo must
give away one of his new garments to each tiger he encounters on his walk
to avoid being eaten. The tigers become jealous of each other's apparel and
chase each other so violently around a tree that they turn into butter. Sambo
retrieves his outfit and goes home, where his mother, Black Mumbo, makes
pancakes for him and his father, Black Jumbo, with lots of butter. Mumbo
eats 27 pancakes, Jumbo finishes 55, and Sambo consumes 169. *The Story of
Little Black Sambo,* like some subversive stories, contains the positive image
of Sambo outwitting the tigers. The rest of the story, however, perpetuates
and reinforces negative stereotypes about African Americans. The name of
the main character, Sambo, employed a term already established in 1899 as
a symbol of a childlike, lazy, docile African American. Including the term
"black" as part of the parents' names also expanded upon the negative racial
connotation.

The success of the Bannerman book led to its printing by various
publishers, who produced more than twenty-seven different versions in
the United States between 1905 and 1953.[123] Each of these publications
offers a variety of illustrations, but overwhelmingly American publishers
set the story in the South, drawing on African American stereotypes to
portray the characters. American illustrators portrayed Black Mumbo as
a "Mammy" figure with a large girth and bandanna, while Jumbo became
an "Uncle Tom" with bare feet and overalls (see page 56). Illustrators often
gave the characters grotesque and distorted facial features, particularly
the lips and eyes.[124] A 1934 version of *The Story of Little Black Sambo*
contained "pop-up" illustrations by C. Carey Cloud. In this version,
Sambo is very clearly African American; he is not in India anymore.
When he climbs a tree, his face and limbs contort to make him appear
like a monkey. In another image, Sambo clearly looks like a black-faced
minstrel, with huge white eyes, dark skin, and a white ring around his

"Black Mumbo" character from *The Story of Little Black Sambo* by Helen Bannerman (Chicago: Reilly and Britton, 1908).

mouth.[125] This image of Sambo and his parents as minstrel-type characters dominated many publications, and some lists remarked upon the "crude, but attractive humorous pictures."[126]

The Story of Little Black Sambo appeared on the recommended reading list for all of the states examined, and was overwhelmingly suggested for the first through third grades. Some states, such as North Carolina, included an asterisk next to *The Story of Little Black Sambo* to denote that its purchase was a minimum requirement "for an accredited elementary school."[127] Florida indicated that the story offered a wider appeal than its suggestion for lower elementary grades would indicate.[128] *Little Black Sambo*'s reach extended into southern child-rearing literature. Mary Clemens, in her parenting book *Our Little Child Faces Life*, mentioned that her son Dicky "became just as much at home with the story of baby Moses as he was with 'Little Black Sambo.'"[129] She recalled that he often played "Little Black Sambo" outside and then came inside for a cookie, which represented the 169 pancakes Little Black Sambo ate.[130] For the young white children who read *The Story of Little Black Sambo*, the actions of the characters reinforced the stereotypes of African Americans surrounding them. The impression of Black Mumbo as a "Mammy" figure and the devouring of hundreds of pancakes—a representation of gluttony and greed—offered white youth an amusing way to imagine African Americans. This humor is predicated upon white children's understanding of African Americans' inferiority in relation to their own superiority; indeed, the story would not be as humorous had the author and illustrator replaced the main characters with whites.

For older youth, Hugh Lofting's *The Story of Dr. Dolittle* (1920) offered lessons on ideal white behavior by reinforcing white patriarchy.[131] *The Story of Dr. Dolittle* was one of the most popular children's books in the early twentieth century. The story appeared on the recommended reading list for Alabama, Arkansas, Florida, Kentucky, Louisiana, Virginia, and West Virginia.[132] Its drawings, also created by Lofting, received praise as well. Louisiana's list described the book as having "much droll humor, especially in the illustrations."[133] The story begins with Dr. Dolittle as a mediocre physician who becomes a successful "animal doctor." The Doctor lives with his sister, Sarah, whose constant worrying about finances leads her brother to his new occupation, which allows her to buy "a new dress" and be "happy."[134] She is portrayed as stereotypically feminine: not only does her life revolve around clothes, but she refuses to allow a crocodile to live in the house. Losing patience, she yells at Doctor Dolittle: "I tell you I *will not* have him around. . . . He eats the linoleum. If you don't send him away this minute I'll—I'll go and get married!" Sarah's pleasure at new clothes and displeasure at a disorderly household, as well as her threats to marry, are intended to appear uniquely feminine. When the crocodile stays, a miffed Sarah leaves.[135]

Doctor Dolittle then hears from Chee-Chee, a monkey he rescued, of an epidemic affecting the monkeys in Africa. The Doctor, Chee-Chee, Gub-Gub the pig, Dab-Dab the dog, and Pollyanna the parrot all set out on a grand adventure to save the monkeys. Upon their arrival in Africa, dark-skinned natives capture the party and take them to their king and queen. Recalling bad experiences with the white race in the past, the natives lock up Dr. Dolittle and his animal companions in a dungeon. The king and queen of the natives are not described in the text, but Lofting's illustration of the king and his sleeping (read, lazy) queen offers all the knowledge a white reader would need to see the similarities between southern blacks and Africans.[136] The illustration shows the queen's proportions as similar to those of a "Mammy" figure, and both the queen and king share exaggerated facial features including an elongated chin, large lips and noses, as well as monkey-shaped heads. For many readers, the connection between these Africans and the stereotypes of southern blacks would have been clear.

Pollyanna the parrot, who taught Doctor Dolittle animal languages, throughout the book utters blatantly racist remarks intended to carry the weight of wise teachings. Pollyanna notes the racial inferiority of the natives and uses this knowledge to devise their escape. She reminds Gub-Gub the pig, "do not forget that although I am only a bird, *I can talk like a man*—and I know these darkies"[137] (emphasis in original). After their successful escape, the group finds the sick monkeys, only to realize that they need help from other animals in the jungle in caring for them. When the Doctor asks the lion, king of the jungle, for help, he refuses, and his wife scolds him, for their cub is sick. The lioness connects obeying a white man with the labor of black peoples as she orders: "Go back to that white man at once . . . and tell him you're sorry. . . . *Then do everything the Doctor tells you. Work like niggers!*" (emphasis added).[138]

When the Doctor and his entourage prepare to leave Africa after successfully saving the monkeys, the king captures them again, and Pollyanna devises their escape.[139] After observing the king's son, Prince Bumpo, reading a book of fairy tales and overhearing his wish that he could become white so that he could win the heart of a fair princess, Pollyanna, speaking in a "small, high voice like a little girl," suggests to Bumpo that she knows someone who "might turn thee into a white prince perchance."[140] Pollyanna promises that, in return for their freedom and a boat, Doctor Dolittle will turn Prince Bumpo white, a task the Doctor finds daunting: "But it isn't so easy to turn a black man white. You speak as though he were a dress to be re-dyed. It's not so simple. 'Shall the leopard change his spots?'" Pollyanna, frustrated, replies, "But you *must* turn this coon white."[141]

Dr. Dolittle's remark about his inability to change Bumpo's skin color is not simply about the idea of making light something dark. Both Dr. Dolittle and the reader know even if he could change Bumpo's skin color, he would only be "dyeing" him, not making him a member of the white race. That night, Bumpo approaches the Doctor, explaining, "If you will turn me white, so that I may go back to The Sleeping Beauty, I will give you half my kingdom and anything besides you ask."[142] The Doctor concocts a tonic and instructs the prince to place his face into a basin. When Bumpo lifts his head, all the animals cry out in surprise, "for the Prince's face had turned as white as snow, and his eyes, which had been mud-colored, were *a manly gray!*" (emphasis added).[143] Knowing that the effect of the potion is only temporary, the animals and Doctor Dolittle quickly leave Africa, although Dab-Dab the dog offers that if Prince Bumpo reverts to his natural skin tone, it would "serve him right. . . . I hope it's a dark black." Lofting clearly connects whiteness to masculinity and, by inverse, blackness to femininity. His characters note that changing one's skin color does not change race, or inherent inferiority. Dab-Dab continues, "The Sleeping Beauty would never have him. . . . [H]e'd never be anything but ugly, no matter what color he was made."[144]

The sequel, the *Voyages of Doctor Dolittle* (1922), which won the Newbery Medal, further reinforces these lessons as the group helps another black group of "childlike people" on Spidermonkey Island, continuing to make the connection between dark-skinned people, inferiority, and monkeys. In *Voyages,* Chee-Chee the monkey tells a humorous anecdote about how he escaped from Africa by disguising himself as a black girl. He dressed himself in the clothes of a "fashionable black lady" and strolled among people in this "disguise." Here the connection between monkeys and the black race is made explicit. Chee-Chee remarks that dressed as a black girl, he "look[ed] just as much like a monkey as I look[ed] like a girl."[145] Furthermore, as the story continues, the lack of civilization of dark-skinned peoples emerges, as the "savages" on Spidermonkey Island worship the Doctor as he solves problem after problem for them. In a model of undertaking the white man's burden, Doctor Dolittle tries to teach those who are "ignorant of much that white people enjoy," and is afraid to leave as "they would probably go back to their old habits and customs," which include devil worshipping. The Doctor concludes this observation by overtly connecting race and paternalism, noting, "They are, as it were, my children."[146]

During the 1960s, the racialized language of these children's books troubled publishers, who were torn between requests to remove derogatory terms and the desire to publish classic titles intact. Ultimately, editors chose to remove the racialized language. In these reprints, the word "nigger" became "native," while publishers deleted "darky" altogether, removed the dialect, and updated the illustrations.[147] The pervasiveness of racist images in children's classics, which lacked positive images of African Americans, troubled African Americans. W. E. B. Du Bois responded by publishing his own children's magazine, *The Brownies' Book,* for black youth. Started in 1919, the magazine focused on positive cultural behaviors and good morals, and featured characters with a variety of skin tones and other physical characteristics. Although short-lived, lasting until only 1921, Du Bois's magazine was the only publication designed for black children until the appearance of *Ebony Jr.* in 1973.[148]

After years without textbooks published in the South, white southerners during the early twentieth century created and regulated educational materials—both textbooks and fiction—to reflect their own cultural beliefs. These works were required to encourage white male supremacy, often in the context of antebellum slavery. White adults sought not to replicate antebellum ideals, but employed historical nostalgia to idealize African American inferiority in order to normalize white supremacy. In 1924, South Carolina students completed an educational test in both rural and urban public schools that revealed how successfully white children had internalized these lessons. Although the test had been designed to measure the progress of children in grasping reading and writing fundamentals, the children's responses revealed not only their scholastic ability but also their racial prejudice. One question read: "Aladdin was the son of a poor tailor. He lived in Peking, the capital city of China. He was always idle and lazy and liked to play better than to work. What kind of boy do you think he was?" The answer choices were listed as: "Indian," "Negro," "Chinese," "French," or "Dutch." Most of the children chose "Negro." The instructor called on one twelve-year-old boy to clarify why he had selected that answer, and the boy responded, "Because he was lazy." Other responses included, "Because Negroes like to play better than to work," and because "most Negroes are lazy."[149] These answers reflected the cultural imagery found in school literature, which further socialized children into the expected racial roles for whites and blacks in the New South and the larger world.

3

Consumerism Meets Jim Crow's Children

White Children and the Culture of Segregation

Eney, meeny, miny, mo, Catch a nigger by the toe! If he hollers let him go!
Eney, meeny, miny, mo.

— Children's rhyme

In the early twentieth century, the emergence of industrialization and mass culture in the South strained the system of racial segregation.[1] Cash made the marketplace an equalizing space, offering at least monetary egalitarianism, while mass culture provided white southerners a public medium in which to reiterate their justifications for white dominance over African Americans.[2] National advertisement campaigns, such as those for Aunt Jemima pancake mix and syrup, Cream of Wheat breakfast cereal, and Czar baking powder, made use of evocative images of the South, especially those of "good darkies," to reinforce the idealized racial roles of southern antebellum society that were also portrayed in public-school instructional materials.[3] Advertisers promoted many of these products in commercial venues all over the country, reflecting the nationalization of white culture and the naturalization of white supremacy. The ideology of African American inferiority lived in the national consciousness, as seen in such events as the mobilization of whites following African American Jack Johnson's defeat of a white man for the title of heavyweight boxing champion in 1908.[4]

Although advertisements containing such images appeared across the country, their impact varied. In the North, these advertisements, seen against the backdrop of industrialization, furthered a historical nostalgia and functioned to keep blackness safely contained.[5] In the South, however, where whites struggled to preserve segregation, these advertisements reflected whites' vision of desirable race relations. Images of subservient African Americans resonated strongly with white southerners, as the rise of mass consumer culture occurred at a time when southern whites were reconstructing their heritage through public commemoration. Throughout the early twentieth century, southern states began funding projects intended to reclaim the South's past. Although part of a larger effort by Democrats to secure and justify their political positions, these state-funded ventures reinforced a white-supremacist vision of southern history in public spaces.[6] In the South the public sphere remained in the control of whites, who quickly quashed counternarratives to white supremacy and contextualized the products of consumer culture within their own race-based society.

White southerners made use of the opportunity popular culture offered to manipulate representations of blacks and whites as a way of perpetuating a social discourse aimed at white control of African Americans. The production of movies such as *Birth of a Nation* (1915) and the creation of organizations such as the Children of the Confederacy supported white southerners' efforts to educate their children in the re-created historical memory of the white South. White southerners crowded their children into theaters to watch movies like *Birth of a Nation* that reinforced lessons the children had learned about the white and black races and that, like other products of consumer culture, offered an additional visual punch. Katharine Du Pre Lumpkin recalled seeing *Birth of a Nation* several times and noted that fellow members of the audience "sighed and shivered, and now and then shouted or wept in their intensity" at the images of the noble southern men and women.[7] Ralph McGill, who saw the movie as a boy in a packed house, wrote that after viewing the film he and his white playmates discussed rumors of trouble in the African American section of town. Empowered by the images of white manhood on the screen, the boys sought to reenact the white male roles within the movie.[8] These early-twentieth-century cultural productions reinforced white power in the Jim Crow South by presenting consumer goods and cultural products in the context of whites' daily lives.

The images and materials mass-produced for children drew on familiar and degrading stereotypes of African Americans—"Mammy," "pickaninnies," "Coons," "Sambos," and "Toms"—that reinforced white dominance and African American inferiority. The cultural media perpetuated a nostalgic vision of race relations similar to the one promoted in the educational materials created for southern schools. Southern white children, therefore, experienced a seamless transition from the view of race relations presented in their school materials to the one they encountered in cultural productions in their daily life. The prevalence of these stereotypes in advertisements directed at children suggests that these images were consonant with the cultural attitudes of most southern whites. Through disseminating caricatures of African Americans, the media dehumanized African Americans. Toys, games, and extracurricular activities such as plays, church pageants, and youth groups, carried this constructed racial nostalgia even further. Not only did white children view these exaggerated race roles in books and advertisements, but white parents encouraged their children to perform them in community activities, allowing the children to enact their dominant roles as whites. Such adult-sanctioned youth activities offered a way for white children to participate in rituals and ceremonies that portrayed white supremacy as normal and acceptable. The transition to enacting social roles mirrored children's development since, by their teenaged years, after successfully merging parental, school, and community lessons, white youth took on an active community responsibility.

By the early twentieth century, mass media played a vital role in the socialization of white youth through normalizing the lessons of home and school. That whites used the medium of advertising to oppress African Americans is perhaps not surprising. What is interesting, though, is the role that white boys and girls played in the emerging mass media culture. Children's placement in advertisements aimed at a youthful audience offered a model of appropriate behaviors for white youth necessary to perpetuate white supremacy. A 1914 Cream of Wheat advertisement reflects the idealized social discourses of whites (see page 64). Harnessed to a cart is an elderly African American, representing the "Uncle Tom" stereotype of an aged, faithful servant.[9] The man in this image is thin, his shoulders drooping as he lights a cigarette. Poorly dressed, he wears grimy, baggy pants and an oversized, ill-fitting jacket. In the cart is a well-dressed, giggling white boy. He holds reins attached to the black man in one hand, while he wields a whip, poised to strike, in the other. The words "Cream of Wheat" are emblazoned on the cart, and the ad's caption reads, "Giddap Uncle!"[10]

This advertisement offers little subtlety in its portrayal of race relations. A white boy whips a subservient elderly black man while uttering a command that reduces the black man to a docile beast of burden. This vivid advertisement reflects the most common themes on which American ad-

Cream of Wheat advertisement, 1914.

vertisers drew in creating a public discourse about race and power. First, this representation links poor hygiene with blackness, which served to reinforce the connection between whiteness and purity. Second, the advertisement portrays a racial fetishism about African American bodies.[11] Advertisers often physically exaggerated black bodies, exhibiting them as underdressed or naked, or giving them animal-like characteristics. As noted, hitching the black man to the cart likens him to a beast of burden. Portraying physical violence against African Americans as entertainment is the third, and most obvious, reflection of racial discourses about power in mass culture. In this case, the white boy enacts his social power over the black body through physical brutality. Even as a child, he is permitted to attack and, perhaps more important, to enjoy assaulting black bodies. In demonstrating his power, the white boy emasculates this "Uncle Tom" and, by implication, all black men. Collectively, these themes functioned to depict both whites and African Americans in roles that supported and justified white supremacy.

Other Cream of Wheat advertisements displayed African American males' inferiority by contrasting black males with wholesome white children. The Cream of Wheat chef, Rastus, a black man in a white cook's hat who emerged as Cream of Wheat's mascot in a series of advertisements, often appeared alongside chubby-cheeked white children. In one placard, he feeds Cream of Wheat to a white toddler above the words "[Cream of Wheat] Is the model children's food, light, nutritious."[12] In another circular, the chef, holding a huge bowl in his arms, speaks in dialect: "Bigges' I could get, Sah! Mo' Wheh Dis Comed Fum, Yas Sah, Cream of Wheat."[13] The use of dialect directed to an unseen white master identified only as "Sir" emphasizes the servile role of African Americans. Another Cream of Wheat advertisement shows the black chef serving Cream of Wheat to a little girl in a fancy frock. The caption of the ad designed to invoke images of "Little Miss Muffet" reads: "Little Miss Muffet, Sat on a Tuffet, Winsome, Charming and Sweet, *Our Fat Darkey* Spied Her, and Put Down Beside Her, A Luncheon of Good CREAM OF WHEAT" (emphasis added).[14] These advertisements reinforced white discourses of social control by showing African Americans serving white children, while the images of the Cream of Wheat chef further emasculated black males by having them take on the traditionally feminine role of a domestic servant. Not only does the caption refer to the chef as "Our Fat Darkey," using the word "our" to suggest whites' possession of African American males, but this image of a "fat" black man dressed in a cook's outfit and holding utensils while happily serving a white child is reminiscent of the caricature of the "Mammy" who devotedly cares for white children.

Historians of imperialism explore how the production and consumption of race in commodity cultures reinforced social realities and justified colonial control.[15] The languages and images created by and spread through mass media advertising share similarities with imperial discourses that conceptualized and labeled dark-skinned peoples as "Others." In the colonial context, advertisers relied on the frequent association in the British Empire of dirt and Africans to degrade blackness and promote the interest of Western, white constructions of race.[16] Just as European advertisements offered empires a way to commodify and consume their colonial subjects, American advertisements presented whites with images of their superiority over African Americans that justified white dominance. The American South participated in this discourse as both a colony and an imperial power. The North's modernization and evolution into a strong industrial society consigned the South to an almost colonial status within the nation.[17] Yet, the white South also functioned like an imperial power, attempting to colonize and control African Americans.

Common themes are identifiable in these colonial discourses and in American advertisements. Two Pears' Soap advertisements, one British and one American, illustrate the similarities between the rhetoric of imperialistic control and that of American racial domination. The first image, from the 1899 *Ladies' Home Journal,* shows a white girl, whose hat, stockings, and ruffled dress identify her as middle class, speaking with an African American child. Her attractive appearance seems intended to suggest that this white girl uses soap daily. Taught that soap removes filth, the white girl is puzzled as to why the African American girl would be unclean, asking, "Oh! Why *don't* you use Pears' Soap?"[18] A similar British 1903 Pears' Soap advertisement shows a white child washing clean a black child, but the African child's face remains black.[19] Although these advertisements are directed to different audiences, the impact of both rests on the white viewer's understanding that blackness, unlike dirt, is permanent. The black child in the picture can never be "pure" because she can never be white. These advertisements served to represent racial and gender roles not only for African Americans but also for white females by depicting them as responsible for upholding society by maintaining their prescribed social roles.

By the 1920s, most Americans' lives included the daily use of soap, and advertisements for hygiene products in particular offer a clear rhetoric about social control, race, and gender. Advertisers primarily targeted women, for females purchased from 80 to 85 percent of household goods.[20] Advertisements displayed white females shouldering the burden of "cleaning up" civilization, offering solutions to both household and social problems by utilizing sanitation products as the symbol of an enlightened and successful white civilization.[21] While American advertisers employed this idea of women wiping away the dirt of society, for white southerners the connection between cleanliness and purity resonated in a specific way. The continuation of white supremacy required white female sexual purity, as white women had a duty to keep themselves both physically free from dirt and sexually free from blackness. In an 1898 advertisement for Fairy Soap, two girls, one white and one black, offer a study in contrasts (see page 68).[22] The African American girl, with her bare feet, unadorned dress with a ragged hemline, and torn waistband, appears unkempt, while the white girl standing next to her appears unsoiled in a ruffled gingham dress. As the white girl approaches the African American child squarely, the black child is looking at the white girl out of the corner of her eye, avoiding direct contact. The image as a whole connects blackness with poverty and dirt. The caption, "Why doesn't your Mamma wash you with Fairy Soap?" reinforces the idea that racial inferiority is permanent, as well as emphasizing the roles that hygiene and mothers play in this cultural process.

Soap advertisements repeatedly drew on the image of the young, well-dressed white girl to depict wholesomeness and cleanliness. One Ivory Soap advertisement from 1932 shows a happy white baby girl immersed in a bath. As an infant, this white female is the ultimate representation of virtue, and her placement in a bath reflects her physical pureness. The copy of the advertisement notes, "A girl can't start out too young doing right by her complexion!" Moreover, "only a clean complexion has a chance to be beautiful."[23] This image of innocence reminded white southern women to retain their childlike virtue, suggesting that only a clean, or pure, white woman could meet white society's expectations for beauty. In addition to print advertisements, Ivory Soap made use of a sales jingle that also connected racial purity with hope for the future. Sung to the tune of "Sweet Adeline," the lyrics note, "Sweet Ivory soap, you are the dope / You make me clean, just like scourine / I love you so, like Sapolio. / You're the idol of my bath, Sweet Ivory soap." At the end of the song, a tenor echoes, "My only hope!"[24] In the South, this advertisement campaign about being clean, targeted at young women, would conjure up additional meanings of racial purity and social acceptability.

Fairy Soap advertisement, 1898. Courtesy of the Warshaw Collection of Business Americana—Soap, Archives Center, National Museum of American History, Smithsonian Institution.

American images of blacks permeated advertisements for many products in the domestic sphere, including baking products, appliances, food, and cleaning supplies. These advertisements often fetishized the black body. Anne McClintock defines a fetish as embodying "crises in social value" or a "social contradiction," and in the system of southern segregation, the black body became a focal point of a race-based society.[25] Images that displayed distorted black bodies for white enjoyment allowed whites to reenact their social power over African Americans. This occurred in the antebellum South when white plantation owners compelled slaves to fiddle, dance, or otherwise entertain them, and in doing so, reaffirmed the slaves' submission. These spectacles are part of what Saidiya Hartman terms "Negro Enjoyment," and they provide a terrifying example of everyday domination.[26] In the New South, whites were prohibited from owning African Americans as a validation of white power, but advertisements allowed a form of this practice to continue by displaying African American bodies in ways that allowed gazing white consumers to reaffirm their own superiority on a daily basis.

Although advertisers portrayed black men in a variety of emasculating ways, fetishism over black bodies often revolved around African American women, limited in popular culture to the "Mammy" figure. The "Mammy" representation most clearly offered white southerners a way to affirm control over black bodies. After the Civil War, white families who desired the services of black women as domestic workers had to employ them. The "Mammy" image assuaged white southerners' feelings of loss of control by recalling slavery and the absolute power white southerners had once exerted over black female bodies. Representations of the "Mammy" evoked the vision of an African American woman who labored not for money, but out of a benevolent love for her white family.[27] The physical depictions of "Mammies" in advertisements also reaffirmed white authority by portraying the black female body with exaggerated physical characteristics.

An advertising card for Czar baking powder drew on both the "Mammy" figure and the stereotypical "pickaninny" image.[28] In this advertisement, the illustrator has drawn both of the figures with exaggerated noses, ears, and lips. Together the black woman and the youth gape in amazement (and perhaps greed) at the enormous loaf of bread created by using this product. A campaign for Arm & Hammer baking soda drew upon similar imagery. These cards show a "before" and an "after" image of the product's rising power (see page 70). In the "before" image, a large black "Mammy" and a small naked "pickaninny" prepare for a bath when a cat jumps atop a baking

"Now, 'Zekiál, chile, stan' right in dar,
I'll wash you clean an' curl yo' ha'r,
But I tell you chile 'f you don' take care,
Yo'll feel yo' mammy's hand."

"My sakes aiwe, what noise was dat,
Git down from dar, you durned ole cat,
Oh! Lord! she clean done gone upsat,
Dat ARM & HAMMER BRAND."

Arm & Hammer baking soda advertisement. Courtesy of the Warshaw Collection of Business Americana—Baking Soda, Archives Center, National Museum of American History, Smithsonian Institution.

soda box. The caption, in heavy dialect, confirms the female figure's identity as a "Mammy" figure: "But I tell you chile 'f you don' take care, Yo'll feel yo' mammy's hand."[29] Both African Americans' features are monkeylike, with large white lips and eyes, reminiscent of blackface minstrelsy. In the "after" image, the startled cat has jumped off the ledge, knocking the powder into the bath. The rising suds reveal Mammy's ample breast, while the black child has little protection against his nakedness.[30] His unclothed body is the center of the image, where the whiteness of the rising bubbles contrasts sharply with his dark features. The nakedness and physical distortion of African Americans' bodies within these advertisements encouraged the white audience to enjoy gazing at the black body for both its entertainment value and the sense of racial domination it supplied. In fetishizing black bodies, white southerners sought to displace their social anxieties. As the nostalgic fantasy of passive, deferential, and controllable African Americans increasingly clashed with the reality of African American resistance to whites' social control, exaggerating African Americans' physical features, often to the extent of making them subhuman, offered white viewers a chance to enjoy African Americans' inferiority and their own race-based power.

While using caricatures of blacks as entertainment allowed whites to express or imagine their domination, it also degraded African Americans, suggesting the acceptability of violence against blacks. The portrayal of the smiling white boy whipping the "Uncle Tom" in the Cream of Wheat advertisement reflects the larger desire of white southern society to reenact that power relationship. For white southerners, these advertisements mirrored their sense that the enforcement of white supremacy often required physical brutality. Several advertisers centered their campaigns on violence to black bodies, usually those of males. A series of placards for Gold Medal baking powder portray a young black male in striped pants, tattered clothes, and bare feet, with exaggerated facial features including oversized lips and ears. In a series of images, animals attack the boy: on one card, a lobster bites his toes; on a second one, a muskrat nips at his behind (see page 72); and on a third, a fox chases the terrified youth away. On each of the cards, the African American carries a heavy box on his back that proclaims Gold Medal baking powder to be "the best."[31] The success of the advertisement requires that a white audience would find this violence humorous and enjoyable.[32]

Other advertisements took physical attacks against black males even further, actively dismembering their bodies and literally reducing them to objects. A two-scene fold-over H. Sears & Co. Fine Cutlery advertisement for a pocketknife executes a black man for white male entertainment. In the first image, the smiling African American man is well-dressed, if ill-fittingly, in a white, wide-collared shirt and black pants. He is, the copy exclaims, thrilled with his purchase of a pocketknife: "This darkey never was before / So happy in his life / He bought a 'Henry Sears & Son / Well known, new Pocket Knife / Then homeward hied with gleesome pride / with joy almost exploded" (see page 73). Below the copy, the man, excited by his acquisition, pulls the knife halfway open and positions his head between the blade and handle. A curious dog looks on from the side. As one might predict, in the second scene the blade snaps shut. The man's headless body, with arms spread in surprise, occupies the background while his severed head rests in the foreground. The copy explains: "The Knife shut up / His head dropped

Gold Medal baking powder advertisement. Courtesy of the Warshaw Collection of Business Americana—Baking Powders, Archives Center, National Museum of American History, Smithsonian Institution.

Henry Sears & Son Cutlery advertisement. Courtesy of the Warshaw Collection of Business Americana—Cutlery, Archives Center, National Museum of American History, Smithsonian Institution.

off, / He did'nt know twas loaded."[33] This violent imagery depicting the dismemberment of a black body in an advertisement directed at white men demonstrates how racialized violence was used to sell products. Further, the copy mocks the black man for not knowing how to use the knife properly. The joke rests on African American ignorance, suggesting that the black man failed to understand a knife could be spring-loaded, or alternatively, that he thought the knife, like a gun, required loading. The humor inherent in African Americans unsuccessfully trying to imitate whites is a theme found in many advertisements and functioned to downplay white anxiety about an equalizing marketplace. Even if African Americans could afford these middle-class products, such advertisements suggest, blacks could never truly reproduce white behaviors.[34] Such images entertain whites by portraying African Americans as unable to perform the most basic tasks, such as using soap or a knife properly. The H. Sears & Co. advertisement dismisses black manhood as a physical threat—how menacing is a black man who cannot even use a pocketknife?

Mass culture offered white southerners an alternative way to dominate African Americans. Through perpetuating discourses about African Americans' need of civilization as seen by a lack of hygiene; demeaning black bodies through fetishism; and presenting physical violence against blacks as entertaining, mass advertising worked to reduce African Americans to inhuman caricatures. Controllable mass-produced images of African Americans represented southern whites' conceptions of ideal race relations, and the degrading stereotypes these images contained of passive, unintelligent African Americans reinforced southern whites' sense of superiority and tightened their control of the public sphere.

Enacting Race

As southern white children matured, their parents encouraged them to be active participants in their own socialization. Most white children grew up as part of a public and interactive communal culture, which was reflected in the toys they played with as well in their participation in schoolyard games, community pageants, and southern parent-organized youth groups such as the children's Ku Klux Klan or the Children of the Confederacy. White children were encouraged to actualize white supremacy through performances focused on reproducing the idealized model taught to them in their homes, observed in their school texts, and reflected in consumer culture.

Children's play is the opposite of work. Although scholars identify various functions that play serves for children, most agree that childhood amusements are a form of socialization into adult behaviors. Plato philosophically considered play the ideal way to socialize free citizens into society.[35] In the seventeenth century, the Enlightenment philosopher John Locke discussed recreation for children as a site where parents could encourage the acquisition of social virtues. He suggested that parents consider play a business task for their child and require children to play every day.[36] Locke wrote that parents should not provide toys, but that children should create their own amusements. Like Plato, Locke ultimately promoted play for the development of "good and useful habits" in the next generation of citizens.[37] In the newly industrialized twentieth-century society, play continued to serve social purposes.[38]

By the close of the nineteenth century, families had become smaller, parents were more focused on child rearing, more children attended school, and fewer labored in factories. Boys, especially, gained playtime, as those between the ages of fourteen and eighteen spent only 40 percent of their time toiling in 1930, down from 61 percent in 1890.[39] After the Civil War, industrialization changed toy manufacturing, with newer, cheaper materials allowing the production of inexpensive toys.[40] By the twentieth century, children were taking advantage of their longer playtimes to enjoy their mass-produced toys. Advertisers, however, marketed to parents, not children, as nineteenth-century youth did not yet have the pocket money to purchase their own toys.[41] Catalogs and children's magazines from the late 1800s, therefore, advertised items to parents that reflected the lessons adults would find appropriate for their child's social class, race, age, and gender.[42]

Much like southern history books, many toys portrayed African Americans as entertainment, reinforcing the idea that African Americans enjoyed subserviently performing for whites. In 1921, the Sears, Roebuck and Company catalog, which generally exemplified mainstream American culture, advertised the "Famous Alabama Coon Jigger" toy, described as "a realistic dancing negro who goes through the movements of a lively jig. Very amusing and fascinating."[43] This catalog description and others like it show a preoccupation with convincing the audience of the realism and authenticity of the black bodies portrayed by toys. A year later, the Sears, Roebuck and Company catalog included another dancing amusement for white children, the "Colored Minstrel Boys, Oh, What Music!" toy. This product pictured "two coons with the exaggerated head and foot movement of real darkies."[44] Even the language describing these toys demonstrated the manufacturers' awareness of the mainstream white culture's stereotypes of blacks and the desire of whites for authenticity in their idealized vision of race relations.

The mass production of these items reveals their appeal to the values and culture of a national audience. These toys reflected the racial beliefs of the dominant group at the turn of the twentieth century—whites. Toys, as an indication of prevailing ideals, legitimized these racialized images of African Americans and created a feeling of superiority for the white consumer or owner.[45] These products resonated distinctly with white southerners, who interpreted these toys not as historical nostalgia, but as reflective of a desired social reality. The toy "Colorful Darky Dancer Does a Lifelike Buck and Wing" encouraged children to "wind up the spring and start him off," with its description noting that "this happy darky just can't keep from dancing! He seems to like it too."[46] The "Charleston Trio," another windup toy, included a dog that expressed its enjoyment of the music produced by the black musicians, "Charleston Charlie dances while the small negro fiddles and the animal nods his approval."[47] In playing with these toys, white children reenacted the roles of slave masters who forced African Americans to perform for whites' enjoyment, a recital, the copy reassured its readers, that blacks enjoyed. As Patricia Turner notes, manufacturers who created items with the images of African American stereotypes such as "Coon," "Sambo," and "Mammy" devised a way for consumers to continue to buy and sell African Americans, keeping the nostalgia of slavery alive.[48] In marketing images of African Americans, manufacturers allowed whites to consume, and therefore control, blackness by commodifying black bodies in products. These entertainments also kept the power relationships of slavery alive, for unlike the images in advertisements, mass-produced toys were three-dimensional objects with stereotypical racial characteristics, which allowed white children to physically possess, and interact with, representations of African Americans.

After 1920, when advertisers began to target children as consumers, they did so primarily based on gender, with toys for boys emphasizing technology and the values of competition. Mechanical toys encouraged male dominance and rewarded aggression, placing white boys in control of stereotypical figurines of black bodies. One toy, a mechanical bank, "Always Did 'Spise a Mule," rewarded the saver by bucking off the rider, a caricature of an African American with grotesque features. This toy required that the child instigate the pretend violence and thus encouraged racial violence as entertainment.[49] Amusements for boys often followed the theme of finding humor in the harming of African American bodies. In 1936, the Sears, Roebuck and Company catalog introduced the "Chicken Snatcher." Described as "one of the new, most novel toys of the year," it included a spring-action motor that caused a "scared looking negro" to dance with "a chicken dangling in his hand and a dog hanging on the seat of his pants." The catalog description concluded that this was a "Very funny toy which will delight the kiddies."[50] The windup feature of the toy allowed the violence to occur repeatedly so the viewer could savor the humor of a dog attacking a black body and exercise control over the replicated body of an African American.

Physical games encouraged white boys to harm black targets. "Dump the Nigger" and "Coon Dip," both carnival dunk-tank amusements, required participants to hurl projectiles at live African Americans or painted facsimile targets. Another popular children's entertainment, "Bean-em," encouraged children to fling beanbag targets at cartoonish African American faces with exaggerated features. Both games, the objective of which was to hit an African American, rewarded racialized physical abuse. Similar games required male aggression against African American targets with guns, such as the "Little Darky Shooting Gallery," advertised in the 1914 Butler Brothers catalog, which contained cardboard cutouts of stereotypical African Americans for target practice, including one depicting a "Mammy" figure.[51] These pursuits promoted violence against black bodies and fostered competitive male physicality. In 1929, the Sears, Roebuck and Company catalog advertised the game "Can You Tip the Bell Boy?" which required boys to shoot wooden balls at a cutout representing an African American bellboy. This activity contained a "double score feature so all can have real fun."[52] A similar game produced by Parker Brothers, "Sambo Five Pins," consisted of a bowling set with black faces on the pins; included within the game's packaging was the story of Sambo, "a good ole Southern Darky." The story was intended to help white children connect the caricatured images of blacks in advertisements and toys to images in children's fiction and textbooks.[53]

While the toys provided for boys encouraged physical and even violent play, toys for girls remained unchanged, with dolls as the primary plaything throughout the late nineteenth and early twentieth centuries.[54] In the antebellum period, dolls developed girls' domestic skills, and, in true Lockean fashion, girls made their own playthings.[55] Adults expected girls to use dolls to imitate adult females' social rituals, and this formalized play trained girls in their future domestic roles.[56] After the Civil War, although society continued to consider dolls as training aids for future wives and mothers, dolls began to be marketed differently. By the early 1900s, manufacturers were promoting their dolls as being true to life, with manufacturers likely expecting that white girls would mimic the etiquette required of white "ladies" and purchase the accoutrements needed to "play house" and host tea parties.[57] In this vein, manufacturers developed a second type of doll, the African American servant doll. Advertisers assured readers that the black doll would assist the white mistress doll in her domestic duties.[58] The 1924 Sears, Roebuck and Company catalog introduced the "Aunt Jemima Doll with Ma-Ma voice." This doll, the catalog declared, would "delight" girls who could pretend the "Aunt Jemima doll is making delicious pancakes or taking care of other dollies." Dressed in a "costume of floral pattern cotton material with large white apron and collar; also red bandanna and Aunt Jemima label," this doll represented the "Mammy" caricature.[59] The idea that a girl would own a black doll in order to have it care for her white dolls reflects the continuity of antebellum ideals for white females, who depended on receiving the benefit of subservient blacks' domestic labor. Although African American dolls were widely introduced, the monetary and collectable value of African American dolls remained low until the late twentieth century. *The Standard Antique Doll Identification and Value Guide* lists values for dolls manufactured between 1700 and 1935, yet it contains only one entry for a "Negro" doll. This doll, listed as being produced in 1885 and clothed only in a grass skirt, is the one wearing the least amount of clothing in the entire catalog.[60] Playthings that employed racial stereotypes, such as subservient dolls and violent mechanical toys, remained in circulation into the mid-twentieth century, when cartoon characters began to replace the caricatures so prevalent at the turn of the twentieth century. Mickey Mouse and his associates replaced "Coon Jiggers," and American manufacturers began to step away from overtly racialized toys.[61]

Games and playground amusements also make up the informal culture of play. Jump-rope chants and schoolyard verses are oral traditions with local or regional variations. The chants, or doggerels, that children recite fall into two categories: gibberish rhymes and descriptive stories.[62] References in these chants to African Americans are uniquely American and often reflect local cultures.[63] Perhaps the best-known of these chants, documented in one variation or another in every state, is "Eney, meeny, miny, mo, Catch a nigger by the toe! If he hollers let him go! Eney, meeny, miny, mo."[64] Rhymes traveled from child to child, school to school, and region to region and were often changed at each new location.[65] This resulted in variations of the same rhyme in different locales; for example, one southern version rhymed: "Eney, meeny, miny, mo, Catch a darky by the toe. If he hollers, make him pay, fifty dollars every day."[66]

Many of lyrics from schoolyard games that reference African Americans utilized the stereotypes found in southern educational literature and toys. Southern children's rhymes included such derogatory lines such as: "Did you ever, ever, ever, In your life, life, life, See a nigger, nigger, nigger, Kiss his wife, wife, wife?"[67] There is also the descriptive, "Nigger, Nigger, never die, Black face and shiny eye, Kinky hair and crooked toes, That's the way the nigger goes," which details the physical exaggerations found in representations of blacks in mainstream white culture.[68] The rhyme, "Teacher, Teacher, don't whip me; Was that nigger behind the tree; He stole peaches, I stole none," draws on the stereotype of the thieving African American.[69] Jump-rope rhymes often contain a "mini-drama," such as, "Some people say that niggers don't steal, I caught some in my corn meal." Other rhymes reinforced African Americans' servile status. One jump-rope counting rhyme claimed: "I know something I shan't tell, Three little niggers in a peanut shell; One can sing and one can dance, And one can make a pair of pants. O-U-T spells out goes she."[70] These rhymes portray African Americans as thieves, servants, or entertainment for whites. In contrast to the portrayal of African Americans in the chants, the white is presented as blameless, a victim who does not deserve punishment. Like the images in advertisements and toys, some rhymes contain descriptions of violence against African Americans, such as "Boil Black blood of big black man; Boilika, bublika, Ku Klux Klan!"[71] Another rhyme refers to the violent practice of lynching, beginning "Nigger on the woodpile, Don't you hear him hollar?"[72] These informal chants strengthened the larger social beliefs about the relative positions of southern whites and African Americans as well as the necessity of using violence to enforce these roles if required.

Community Culture

Playacting with toys helped white children across the nation to imagine themselves as racially superior, but, besides pretending with toys or games, southern children also engaged in activities such as plays and youth organizations that encouraged them to fantasize about dominating black bodies. Adults organized and sanctioned these activities, using role-playing and social rituals to prepare children to uphold their future gender and racial roles. White southern children could act out both white and black roles in plays, reinforcing their own position against the stereotypical images of African Americans. Even today, children are encouraged to perform in plays as it allows them to enact different roles and characters.[73] The University of North Carolina Extension Bulletin in 1925 published a booklet of historical pageants of North Carolina for youths, the *Children of Old Carolina,* by Ethel Theodora Rockwell. Information on royalties revealed the play's intended use in elementary classrooms, for any school in North Carolina wishing to perform the play was obliged to send ten dollars for each performance, while those outside North Carolina had to pay twenty-five dollars. The cast of *Children of Old Carolina* included a group of "colored" characters who were played by children, presumably in blackface. When the character of a "negro boy," playing a lively tune on a banjo, enters, the "colored children carrying baskets and bags of cotton" join him onstage singing, "Dis cott'n want a-pickin' so bad."[74] When they reach center stage, the group puts down their burdens and "begin[s] to sing, pat juba, and dance" the "Cotton Dance Song." The lyrics focus on the joy of picking cotton; "A'll pick a hundred by an' by, Way down- in de cot'n fiel'." In its depiction of a contest to see who could pick the most cotton, the play demonstrates the enthusiasm slaves purportedly possessed for this activity: "Jim he bet me a tater pie, Way down- in de cot'n fiel', Dat he could pick mo' cott'n dan I."[75] The play encourages children to act out the revised history of an Old South populated by happy African American slaves who cannot wait to pick cotton.

The State of Alabama also created a play to encourage elementary students to act out the history of great white men that they learned in their textbooks. The third in a series of children's dramas about statehood published in 1919, *How Alabama Became a State* included costume direc- tives for the character Lucy, "A Negro Mammy," which instructed the actor to wear "a dark blue dress, a big white apron," and to be "turbaned with a red bandanna handkerchief." She must also "be blacked to represent a real negro slave woman."[76] Mammy, whose lines are in heavy dialect, begins the play on her knees rolling up her bed, while her "lil'le honey" cries nearby. As the play unfolds, Mary, a character from North Carolina, describes her journey to Alabama. She narrates how "the slaves worked and had such fun around the camp fires at night."[77] All of the young female characters in the play order their "Mammies" around, taking on the role of plantation mistress, while the boys act out the role of adult men by pledging to help the great state of Alabama.

White southern youth continued to act out gendered and racial roles in a dramatic way through high school and into college. Recommended in the approved book list for southern secondary school teachers and dramatic coaches, *Easily Staged Plays for Boys* contained the script *The Scary Ape*. The introductory notes describe Tom, the main African American character, as "a very black Negro butler." Tom has no last name, which is common for African American characters. Throughout the play, Tom speaks in heavy dialect, and various whites scold him for his lazy ways. The humor of the play centers on Tom's simplistic understanding of the world. The similarity, in name, appearance, and actions between Tom and an escaped ape named Tom-Tom offers most of the play's humor. The house's master, Mr. Thom, observes that the monkey treats Tom like a brother, and that the butler resembles Tom-Tom the ape "a great deal."[78] This may be because the direc- tions for Tom's and the ape's makeup are very similar; both characters are to wear dark paint on their faces with large light circles marked around the lips and eyes, similar to the makeup applied in blackface minstrelsy. The end of the story reveals Tom-Tom the ape to be a female, and she devotes herself to Tom. Tom then offers Mr. Thom to be "yo' slab fo' life ef yo' gits me ob dis heah 'tachment" and promises not to steal any more gin.[79] The play concludes with Tom offering himself as a lifetime slave, creating a parallel between sharecropping and slavery and suggesting that black subservience and white ownership should occur in practice, if not legally.

Churches also sponsored children's plays to promote fellowship, and like their counterparts in southern schools, they chose stories that modeled ideal behaviors for whites. The overall message of church plays, as in racialized advertisements, was that the uncivilized nature of African Americans justified white benevolence, linking white morality to the control of African American bodies. As studies on morality demonstrate, sets of common ethics transcend spiritual divisions, and in the Jim Crow South, the aspiration of keeping whiteness separate from blackness overcame denominational differences.[80] *Phunology: A Collection of Tried and Proved Plans for Play, Fellowship, and Profit* published in Nashville for southern Sunday schools, suggested a list of plays that included *Mirandy's Minstrels, The Thread of Destiny,* and *Hunker's Corner* as suitable for children to put on for their church.[81] In addition to being popular selections, these plays all contain white and African American characters that represent the power relations of segregation. Although it is unclear if the children performed all of these plays in blackface, the depictions of African American males within these plays are consistent with those found in minstrel performances.[82] These representations of black bodies paraded for whites' pleasure offered the audience a way to imagine themselves dominating black bodies.[83]

Hunkers' Corners: An Entertainment in Three Scenes included in its cast of characters Tom, the "colored assistant." The directions for the opening scene introduce Tom as a "Colored boy lazily sweeping." He provides the comic relief in the story, as the main characters repeatedly remark upon Tom's slothfulness, and his lack of basic knowledge is the punch line for many jokes. He speaks in dialect punctuated by yawns that represent his laziness: "Mistah Hunkahs, ef dem stunnin' young ladies boadin' down to de Cohnahs takes it into dey haids to come to de sto' dis yere day, d'ye reckon yer kin sar' me to hol' dey hoss and shoo de pesky flies off? [Yawns and stretches]." Bill Hunkers, who owns the store at which Tom works, replies, "You lazy nigger, you're forever studyin' up some scheme to get shot o' work."[84] *Hunker's*

Corners not only portrays Tom as ignorant and lazy, but Bill Hunker, the store's white owner, keeps Tom in his place for Tom's own good by giving him a "hard time," a phrase with a violent undertone.

The Thread of Destiny, a pro-Confederate play set during the Civil War, tells a story about a plantation that "goes to waste" when only a few "faithful negroes remain with the women."[85] Those remaining loyal slaves are Uncle Billy and Mammy Dinah. Mammy Dinah, described as "A Faithful Servitor," is "always displaying her loyalty to the family she serves and her devotion to their cause." She is "always cheerful in the midst of misfortune" and wears "the conventional servant costume—calico dress, white apron, and red bandannas around neck and head." The author characterizes Uncle Billy as an "Uncle Tom," as seen by his "absolute devotion to his master and his master's family; unselfish in his service to them." Uncle Billy wears "baggy trousers, old frock coat and colored vest; carries red bandanna."[86] Similar characters pepper *Mirandy's Minstrels,* which suggests "blacking" performers' faces and hands and practicing delivering lines in dialect.[87] These descriptions further reinforced the reenactment of power relations that these plays offered. The plays replicated the power relationships of slavery when whites compelled slaves to perform for them and allowed white youth to playact the power of their whiteness. As children performing in plays portrayed African Americans as comical, entertaining, and loyal, they participated in a form of everyday racial domination.[88] As a popular form of entertainment, plays made instruction in white supremacy more dramatic and real for white southern children, drawing on cultural images of African Americans as uncivilized and in need of white control. This role-playing, like other activities, allowed youth to perform nostalgic racial roles.

Community Youth Groups

As southern society modernized, parents were concerned that a generation experiencing great social change might be less able or inclined to maintain white supremacy.[89] The Ku Klux Klan and the Children of the Confederacy were the most prominent youth organizations that emerged in the New South; both were dedicated to preserving white supremacy. In 1915, the Ku Klux Klan's Invisible Empire was reborn out a fear that racial egalitarianism would result from African Americans' experiences as soldiers in World War I. This fear was pushed to the forefront by D. W. Griffith's 1915 movie *The Birth of a Nation.* The core values of the faction, founded in 1868, remained intact, for the Klan continued to support white-supremacist policies and employed violence to terrorize African Americans, but in its second incarnation, the Klan adapted and expanded its messages in response to changing times. The reborn Klan, with a new national focus, added an anti-Catholic, anti-immigrant agenda to its anti–African American stances. Despite the Klan's new national focus, though, its stronghold remained the South.

In 1915, as part of the Klan's reemergence, women were recognized through the formation of the Women's Ku Klux Klan (WKKK). Although the WKKK was implemented as independent from the men's group, WKKK members bound themselves to the Klan's ideals.[90] Their oath reflected members' goals to create white, Protestant, Anglo-Saxon dominance: "I, the undersigned, a true and loyal citizen of the United States of America, being a white woman of sound mind and a believer in the tenets of the Christian religion and the principles of 'pure Americanism,' do most respectfully apply for affiliation in the Ladies of the Invisible Empire."[91] As Klanswomen, members marched in parades, organized community events, and recruited new Klan members.[92] As part of their quest for members, the WKKK began a "cradle roll," enlisting white youth from birth through the age of twelve into their auxiliary. At the child's dedication, a Klanswoman presented each baby with a Bible.[93]

Katharine Du Pre Lumpkin's parents enrolled her in the children's Ku Klux Klan. She recalled, "We were happy in it for the aid and the blessing it won from our adults." Seen as an "offspring of our warm Southern patriotism," the group held secret meetings and made Klan costumes, complete with hoods and masks. Lumpkin remembered making her robes from old sheets and the crosses with cheesecloth.[94] The renowned movie director D. W. Griffith also reminisced about his mother making KKK robes during his youth, and about the sense of historical duty his parents imparted to him. In an interview he recalled, "you heard your father tell about fighting day after day [in the Civil War], night after night, and having nothing to eat but parched corn, and about your mother staying up night after night sewing robes for the Klan."[95] Not all children viewed their participation in the group solely as fulfilling their responsibilities to their parents or heritage. One girl considered the group social entertainment: "It was just something to do and somewhere to go and nice little cookies and tea or cookies and Kool-Aid or something." The group utilized the secrecy of the society to promote the young children's feelings of privilege, as she recalled: "You knew very much it was a secret." This mystery is what "was fun" about the club.[96]

Although recalled fondly by southern youth as a social organization, the children's Klan had serious functions that included discussing imaginary violence against African Americans. Lumpkin remembered that "a chief topic of business when ceremonies had ended was the planning of pretend punitive expeditions against mythical recalcitrant Negroes." The significance of these conversations, however, often "went far beyond pretense." Lumpkin concluded that her participation was a significant matter for "it was truly a serious game, and in a sense we were serious children bent on our ideals."[97]

As white children began to outgrow the children's KKK, the Klan undertook to continue white children's education into their teenaged years. In 1923, the Ku Klux Klan voted to create two auxiliaries, the Junior Ku Klux Klan for adolescent boys, and the Tri-K-Klub for teenaged girls. As a member of the Tri-K-Klub, under the umbrella of the WKKK, girls learned the messages of the Klan and the skills required for marriage and motherhood. The WKKK upheld the overall goal "of all Klan bodies" to preserve America as "a great, free, Protestant country," keeping the United States under "the control of the White, American born, Anglo-Saxon leadership."[98] Told to picture themselves as wives and mothers, girls repeatedly read that their actions would affect the future of white America: "The hope of the next generation lies within your hand, young women. You are the mothers of tomorrow. You are the wives of tomorrow. You are the voters and the Christian women of tomorrow. You must be right in your thinking if conditions are to be kept secure for the traditions of a great democracy."[99]

The WKKK disseminated the messages of the Tri-K through pamphlet lesson books aimed at young women. In these materials, each letter of "Tri-K-Klub" was identified as relating to a quality or behavior that members of the Tri-K-Klub should cultivate: Trust, Races, Influence, Knowledge, Kindling, Leadership, Unity, and Brains-brawn-breadth. Each of these terms was featured in a corresponding pamphlet explicating the related behavior expected of a Tri-K member in society. In the *RACES* pamphlet, the authors presented the three major race problems affecting America: southeastern European immigrants, Catholics, and, of course, African Americans. Using rhetoric similar to that presented in textbooks justifying slavery, the anti-immigrant discussion noted the predisposition for some nonwhites to work, eat, and live in a specific manner. One described a southern European immigrant who endangered whites because of his "racial training." Although he had come to America, his way of life remained unchanged: "He can live on garlic and a little cheap meat. He was never used to more than that, so why does he want it here?" The section ends by expressing fear for the future, for his wife (if he has one) "will keep the little dingy hut for him and they will raise from three to five times the number of babies the Anglo-Saxon mothers will raise."[100] This declaration reiterates the text's core message to white girls: they must protect the future of white America by upholding Protestant, Anglo-Saxon values through marriage to a white man and rearing "a family for God."[101] As for Catholics, "a little study of the Mexican situation will forever put you on guard against Catholic influences."[102]

The Tri-K-Klub employed little subtlety in teaching about African Americans: "The Klans believe in white supremacy. . . . We teach this, practice this and urge at all times no entangling alliances with the negro race." The central message was that white girls should remove themselves from all contact with blacks, a passive way of preserving white supremacy. The phrase "entangling alliances" contains an undertone suggestive of sexual contact between white girls and black males. The message that white girls must never consider a liaison with an African American man is explicit in the *RACES* pamphlet, which justified black and white separation in the conclusion: "The Klans have always considered the problem of the negro race, one worthy most careful consideration [*sic*]" after the Emancipation Proclamation freed "a great band of negroes who did not know the first thing about caring for themselves, and many of whom did not want to be free."[103] Beyond the instruction offered in these pamphlets, parades sponsored by the Klan offered a highly visible way to draw attention to the issue of racial purity and white womanhood. In their role as members of a Klan auxiliary, Tri-K girls often marched in parades to show support of their male counterparts. In one parade, pretty, young white girls waved to the crowds on a float bearing the banner "Miss 100 percent America."[104]

The next booklet in the series, *INFLUENCE,* focuses on how girls can attain the goals set by the Klan. As young women, they should be cheerful in order to gain the confidence of others, as well as energetic, helpful, and determined. For emphasis, the authors capitalized part of the following message: "DON'T HOPE TO GET ALONG WITHOUT TAKING SOME STRONG POSITIONS ON THE QUESTIONS OF THE DAY. This is why the Tri-K-Klub came into existence. That is why you are a member. That is why we are talking to you in this way. We need girls of determination, who are correctly informed, will not yield one step to the arguments and working of un-Americanism."[105] This meant that girls must keep themselves "free from even the suggestion of immodesty and wrong," for if they failed, the "womanhood of the nation tomorrow will suffer irreparable loss." Girls, the pamphlet demanded, "must be militantly and aggressively good."[106] The WKKK repeatedly stressed that white girls bore the responsibility for the future of white supremacy, which they could accomplish by keeping themselves racially clean through sexual purity: "We would not be in any sense irreverent in telling you again that the Tri-K-Klub exists to deliberately destroy many evil influences that are running riot in America. We expect you to plan as to how you can overthrow such evil influences."[107]

While the Tri-K focused on social lessons and appearance, male members of the Junior Klan learned masculinity through action and tradition. Established in 1924, the Junior Klan sought to "aid and assist in promoting and fostering the precepts and principles of the Knights of the Ku Klux Klan" for boys between the ages of twelve and eighteen.[108] Teenaged boys, in a mixture of patriotism, religion, and ritual, mimicked the actions of adult Klansmen, for the Junior Klan "was a preparation for the responsibilities of adult clannishness."[109] The Kloran, or the "sacred book" of the Junior Klan (whose "contents *must* be safeguarded and it's [sic] teachings respected"), detailed the group's opening and closing rituals, constitution, and by-laws.[110] The titles of officers in the Junior Klan reflected the medieval notions and depictions of honor found in the film *The Birth of a Nation*. The president, known as the Worthy Knight (and assisted by an Honorable Squire), oversaw his junior officers: the Worthy Captain, Worthy Lieutenant, and Worthy Counselor. Membership required the applicant be "a native-born, white, Gentile CHRISTIAN boy of good character" with parental consent and vouched for by two members of the Junior Klan.[111]

The opening ceremony, which was restricted to members, began with a ritual in which each boy whispered a password and gave a signal, followed by a salute. The Worthy Counselor then placed the Bible, open to the twelfth chapter of Ecclesiastes, on the center of the sacred altar. These verses of Ecclesiastes note that the young do not know of the hardships of the world ("in the days of thy youth, while the evil days come not" [12:1]) or the eventual end of the world ("Then shall the dust return to the earth as it was" [12:7]). This is followed by acknowledgment of God's judgment of all things ("For God shall bring every work into judgment, with every secret thing, whether it be good, or whether it be evil" [12:14]). These lines may have been chosen for use in the opening ceremony because they reflect the goals of the Junior Klan. Youth cannot remain ignorant, but instead must be prepared for the challenges they face. The Klan, like God, must secretly prepare to restore order. As future leaders, young men must stand firm "for God, the Holy Bible, the American Constitution, the American flag, and public schools."[112]

After all members were verified and the Bible placed on the altar, the opening ritual continued with members saying a devotional prayer, singing "America," and reciting the Pledge of Allegiance. The devotional prayer emphasized the masculine nature of the Junior Klan, asking God to "keep us in the bonds of fraternal union" and to "help us to understand that Honor is the crowning virtue of manhood." In addition to presenting manhood as related to honor, the devotional underscored loyalty, and Junior Klansmen prayed to "observe Klannish fidelity, one toward another, and a devoted loyalty to our great Organization." The prayer ended with, "God save our nation!"[113] The end of the meeting mirrored this lengthy opening ritual. During the closing ceremony, members saluted the flag, repeated the Pledge of Allegiance, recited the Lord's Prayer, and sang "Onward Christian Soldiers," reinforcing the idea that these teenage boys served a God-given cause. The meeting concluded with a call-and-response, as the Worthy Lieutenant recited, "I would have all Junior Klansmen remember that Honor is the crowning virtue of American manhood," and members responded, "On our honor as Junior Klansmen, we will heed well these lessons," repeating the connection between manhood, honor, and loyalty.[114] This emphasis on faithfulness was, of course, necessary for a secret organization. Failure to uphold the promise of the Junior Klan meant "Disgrace, Dishonor and Expulsion from the great American organization." Any major offense such as disloyalty to the Klan, country, or flag resulted "in *banishment forever* (emphasis in original)."[115]

The Junior Klan did not record the content of their meetings due to their confidential nature, yet the constitution and by-laws of the organization demonstrate the rituals and vision of ideal white manhood. These Klan documents reveal the gender differences between young men and women. The Tri-K encouraged girls to do their duty to uphold white supremacy in passive ways, through marriage and motherhood. Tri-K members' public activities, limited to marching in parades, exhibited white females as examples of public virtue, not active social agents. In contrast, the males in the Junior Klan were prepared, as the passage of Ecclesiastics suggested, to fight for their ideals, and the group's meetings centered on taking oaths and expressing allegiances, ceremonies similar to those that attend soldiers going off to battle.

Formed by adult men and women for their children, the Klan's auxiliaries created a space for white children from birth to adulthood to learn the rhetoric of white supremacy. Although the South was the stronghold of the re-created Klan, the group also addressed national issues, offering, for example, an anti-immigration platform attractive to many northerners and midwesterners. Another children's group organized to foster both white supremacy and southern patriotism, the Children of the Confederacy, emerged by the early twentieth century under the umbrella organization the United Daughters of the Confederacy (UDC). Founded by Caroline Douglas Meriwether Goodlett and Anna Davenport Raines in 1894, the UDC sought to keep "alive the sacred principles for which Southern men and boys fought so bravely."[116]

The UDC quickly became the most prevalent women's memorial association.[117] Within three years of its founding, it boasted 103 active chapters, and by 1905 its membership had risen to more than one hundred thousand.[118] The goals of this distinctly southern group focused on creating a social network, memorializing the war, maintaining a "truthful record of the noble and chivalric achievements" of their veterans, and teaching the next generation "a proper respect for and pride in the glorious war history."[119] Mary Nowlin justified her participation at the first chapter meeting in Lynchburg, Virginia, in June 1915, noting, "I am a Daughter of the Confederacy because I was born a Daughter of the Confederacy" with "a heritage so rich in honor and glory that it far surpasses any material wealth that could be mine." To Nowlin, the UDC represented the "continuance and furtherance of the true history of the South and the ideals of southern womanhood as embodied in its Constitution."[120]

One year after its inception, in 1896, the United Daughters of the Confederacy founded the Children of the Confederacy to teach children the truth about the "War Between the States." Formed in Georgia, the first chapter of the Children of the Confederacy began with fifteen members.[121] The object of the organization included uniting "the children and youth of the South in some work to aid and honor ex-Confederates and their descendents."[122] Membership consisted of southern children from birth to age eighteen whose ancestors had "honorably served the Confederate States of America."[123] Concerned about increasing membership numbers, at the 1909 convention, Cornelia B. Stone urged "greater activity in the organization. . . . For upon the training of these our boys and girls, our citizens and patriots of the future—depends the perpetuity of the organization."[124] This fear proved unfounded as the organization grew quickly; between 1924 and 1929, women organized 107 new chapters, and by 1929, the UDC convention reported children's membership to be 22,507.[125] This rapid growth showed the increased support for the Children of the Confederacy. Despite this growth, the association did not include every white in the South, and many failed to gain membership when they could not definitively prove their Confederate ancestry. Regardless, the UDC's influence through the Children of the Confederacy was widespread. Their preservation of southern culture and efforts to socialize southern youth into their crusade of glorifying the Confederacy helped to perpetuate sectional differences and prevent reconciliation between the North and South.[126] The Children of the Confederacy produced, through their memorialization of the Civil War, an image of southern society that had concrete political and social implications. Not only did this mythical depiction created by white women and children of the New South uphold contemporary white racial convictions, but it rewrote the history of the southern defeat in the Civil War period, creating the image of an independent and indomitable South.[127] The Children of the Confederacy still exists today, maintaining its mission through its sponsorship of essay contests and scholarships, and remains a component of their educational experience for many southern white youth.

Like the KKK's children groups, the UDC utilized the Children of the Confederacy to impart to the rising generations their own white-supremacist vision of the future. Although the UDC found a number of ways to educate white youth, including creating playing cards, games, reciting poetry, and plays, the typical way of teaching Confederate history remained catechisms.[128] At their meetings, after members had saluted the Confederate Flag and recited their creed, the ritual of the catechism began. The chapter leader asked a series of historical questions about the South. If a child knew the answer and was acknowledged by the leader, he or she stood and delivered the answer. A correct answer earned the youth three points. If none of the children knew the answer, the leader would say, "Books," a signal that the children were allowed to search for the answer, but for the reduced reward of one point.[129] Like the ceremony-heavy meetings of the Junior Klan, the ritualized meetings of the Children of the Confederacy provided a repetitive structure for white youth, teaching them a historical construct that glorified the antebellum South and slavery as representing the desirable and natural order of the world.

Although each chapter might write its own catechisms, the central theme was a racialized and romanticized nostalgia for the antebellum and Confederate South. One publication, written by Mildred Lewis Rutherford, contained a program for youth for every month of 1915. A twenty-five-dollar donation intended to further "the systematic study of Southern history by the children" funded the printing of one thousand copies of Rutherford's work.[130] February's session on secession began with the song "The Bonnie Blue Flag," which contained the lines: "Then here's to our Confederacy, strong are we and brave / Like patriots of old we'll fight our heritage to save / And rather than submit to shame, to die we would prefer." The refrain, "Hurrah! For Southern rights, hurrah!" reflects the nostalgia and idealization at the core of the beliefs promoted by the Children of the Confederacy.[131] After the song, the competition began with questions framed to elicit answers sympathetic to the white South. Questions included, "Was succession a rebellion?" and "Was the war fought to hold the slaves?" with the correct answer to both questions being a negative.[132] Another catechism, created by Cornelia Branch Stone from the Texas UDC, asked, "How were the slaves treated?" The correct answer, according to the students' text, was, "With great kindness and care in nearly all cases."[133] The issues of slavery and the treatment of slaves form the cornerstone of many auxiliary texts, emphasizing how both blacks and whites reaped benefits from slavery. Rutherford's auxiliary in July asked members to "describe the happy life of the slaves in the old Plantation" and to read an excerpt from the fictional and highly romanticized book *Diddie, Dumps, and Tot* to gain an understanding of life under slavery.[134] Such connections to fictional literature encouraged the creation of a dominant narrative that idealized black subservience as natural.

Some chapters' catechisms display the passion of their authors. The John Phifer Young Chapter of Children of the Confederacy in North Carolina offered an example of particularly zealous questions and responses, including, "Did we kill many Yankees?" with the answer, "Yes, thousands and thousands of them." To the modern reader, some of the questions and answers may seem humorous: "What reason did one Confederate soldier give for giving up? He said, 'we wore ourselves out whipping the Yankees.'" Other questions use repetition both to emphasize the answer and to excite the passions. The correct response to the question, "Were our Confederate Soldiers and our relatives who fought in the Confederate army traitors?" was a resounding "No! No! No!"[135] This requirement to affirm a southern version of historical knowledge, seen as necessary to counter the northern narrative of the Civil War—or, as materials for the Children of the Confederacy, termed it, the "War Between the States"—justified southern history as part of a larger just and glorious cause. As the Creed of the Children of the Confederacy noted, the youth of the South pledged "to study and teach the truths of history (one of the most important of which is, that the War Between the States was not a REBELLION, nor was its underlying cause to sustain slavery)."[136]

Adults' efforts to engage southern youth in imagining themselves as children on plantations or in answering trivia questions about the number of southern slaveholders who fought in the Civil War reflected the mission of the United Daughters of the Confederacy to teach a specific vision of their heritage. Anita McCarty, Anne Braden's mother, enrolled her in a local chapter of Children of the Confederacy, an organization she describes as designed "to indoctrinate southern youth into the culture of the Confederate 'Lost Cause.'"[137] The organization's goal was clearly stated: to counter the "false" history taught in schools. At the 1912 conference, the first Children of the Confederacy event was held separate from the United Daughters of the Confederacy; two of the major issues included the promotion of the Children of the Confederacy and "how to meet and correct false and slanderous statements concerning the South and Southern history" in children's literature. During the meeting, "it was determined to seek a constructive policy and a resolution was passed: 'That the study of Southern authors shall be considered a part of the regular work of C of C chapters.'"[138]

To achieve their goal, the Children of the Confederacy leaders took local action. In 1931, one division protested the actions of a local junior high school teacher who had "required her students to prepare booklets with Civil War in large letters across the front."[139] Members attending an annual national convention were proudly told that, during the 1934–1935 school year, "313 books were placed in libraries and 10 pictures were placed in schools."[140] This attempt to reframe history continues, as the director of the Florida UDC, Mary Alice Geary, explained in 2008 that one of the current goals of the Children of the Confederacy is to combat public-school teachings: "As you probably suspect, children do not get the truth about the Confederacy and the War Between the States from their schools. . . . Unless we intervene, our children will grow up hating their Confederate ancestors based on the myths being perpetrated in schools."[141] By creating the KKK's auxiliaries and the Children of the Confederacy, white southern adults instituted a ritualized way for white children to learn songs, chants, salutes, prayers, and catechisms—all activities focused on making children active social performers. Through these youth groups, adults taught, modeled, and promoted a historical nostalgia that encouraged children to uphold the social roles their generation needed to maintain white supremacy.

Advertisements, games, and toys that reduced African Americans to inhuman caricatures provided white adults and children throughout the nation with a space in which to negotiate and affirm their racial roles. In the South, white adults created youth groups intended to perpetuate this portrayal of African Americans and to impart to children a revised version of southern history. Through these groups, children participated in public performances and social rituals that reinforced a revisionist history. By mimicking the system of white supremacy, children visualized themselves as part of the dominant race. As children grew older and experienced the world on their own, sometimes this idealized southern history clashed with reality. Katharine Du Pre Lumpkin remembered the shock she received when she discovered that the African Americans around her behaved differently from what her cultural socialization had led her to expect. She had anticipated seeing "jolly black laborers" working between the cotton rows and thought she might "hear jokes bandied back and forth and see 'white teeth gleaming with happy grins.'" When Lumpkin listened for such banter, she "could seem to hear little of it." She expected friendliness and deference, but her encounters with African American sharecroppers dashed her expectations: "I had thought they would treat me . . . deferentially, of course, as would be right to the white landowner's daughter, but also outgoingly, responding with hearty pleasure to my little attempts to be friendly. . . . They were polite when I spoke to them, but so reticent, it seemed, so very remote. A 'Yes, ma'am' or 'No, ma'am' and nothing much besides."[142] Taught her entire life that African Americans enjoyed manual labor, Lumpkin lacked the context in which to frame this exchange. Her socialization into the idealization of white supremacy had left her unprepared to face the reality of segregation.

4

"THE COURSE MY LIFE WAS TO TAKE"

The Violent Reality of White Youth's Socialization

> It brutalizes children who frequently witness its orgies, and particularly the youth, who are usually conspicuous participants.
> —United States antilynching report, 1937

Harry Leland (H. L.) Mitchell, born in 1906, begins his autobiography, *Mean Things Happening in This Land* (1979), with vignettes of his early encounters with race. As a child, he viewed the corpse of a white man, heard his uncle's story of killing a black man, and witnessed a mob burning an African American man alive. Of the incidents, Mitchell writes, "I could never forget these killings, the violence between blacks and whites, the savagery of mob spirit." Mitchell, in his autobiography, reflects on these events, noting, "certainly these early impressions helped to determine the course my life was to take."[1]

White children in the South often accepted incidents of racial violence as natural and inherent to the racial order of Jim Crow, as parents and the community indoctrinated white youth to believe in white male supremacy through parental stories, schoolbooks, toys, playacting, and children's organizations. White southerners sought to maintain white supremacy by teaching their youth that whites and African Americans who failed to uphold segregation threatened the entire power structure of the white South. As a result, white children learned that African American violations of the dictates of segregation required punishment, primarily through physical brutality. Examining children's experiences and reactions to racial cruelty reveals that many white children accepted their socialization and viewed violence as a necessity of daily life in the Jim Crow South. A few white youths, however, reacted with revulsion to their contact with racial aggression and proved unwilling to commit the brutality required of them.

As southern white children matured, the idealizations of white superiority began to assume more concrete form, a shift often hastened by their experiences with white violence toward African Americans. Racial brutality became the site in which boys and girls either upheld their youthful lessons by taking on their predetermined adult roles or rejected them and the larger system of white supremacy they represented. Those who abandoned their youthful lessons did so primarily when faced with racial violence, which triggered an epiphany that allowed them to recognize Jim Crow as a system of oppression and to comprehend that whites had falsely justified segregation as beneficial to both whites and blacks. As they recognized the personal and social repercussions of the racial lessons they had learned from an early age, they rejected their role in maintaining segregation, often in adult years, chronicling their childhood experiences in order to demonstrate their denunciation of Jim Crow. The autobiographical works by writers who detail the process of renouncing their youthful socialization reveal the inner workings of a system that rested upon violence, cruelty, and dehumanization. Many white children witnessed events of racial hostility without experiencing a racial awakening, however, perhaps because they accepted that segregation required their participation. Their partaking in racial brutality affirmed the messages they had learned since birth about their rightful power over African Americans.

White culture desensitized children to racial violence so they could perpetuate it themselves one day. Racial brutality was clearly a part of daily life for many white youths: in autobiographies written throughout the nation between 1820 and World War I, 53 percent of males and 20 percent of females recall occurrences of violence.[2] Nearly every southern autobiography focusing on segregation, regardless of the author's race, discusses an episode of racial violence, whether the actions inflamed the author or not. These authors describe such disturbing events in order to share the experiences that changed their conceptions of self and racial identity and thereby helped them to resist racial inequality.

In its simplest form, a memory is what an individual learns from an experience. Autobiographies, constructed by adults from their childhood memories, demonstrate a strong connection between the strength of writers' recollections and their reactions to the event recalled. This is especially true regarding witnessing violence, which tends to leave durable and vivid memories.[3] Adult writers revisit the experience of viewing a traumatic incident, often within the household, in an effort to trace their personal development. A graphic description of such pivotal events in a writer's life allows the reader of racial awakening narratives to understand that the author had no choice but to fight this system. Yet, only a few white southerners depicted their experiences with racial violence as instigating their abandonment of segregation. The majority of white southerners quietly internalized their childhood socialization in race relations. For white males, this socialization required using violence when necessary to uphold segregation, while females were called upon to maintain racial boundaries and report any infractions to white men.

The turning point in narratives of awakening racial consciousness is the moment in which the meanings and purposes of constructions of whiteness and blackness crystallized. For many, this understanding dawned instantaneously, triggered by a single event. In general, stories of sudden racial awakening follow a basic pattern in which an idyllic childhood ends abruptly with the realization of extreme inequality or the experience of an incident of brutal racism. For example, Katharine Du Pre Lumpkin's conversion moment occurred when she witnessed violence as an affirmation of male white supremacy. This insight shattered her pleasant childhood by opening her eyes to the brutality surrounding her.[4] Others, like H. L. Mitchell, describe their awakening as occurring more gradually, tracing multiple events that laid the groundwork for their transformation. The common denominator of both types of such narratives is the writer's realization that a world exists outside of the culture of segregation.

One of the formative experiences H. L. Mitchell relates in his autobiography occurred when he was five years old. He describes an altercation between his father, Jim Mitchell, and an African American man during a workday at the lumber camp. Angered for some reason, Jim Mitchell picked up an axe to attack a black coworker, and in self-defense, the black man struck Jim on the head with a board so severely he nearly died. While his father recovered, relatives called on the family to offer support. During one visit, his uncle revealed to H. L. and his mother the punishment that had been meted out to the offending black man. A group of white men, including his uncle, caught the African American, tied him to a tree, and shot him "to pieces." They then weighted down the black man's remains with log chains and dropped him into the Obion River.[5] Mitchell reveals little emotion as he relates this story, and he concludes the episode by informing the reader that his father recovered from his wounds. There is no mention of his uncle or the other white men facing criminal prosecution after committing this murder. Throughout the account, Mitchell refers to his father as "Jim" rather than by any familial term. While this may have been the custom in his family or a sign of respect, it also allowed Mitchell to distance himself from the experience and the violence.

Similar to H. L. Mitchell, Katharine Du Pre Lumpkin was a child when she first encountered racial violence performed by a family member. Both Mitchell and Lumpkin make it clear in their narratives that as children, before experiencing racial brutality firsthand, they believed that the maintenance of white supremacy ultimately depended upon the threat or use of violence. Neither Lumpkin nor Mitchell questioned their childhood lessons of white supremacy until confronted with the consequences of physical violence. The similarities of the childhood accounts written by a white boy from limited circumstances and a white girl from an elite family of former slaveholders indicate that the experiences described transcended social class and geography. Katharine Du Pre Lumpkin's entire childhood immersed her in lessons of racial behavior from her father, a member of the Klan. Her sister became a renowned speaker in support of the Confederate "Lost Cause," reflecting their father's successful socialization of one of his children.

When Lumpkin was eight years old, she heard a commotion coming from her kitchen window. She peeked in and observed "the white master of the house," her father, beating their African American cook. Lumpkin sensed the cook's fear, watched her try to avoid the blows, and heard her screams. Horrified, Lumpkin covered her ears and crawled away. Later, she learned that the servant's "impudence" had prompted the attack.[6] Such boldness challenged white control, and, as a white, Lumpkin knew whites must always guard against African American impertinence in order to uphold the position of her race. In recounting the event, Lumpkin continually repeats the word "I." This, together with her describing her father as "the white master of the house," indicates her emerging autonomy.[7] This passage clearly illustrates that Lumpkin views her father as a patriarch, the former slaveholder enforcing his will through brutality, and like Mitchell, she elects not to refer to him as her father. Lumpkin's distancing of herself from a family member who engaged in racial brutality foreshadows her later alienation from the system of white supremacy. After watching her father attack the family cook, she became fully aware of herself "as a white, and of Negroes as Negroes." Lumpkin uses a violent metaphor to depict this shift in her awareness, writing that, in the aftermath of beating, her new knowledge was "battering against [her] consciousness."[8]

It was viewing a white man's attack of a black man that changed southerner Marion Wright's previously "conventional" views on African Americans. The attack occurred while Wright was working as a young clerk in a store in Trenton, South Carolina. One day a well-dressed black man came into the store and asked Wright, a white teenager, if he could wash his hands. Wright retrieved a basin and some soap from the back room, but as the black man began to wash, the storeowner, Walter Wise, walked in and "went berserk." He grabbed a buggy whip from a rack and "shouted something about a 'goddamn nigger using my washpan' . . . and ran the Negro out of the store." Several factors came into play in the shopkeeper's attack on the African American man. Wright, in allowing a black man to wash his hands in the front of the shop, had violated the social code requiring separation of the races. That the African American man was a stranger exacerbated the owner's response, for as an outsider, the man needed to be educated in what the local white community considered proper behavior. The stranger's mode of dress also implied a higher social standing, perhaps suggesting that he was unaccustomed to being deferential and submissive to whites. After his attack on the African American man, Mr. Wise delivered a lengthy lecture to his young clerk about race relations.[9] Instead of being regretful or embarrassed at having failed to enforce racial bounds, Wright felt indignation at his employer's behavior and sympathy for the black man.[10] This confrontation proved to be a clarifying moment in Wright's understanding and rejection of his role in upholding the practices of white supremacy; as the shop owner demonstrated, a white man was expected not only to patrol black behavior but also to police other whites who allow transgressions to occur. Upon adult reflection, Wright realized that his reaction of sympathy for the black man being assaulted with a buggy whip represented a turning point in his life, triggering his lifelong activism for racial equality. As an adult, Wright attended the University of South Carolina and became a lawyer and prominent civil rights activist.

Like Marion Wright, some white youths who encountered African Americans in their homes and community recognized them not as dehumanized cartoons or animals, but as fellow humans. In 1946, Anne Braden moved to Birmingham, Alabama, and took a job covering the courthouse beat for the *Birmingham News* and the *Age-Herald* newspapers. Her experience on the job reinforced the message that a different set of rules applied to blacks than to whites since the law, which defined the killing of a white man by an African American as a capital crime, failed to classify the murder of an African American by white hands as a major offense. Similarly, white men who raped black women rarely faced criminal prosecution, but if a black man "so much as looked at a white woman," the police charged him with the capital offense of "assault with intent to rape."[11]

Although aware of the inequities in this system, Braden did not recognize her own role in upholding it. Her racial awakening occurred when she met a friend for breakfast one morning, during which she briefly excused herself to telephone the newspaper office. When Braden returned to the table, a black waitress served their meals. "Anything doing?" her friend asked. Braden replied, "No, everything's quiet. Nothing but a colored murder." In telling the story, Braden justifies her answer by noting that the reporter in her responded first. When she looked up at their server, however, that rationalization failed her. The young black woman's "body was stiff; and her hand on the coffee pot jerked. But her face was a stony mask, her eyes cast down." Braden, in parroting the words she had heard applied to blacks her entire life, suddenly realized the callousness and implications of her language, which shocked her into recognizing the humanity of African Americans. Braden remembers that she wanted to say: "I'm sorry for what I said. . . . It's not that I don't care if one of your people is killed. I am not part of this thing that says a Negro life does not matter. It isn't me." At that moment, like "a shaft of morning sunlight over the breakfast table—the truth dawned on me. . . . [I]f what I said had not been in my mind, I wouldn't have said it. I could not shift the blame to my newspaper; I was part of this white world that considered Negro life not worth bothering about."[12]

Seeing herself through an African American's eyes allowed Braden to recognize her accountability in the inequality she witnessed every day. She realized that by not opposing segregation, she implicitly became a part of the violence underpinning race relations and could not escape responsibility for segregation's sins. Throughout the 1940s and 1950s, Braden worked as a crusader for social justice. She and her husband became famous on May 1954, when they bought a house in a white neighborhood and signed it over to Andrew Wade, a black man, and his family who were unable to purchase housing in suburban Louisville due to Jim Crow housing decrees. Braden also became a member of the Southern Conference Educational Fund, edited antisegregation newspapers, and participated in a variety of political demonstrations. After her husband's death in 1975, she continued to work toward racial justice by forming the Southern Organizing Committee for Economic and Social Justice.

Lynchings

Reformers such as Mitchell, Wright, and Braden wrote about their childhood lessons about race to demonstrate their successful triumph over their youthful indoctrination into white-supremacist society, and in doing so, revealed racial violence as a central response of whites to challenges to white supremacy. Lynchings became one of the most public methods of violently controlling African Americans in the Jim Crow South. Many white youths encountered this form of racial brutality through witnessing or participating in a lynching, or indirectly through pictures and newspaper reports. The mass mob lynching, directed at blacks for trespasses against segregation, vividly displayed to white children the reality of Jim Crow and the violence that underpinned it. Countless children attended lynchings, yet only a few wrote about their experiences as exceptional or memorable, and those who did so described their witnessing of this bloodshed as resulting in their inability to participate in the racial brutality their community required of them.

At the age of eleven in Arkansas, H. L. Mitchell witnessed his first lynching. At first, he excitedly pushed and shoved his way through the crowd of five hundred men, women, and children to view Scott Lingon, a black man, being burned alive. At the front of the mob, Mitchell stared as the flames rose and Lingon's dead body sagged against the iron post and chains holding him. Then the image of Lingon's corpse, combined with the smell of burning flesh, suddenly shocked Mitchell, and he ran back through the crowd to the railway station. There, feeling nauseated, he "stretched out trembling on the cold ground."[13] In his narrative, Mitchell follows this story with the details of an incident that had occurred earlier in that year, when two African American men escaped from prison and killed Jeff Yarbrough, a white man, after which Mitchell viewed the corpse, displayed by the local hardware store as a reminder to whites of the necessity of maintaining white supremacy. Mitchell presents his childhood experiences of incidents of violent death as awakening him to the brutality required to maintain segregation.

Other white boys also witnessed lynchings that deeply affected them and instigated their rejection of the social hierarchy of the South. As a nineteen-year-old student at the University of Georgia in Athens, Clark Foreman participated as a mob member at the lynching of John Lee Eberhart. Legal authorities endorsed the lynching, described by the *Atlanta Constitution* as "the most horrible in the history of the state," as retaliation for the death of Mrs. Ida D. Lee, who had been killed by two shotgun blasts while caring for her cows the morning of February 16, 1921.[14] Eberhart, a laborer for the Lee family, became the prime suspect, and authorities arrested him. After taking him into custody, a mob of hundreds began to form, which by eight o'clock in the evening had grown to an estimated three thousand people. Then, incited by several white men who smashed the front courthouse windows, the mob overpowered the law-enforcement officers, seized Eberhart, and drove their hostage to the murder site, where mob members chained him to a tree. The crowd encouraged Eberhart to confess his guilt and then proceeded to stack wood under him, light the pyre, and burn him alive.[15] In a letter to his parents, Foreman provided details about the savage behavior of the mob, which, he specifically noted, included many children. This "sadistic orgy," Foreman recalled, brought him face to face with the barbarity that underlay race relations in the South and made an "indelible impression" on his mind.[16] Later, evidence surfaced that proved Eberhart's innocence.[17]

As a boy, the historian C. Vann Woodward encountered a lynch mob in Morrilton, Alabama, an experience that affected him deeply. Even though he did not see the body of the victim, Woodward witnessed the mob and knew they had executed a black man. After this, Woodward became racially conscious, awakened by the differences between his conceptions of morality and those of his world. Woodward recognized the incongruity between the religious teachings of his youth and the "grisly death of a black man destroyed by a white mob."[18] After having his trust in the church temporarily restored by the activist Charles Hillman, who stopped the Elaine Race Riot, a visit from Woodward's uncle demonstrated to him that his family's white-supremacist beliefs did not exist in isolation, but rather permeated all southern institutions. As a result, Woodward refrained from attending church because of what he now perceived as its hypocrisy.[19] Although all three white boys' encounters with lynchings resulted in their rejection of such violent practices, their reactions were not typical. Many white boys and girls across the South participated in various ways, willingly and without reservation, in public lynchings of African Americans. Obviously, not every white child in the South attended or participated in a lynching, yet those without direct experience of a lynching likely became acquainted with similar events through radio, newspapers, or souvenirs.

The ritualistic character and widespread nature of lynchings during segregation distinguish these events from earlier historical killings. In its earliest form, the word "lynching" referred to executions by vigilante committees in the West, but during the Civil War and Reconstruction, "lynching" took on its modern meaning of a mass mob killing.[20] During the Jim Crow period, lynchings, as a circumvention of legal action, functioned to demonstrate to African Americans, in a public forum, the deadly consequences of violating white-supremacist codes of racial behavior.[21] As Michel Foucault notes, the formalized legal system hid from view the punishment that had been so widely publicized in the sixteenth and seventeenth centuries, making judgment more time-consuming and abstract. White southerners, however, desired an immediate action, and viewed their mass mob brutality as part of a larger public responsibility.[22] Many whites justified the extralegal nature of lynchings by claiming that the legal system would fail to fully prosecute African Americans.

By the early twentieth century, the lynching of African Americans by whites had evolved as earlier southern cultural practices came in contact with new methods for disseminating information such as radios, photographs, and newspapers.[23] These technologies spread advance knowledge of a lynching, creating a spectacle out of what would otherwise have been a local event.[24] The transmission of news of racial violence across the South created the collective expectation that such violence would follow particular patterns.[25] Although it is often difficult to define lynchings during Jim Crow, with various classifications resulting in discrepant statistics, the designation of lynch mobs as three or more people who intend to inflict bodily harm on their victim based on the victim's race or heritage encapsulates the race-based lynchings that occurred throughout the New South.[26]

Although vigilante violence occurred outside of the South, especially in the Midwest, the motives behind lynchings differed regionally. Northern lynchings offered working-class whites a vehicle for "rough justice" aimed at repressing crime, while the objective of southern mass mob violence was the control of the African American population.[27] Outside the South, vigilantes principally targeted whites, often ethnic or religious minorities, only occasionally lynching an African American. Conversely, southern lynch mobs targeted African Americans 80 percent of the time.[28] Mass mobs formed in the New South for only the most atrocious of crimes, overwhelmingly those considered violent and committed by African Americans, primarily the rape or murder of a white. Statistics support this, as between 1882 and 1889 the rape of a white woman was the alleged motivation behind the most lynchings (38.1 percent). The accusation of rape, often coded in various accounts as "assaults" or "attacks" on white females, remained more prevalent than any other allegation against blacks in the early twentieth century except for the murder of a white. Overall, between 1882 and 1930, rape is the second-most prevalent charge leveled against African Americans by lynch mobs, at 31.1 percent; only the charge of a black murdering a white occurred more frequently (37.3 percent).[29] When southern whites executed other whites, it rarely involved a mass mob, nor did the execution include elements of ritualistic torture. In addition to public spectacle lynchings, other extralegal approaches included terrorist mobs, such as the Ku Klux Klan or the Nightriders, groups that carried out relatively private acts of violence aimed at limiting African American political activity and controlling black labor.

Performed as public acts with hundreds and in some cases thousands of participants, mass mob lynchings involved the entire spectrum of the white community, regardless of class, age, or sex.[30] For the white population, public lynching rituals functioned to create a collective sense of race-based identity established on the understanding that virtually all whites, regardless of economic or social standing, who committed acts of racial violence would go unpunished.[31] This bonded whites along racial lines, minimizing class distinctions, and prevented poor whites from recognizing that they had more in common with poor blacks than they did with elite whites.[32] For this reason, the social elite often attended lynchings, most of which would not have occurred without their consent. This ritual downplayed the economic strains that began between 1870 and 1910 and resulted in a generation of white men failing to achieve the financial success of their fathers. As the economic decline continued into the twentieth century, white men used lynching, usually of a black male victim, to overcome their economic anxiety by expressing their power as white men.[33] As poor whites participated with more affluent whites in a form of public domination of blacks, they avoided confronting their financial issues, choosing instead to express white solidarity through lynching.[34]

Public lynchings developed dramatic patterns of symbolic communication, and followed a set order of specific procedural rules.[35] An example of this highly ritualized public performance occurred on February 1, 1893, in the town of Paris, Texas. After a manhunt ranging from Arkansas to Michigan, a train returned Henry Smith, an African American accused of murdering white four-year-old Myrtle Vance, to Paris. In celebration of his arrival, the mayor granted the town's children a holiday from school, and they joined their families in waving handkerchiefs at Smith as he was paraded through town on a carnival float drawn by four white horses. After this display, the mob took Smith to a field outside of town, placed him on a scaffold, and tortured him with hot pokers wielded by Myrtle Vance's father, brother, and two uncles. For almost an hour, her relatives scorched Smith's feet, legs, stomach, back, and arms; they burned out his eyes and thrust the hot pokers down his throat. During this, the crowd, including the white schoolchildren, shouted their approval. Ultimately, the mob doused both the scaffold and Smith with oil and set him on fire. After the burning, the crowd scavenged the body and site for souvenirs.[36]

As in many rituals, the violence within mass mob lynchings included religious overtones of sin, punishment, and sacrifice.[37] Sunday was the preferred day for a lynching since it both suggested the act's religious meaning and allowed participants the time to perform and view the violence.[38] Once the mob brought the victim to the chosen site, they charged their hostage with the alleged crime(s) and often offered him a chance to confess his "sins." In churches across the South, whites heard in sermons and repeated in prayers and hymns that sin deserved punishment. This possibility for redemption within the ritual maintains the religious ideology that retribution and suffering are part of salvation. A mob's attempt to gain a confession from the accused was intended not only to determine the lynch victim's guilt or innocence, but also to extract a degree of salvation through pain.[39] A lynch victim's failure to admit to the alleged crime often led to torture in an effort to gain a confession. Of course, admission of the crime resulted in continued suffering as punishment was inflicted. In cases of the rape or murder of a white woman, male relatives of the victim, as self-appointed avengers of the degraded white female, often carried out this retribution. Torture as punishment was part of the triumph of the lynching ritual; it controlled the level of pain, branded and marked the body to purge the crime, and provided a celebrated spectacle.[40] The climax of the ritual arrived with the killing of the victim, and this culminating act imposed justice and unified whites against a black aggressor, with men posed as the protectors of white womanhood and women as the dependents in need of safeguarding.[41]

White children's presence at incidents of public racial violence allowed white adults to demonstrate how to dominate African Americans. Thus, the white community did not see having children witness racial killings as barbaric, but instead embraced the experience for their children as part of a larger protective duty. Many media and first-person accounts of white mob violence against African Americans note the celebratory atmosphere and remark that the community often viewed the event as a leisure activity. Some families approached lynchings as a Sunday outing similar to a picnic and considered the occasion as entertainment.[42] In her report on the Waco, Texas, lynching of Jesse Washington, Elizabeth Freeman, secretary of the NAACP, discovered that women and children eagerly watched the proceedings. This included "a little boy" in the tree next to the one where "the colored boy was hung," who observed the violence "until the fire became too hot."[43] This lynching, which occurred in the middle of the day, entertained not just white citizens, but also students who walked from Waco High School on their lunch break to watch as the mob brutalized Washington.[44] At the lynching of Allen Brooks in 1910, one participant wrote of "the great day" he experienced watching Brooks hang: "I saw this on my noon hour. I was very much in the bunch."[45] Weldon Johnson, secretary of the NAACP, testified in 1926 that newspapers often promoted lynchings; one article he recalled advertised that "a negro will be burned at 5 o'clock in the afternoon. That was the language used. And trainloads of people were run to the place to witness the orgy."[46] If the newspaper or radio announced a lynching in advance, parents often sent notes to school asking teachers to excuse their children so that they could attend with the rest of the family.[47] In 1915, for example, schools in Fayette County, Tennessee, delayed their school schedule "until boy and girl pupils could get back from viewing the lynched man."[48]

Parents made every effort to secure their children's presence at lynchings, for this act of communal racial violence applied, in a vividly compelling manner, the lessons related to race relations that whites learned in their youth. In Memphis, Tennessee, in 1892, parents of a twelve-year-old girl brought her to see the lynching of Lee Walker, who was accused of attempting to "outrage" Miss Mollie McCadden.[49] The mob dragged Walker out of jail, and when he fought them, the mob beat and cut at him with knives until he could no longer resist. The crowd then hung Walker from a telephone pole. Members of the mob pulled on his legs until they heard his neck break. Afterward, the crowd swung Walker's naked dead body into a fire in the middle of the street.[50] A similar instance occurred in Sherman, Texas, in 1930, when a grandmother roused her grandsons from bed to observe the mob's treatment of George Hughes.[51] The mob, which reportedly included many young boys, proceeded to sexually mutilate the forty-one-year-old black man before burning him alive. The *Sherman Daily Democrat* eloquently described the fire that "mutely but forcefully evidenced the penalty the inexorable law of racial separation exacts on its violators." The mob continued to riot after Hughes's lynching, destroying three blocks of the African American business district and the Grayson County Courthouse; the Texas National Guard was needed to quell the estimated crowd of five thousand.[52]

Those children who missed the lynching often went later to view the victim's brutalized remains. The *Chicago Whip* on August 20, 1927, recounted the sights seen after a lynching in Bailey, North Carolina. The reporter described the crowd, which traveled through tobacco patches to see the body and take pictures: "Some drove up within a few feet of the man's body in their Fords. Others parked a mile away and walked it." Many adults brought their children, including a five-year-old boy who, apparently fascinated, spent the afternoon standing "at the dead man's head." A minister, Dr. E. C. Manness, also traveled to view the dead body, bringing several white children with him. "'That's enough,' he said, when they had one good look, awed."[53] As these examples reveal, children's attendance at incidents of racial violence was neither accidental nor rare.

The Future of Race Relations

The presence of white children at incidents of racial brutality became a focal point in the campaigns against lynchings. The movement to stop lynchings began in 1882 with Ida B. Wells-Barnett's argument that whites' rhetoric of the bestial black rapist who violated pure white females and deserved torture and death cloaked the primary purpose of lynching, which was maintaining white social power.[54] The roles that white children played in racial violence troubled the black community in the late nineteenth century, as some African American leaders recognized that whites utilized lynchings not only to reassert their authority, but also to perpetuate racial brutality and segregation in the next generation of white southerners. Emanuel K. Love, born a slave, became a prominent clergyman and activist in Georgia.[55] In an 1893 sermon, Love discussed the presence of white children at lynchings, noting, "Mob law is breeding a race of savages," and arguing that "the young men and boys who engage in this bloody business will as surely grow up to be blood thirsty and cruel as the tiger will become a man eater after tasting human blood."[56] Like Minister Love, those who opposed lynching expressed fear that the participation of white children in racial violence would promote continued racism.

As the twentieth century progressed, the antilynching movement became effective at a national level with the formation of the National Association for the Advancement of Colored People (NAACP) in 1909, which set as a primary goal bringing the horror of lynchings into the public eye. Marches offered a visible means to do so, and in 1916, the *New York World* described a Parade of Protest against lynching, led by a boys' drum corps, followed by "fourteen lines of young girls." Along with these children, women marched holding signs, the most visual of which represented "a colored mother crouching protectively over two cowering children."[57] Antilynching advocates employed images of children as they protested racial violence, using the modern idea of a protected childhood to petition for the end of racial violence, noting that the eradication of lynching would benefit both races. Despite these efforts, a new wave of lynchings occurred between 1917 and 1919, coinciding with the NAACP's failed attempt to pass antilynching legislation in Congress.[58]

The rise of lynchings after World War I resulted from white southern fears that African American soldiers might challenge white supremacy after having experienced egalitarian treatment in the military and in Europe. A speech given by Mississippi governor Theodore Gilmore Bilbo passionately encouraged lynchings in order to prevent such attitudes from taking root in the South.[59] Governor Bilbo spoke of the "the social reception and familiarity" African American soldiers had received from "a certain class of white women in France." His speech, described in the *Jackson (Miss.) Daily Clarion Ledger* as "Governor Bilbo Talks Out in Meetin': Gives the Northern Negro-Lovers to Understand Mississippi Will Attend to All Brutes," touched on the central fear of white southern males, that African Americans would seek equality through access to white females.[60] Fears of African Americans gaining sexual, and therefore social, equality spurred white southerners to use racial violence to remove potential problems from the black community. Whites often invoked the protection of white womanhood as a justification for the murder they used to maintain their political and economic dominion. In 1919, in reaction to this upsurge in racial violence, the Commission on Interracial Cooperation formed to counter these outrages.

By the 1920s, the number of reported lynchings had declined, although these statistics may not reflect fewer incidents of lynching but rather white southern responses to larger shifts in social attitudes. As the antilynching movement gained support and popular sentiment began to condemn the barbaric displays, white communities increasingly concealed evidence of lynchings to avoid outside criticism, and officials often failed to report lynchings for fear of legal or monetary punishment. During the economic hardship of the late 1920s and 1930s, another wave of lynchings occurred, resulting in an increase in local antilynching movements, the most prominent of which involved southern white women. In 1930, Jessie Daniel Ames founded the Association of Southern Women for the Prevention of Lynching (ASWPL) to expose how lynchings allowed white men to maintain both sexual control over women and racial supremacy. Jessie Daniel Ames, like Ida B. Wells-Barnett, worked to challenge the rhetoric behind the accusation of rape, employing the antilynching movement as an opportunity to enter public discourses and gain access to the public sphere.[61]

Antilynching advocates pressured for governmental intervention, arguing that as long as lynchings continued to occur, white children would attend scenes of racial brutality and the cycle of violence would remain unbroken. Mary Church Terrell, the first president of the National Association for Colored Women, spoke to a Senate committee regarding the potential effects of lynchings on the white race. Terrell claimed that young women's participation in a lynching harmed not only them, but also their future children: "I think it is going to be more and more difficult to stop lynching, as has been suggested here, because the white mothers of the South are becoming more and more brutalized by lynchings in which they themselves participate." The results, she concluded, would affect not just whites, but also the African American children who would become the victims of future white mobs.[62]

Children became a powerful propaganda tool of the antilynching movement, as northerners and African Americans focused on the harm white southerners perpetuated by exposing their children to what they viewed as horrific acts of violence.[63] One advocate noted that white "men, women, and children who go out to kill, or to look on sympathetically while others kill, may be members of an actual mob but 1 day in a year of a lifetime" but remained "mob minded every day in the year."[64] White children attended lynchings, another supporter observed, in order to be "taught by their peers and neighbors how to treat black people."[65] Images of white families involving their children in lynchings as part of a social ritual became ammunition for the antilynching movement. A 1935 exhibit sponsored by the New York Art Gallery, titled An Art Commentary on Lynching, attempted to bring the issues of lynching into the national spotlight. The introduction to the exhibition catalog, by the author Erskine Caldwell, notes that southern children learned to "practice brutality just as if they were learning to fish and hunt."[66] His comments related both to the sense of indifference that antilynching advocates felt southern whites displayed toward violence as well as recognized southern whites' employment of racial brutality as an educational tool.

Raised in the South, Caldwell had learned a sense of social justice from his father, a minster and reformer, and his writings depict life among the South's poor whites and blacks.[67] The New York Art Gallery likely chose Caldwell to write the introduction based on the recent publication of his short story "Saturday Afternoon," which describes a horrific lynching. Like Caldwell's introduction, much of the exhibit focused on the harm lynching inflicted upon the white race, especially children.

This exhibit contained art that juxtaposed the cruelty of lynching as seen by northern whites with southern acceptance and encouragement of it. Reginald Marsh's satirical drawing entitled *This Is Her First Lynching* shows parents raising their daughter up above a frenzied mob to get a glimpse of the body of a lynched victim.[68] As one author notes, the description of this as the child's first lynching implies that she will attend others throughout her life.[69] This work reflects the inclusive nature of many lynchings, as both the family and the community encourage the little girl to view the violence. Marsh located the actual lynching off-scene, allowing the viewer to contemplate the savage white crowd illumined by flames. This image, which appeared on the cover of the *New Yorker* in 1934, gained praise for its subtlety; it likely also allowed white northerners to feel morally superior to the whites depicted in it.[70] A 1946 interview with Walter White, secretary of the NAACP, by Amy MacKenzie demonstrates the impact of Marsh's drawing on the cultural consciousness. MacKenzie began the interview with a detailed description of Marsh's image, noting the power of the illustration, "drawn with swift, strong strokes that flamed upward and seemed to burn themselves upon my vision."[71]

The goal of the exhibit, to draw attention to the issue of lynching, was accomplished primarily by focusing on the white family as a unit that perpetuated violence and inequality. Another exhibitor, William Chase, played on the inherent contradiction in a white southern God-fearing family participating in racial violence. Chase's drawing shows a father and son walking in the foreground with a lynched black man in the background. The caption reads, "son,—that nigger ain't made us late for prayer meetin!"[72] William Mosby's wood statue *Dixie Holiday* also presented the perceived moral contradictions exhibited by the southern white family participating in a lynching. Mosby carved a white family, including a mother and child, gazing at a hanged naked African American man.[73] Critics praised the black walnut statute as portraying a sense of the powerlessness of the black victim, whose exposure elicits sympathy, in contrast to the white family, shown as expressionless and stoic. Mosby, a student at Virginia Union University, had never carved before creating this foot-tall sculpture, which the NAACP later purchased for its offices.[74] African American activists presented images of southern white women and children participating in mass mob violence to counter the white argument that, without slavery to civilize them, African Americans would revert to their savage nature. Instead, black activists contrasted black nobility with the brutality of the white race.

Print Proof

Beyond autobiographical accounts by southerners and the pamphlets and proceedings of antilynching protest movements, photographic and newspaper evidence offer further testimony to the frequent presence of boys and girls of all ages at lynchings.[75] Photography, a product of modernization, created a consumer object that commodified both lynchings and the mob's African American victims. In 1915, photographers installed a portable printing plant at the lynching of Thomas Brooks in Tennessee and "reaped a harvest in selling postcards showing a photograph of the lynched Negro."[76] At Claude Neal's 1934 lynching in Brewton, Alabama, pictures of his corpse sold for fifty cents.[77] Selling photographs of lynchings developed into a common practice, and those in possession of images of racial violence cherished them as personal artifacts.[78] The photographer Fred Gildersleeve attended Jesse Washington's lynching in Waco, Texas, in order to snap six pictures of the youth being tortured and burned, capturing among the crowd the police chief, mayor, and county sheriff. Gildersleeve, aware of the event in advance, set up his flash powder camera on a corner fence post, hoping to profit from selling his prints.[79] Photographs both preserved the memory for those in attendance and functioned to extend the effect of the violence, as whites often mailed the pictures as a postcard, providing a means for those absent from the lynching to be included in the experience.[80] Taking photographs after the lynching also added to the ritualistic aspect of the event, with the staging of the victim and posing of white families with the corpse conclusively demonstrating whites' triumph over blacks.

A striking feature of many photographs of the aftermath of lynchings is the number of white children visible or posing for the camera. Images from the lynching of Jesse Washington focus on several young boys among the spectators surrounding the body. The boys exhibit pride in their presence at the event; one boy, between twelve to fourteen years old and dressed in a white-collared shirt with rolled-up sleeves, smiles into the camera.[81] This deliberate gaze shows the white youth's awareness of a larger audience.[82] A postcard photograph from the lynching of Lige Daniels, a sixteen-year-old black boy, for alleged murder, shows Daniels's body hanging in the center. Near him, in the front of the photograph, is a young white boy in his early teens, grinning with several other young boys.[83] On the back of the postcard appears a note from Aunt Myrtle: "This was made in the court yard." Images such as these support the 1934 observation that the "most striking feature" in newspaper photographs of lynchings was the presence of children.[84]

Images of children flanking black bodies after lynchings often defied the belief of viewers. One postcard pictured a group of nine- and ten-year-old white boys standing beneath the corpse of Ray Porter, a lynched black man. Handwritten across the back of the image was the message: "this fucking nigger was hung in Clanton, Alabama Friday, August 21, 1891, for murdering a little white boy in cold blood for 35-cents cash." It was signed "lynching committee." The Reverend C. F. Aked, one of Ida B. Wells-Barnett's antilynching supporters, widely circulated this postcard during a visit to England. Such vulgarity and violence, both symbolic and literal, led the English to assume the photograph was a fraud. They "refused to believe that a group of children would pose this way or that such an image could be authentic."[85]

Newspaper descriptions of mobs noted the constant presence and participation of white children. The *Chattanooga Daily Times* headline on February 13, 1918, read, "Thousands of Men, Women and Children Witness Proceedings, Many Crying for the Negro's Blood."[86] During the lynching, white mob members used a heated crowbar to assault Jim McIlherron, an African American accused of killing two white men. At one point during the ordeal, McIlherron grabbed the red-hot crowbar, burning and ripping the skin from his hands. Mob leaders also removed his ears while "children hardly able to toddle" observed.[87] Walter White, an African American who was light-skinned enough to pass as a white, asked James Weldon Johnson of the NAACP for permission to investigate the lynching in Estill Springs, Tennessee, firsthand. White ingratiated himself with the local community and learned that McIlherron had killed in self-defense.[88] White's account detailed the torture the mob had demanded, including hot pokers applied to McIlherron's face, through his thigh and calf, and his castration. After the mob's torture of McIlherron failed to elicit a confession, only "involuntary" groans, they doused their victim in oil and set him on fire.[89]

Similar newspaper descriptions abounded, with children's presence always emphasized to both dramatize the event and illustrate its widespread support. The mob's actions, sensationalized by vivid headlines, such as "Colored Man Roasted Alive" and "Negro Barbecue," testified to the lack of empathy white southerners felt for the mob's African American victims.[90] Like the lynching ritual itself, the reports followed a standard format. Lurid details designed to sell papers were recounted, resulting in a "folk pornography."[91] Detailed newspaper accounts never questioned the guilt of the accused, although by the 1930s, following the upswing in racial violence, a few white papers hinted that lynchings had failed to solve the problem. Most, however, continued to dramatize the violence, voyeuristically describing the gruesome details of the mass mob murder and spreading racial hatred and fear.

Like the larger culture of the Jim Crow South, newspaper accounts and photographs of lynchings dehumanized blacks. For some white youths, hearing, reading, and speaking about the necessity of racial brutality proved markedly different from experiencing in it. A few white children, after witnessing the physical nature of white control, questioned the legitimacy of their childhood socialization; as adults, they rejected the race and gender roles in which they had been instructed as children. Most whites, however, accepted the centrality of racial violence in their daily lives. Many participated, either directly or as observers, in the most prominent form of domination of blacks—ritualized, race-based lynchings, which applied all the lessons about race relations that they learned in their youth.

Children's presence at lynchings became a battlefield for the antilynching movement, as reformers identified children's attendance at ritualized murders as proof of the brutality of southern whites. Many African Americans understood the didactic nature of lynchings as an entertaining form of socialization that functioned to unite whites. At Henry Smith's lynching for alleged murder, an African American minister was among the thousands who witnessed Smith's torture and death. In the crowd, the minister noticed a "little tot scarcely older than little Myrtle Vance," clapping her hands as she perched on her father's shoulders in order to see above the crowd. Outraged by the display, which suggested that white children and their parents considered this brutal murder to be entertainment, he yelled, "For God's sake, send the children home." "No, no, let them learn a lesson," was the impassioned response to his plea.[92] For this white child, partaking in racial violence allowed her to learn the reality of the racial violence that whites deemed necessary for upholding white supremacy.

5

Violent Masculinity

Ritual and Performance in Southern Lynchings

Day dawned, and soon the mixed crowds came to view
The ghastly body swaying in the sun
The women thronged to look, but never a one
Showed sorrow in her eyes of steely blue
And little lads, lynchers that were to be
Danced around the dreadful thing in fiendish glee.
                    —Claude McKay, "The Lynching," 1922

In 1916, authorities arrested seventeen-year-old African American Jesse Washington for the murder and sexual assault of fifty-three-year-old Lucy Fryer. Washington's confession, which he signed although could not read, claimed that he had, "pulled up her clothes and crawled on her and screwed her," after which he hit her in the head twice with a hammer.[1] Washington, the only suspect, stood trial in Waco, Texas. During the hour-long proceeding, a crowd gathered to hear the judgment. After the jury read the "guilty" verdict, the crowd turned into a mob, removed Washington from the courtroom, and dragged him into the town square. Along the way, people tore his clothing and men slashed at him with knives. The crowd, which had swelled to fifteen thousand, nearly half the population of Waco, brought their victim to city hall. Leaders of the mob chained Washington up and cut his fingers off so that he could not grab at his restraints. White men and boys then cut off his toes, ears, and penis. After these attacks, the mob set fire to Washington, who was still alive. Several times, to prolong the ritual, men raised Washington from the flames and then lowered him again. One small boy who was observing from a nearby tree had to be rescued when the heat of the fire spread. After burning Washington until only his head and chest remained, mob members took ashes, body parts, and pieces of chain as souvenirs of the event.[2] During the violence, one white father, when questioned about the propriety of holding his young son on his shoulders so that the boy could get a good view of the mob that kicked, stabbed, castrated, and incinerated Washington, replied, "My son can't learn too young the proper way to treat a nigger."[3] During Jim Crow, similar events occurred repeatedly across the South. As the father's remark suggests, the social hierarchy of the New South rested upon a foundation of brutally enforced race and gender roles.

Concerns about the future of white supremacy prompted white male southerners to show their youth how to maintain white superiority through ritualized aggression against African Americans. In the antebellum South, white men's ability to control those within their household and below them in the social hierarchy, primarily slaves and women, was perceived as reflecting their masculinity.[4] Without the support provided to them by legalized slavery, white male southerners struggled to uphold their supremacy in the face of post–Civil War era challenges that included economic depression and political movements such as populism and women's suffrage. As the New South modernized, it became imperative for white males to locate alternative ways to demonstrate their manhood. Ritualized lynchings allowed the white community to model, produce, and reinforce a distinct masculine identity while also sending a message to the black community and white women and children to obey the boundaries set up by white males.[5]

Whites in the segregated South feared that their society was being polluted, and they aggressively policed racial boundaries. As in all social systems that enforce racial or class inequities, those benefiting from the separation were the ones who feared contamination and who were vigilant in identifying any perceived threats to the status quo. A society that fears it may be defiled requires a communal procedure for purifying itself, as such rituals create group solidarity. In the Jim Crow South, this harmony was achieved at the price of human lives, through lynching.[6] In lynchings, white southerners offered up young African American males as scapegoats in a dramatic, ritualistic sacrifice that created fellowship among the white community.[7] Attacking black men, who represented the underlying sexual fears of southern white men, united the white community along racial lines, repressing whites' own class and political differences.[8] Southern whites viewed the possibility that black males could have sexual relationships with white females as the most serious threat to segregated society. Since whites believed it had the potential to destabilize the racialized social order, this form of interracial sex became the focal point of whites' efforts to maintain the racial and gender hierarchies of the New South.[9] Although black men were the targets of white men's sexual anxieties, whites also feared black men's organized resistance to Jim Crow. Most of the African American males lynched were young, usually in their twenties or thirties, and they often lived outside of the local society; some black victims were simply visiting relatives or passing through town. Lynchings allowed whites to control potential black insurgents and the larger black community through terrorism.[10]

Public rituals such as parades, pledges, and holidays are culturally constructed events and practices that communicate social realities by defining and setting a common social agenda.[11] Mass mob lynchings were intended to define and enforce the boundaries of an idealized view of southern society in which white patriarchy remained intact. This public defense of white masculinity temporarily subsumed any social disorder and contestation of white supremacy. A society must perform its gender roles in order for them to survive, and lynchings offered an ideal forum for such performances.[12] Sharing in a public ritual allowed the participants to assert a conception of their identity to both themselves and those in their larger social context. A performance requires an audience, for the audience's presence endows the performance with social legitimacy.[13] The lynching ritual offered a public space for white male southerners to reassert their idealized view of their own role as, to use the term coined by the anthropologist David Gilmore, "Man-the-Impregnator-Protector-Provider."[14] By lynching blacks, white southern men made the socially constructed and highly romanticized image of white male masculinity a reality, if only for a short time. Spectacle lynchings offered white males a platform upon which to perform their interpretation of masculinity for a communitywide audience.[15] That such a ritual was needed to maintain racial boundaries, however, demonstrates segregation's inherent instability.

The brutality of lynchings and the actions of the white male mob leaders are the subject of many studies. Less often examined is that, while lynching rituals functioned to create and solidify racial identity in white adults, they also became crucial sites for delivering those lessons to the next generation. Thus, it was imperative that white women, children, and adolescents attend mass mob violence, as each had an assigned role to play. Women and young children provided an audience, while teenagers modeled their future adult responsibilities by partaking in actions that reflected their gender roles. While thousands of children and adolescents attended lynchings across the

New South, as documented in photographs, newspapers, and antilynching propaganda, the few firsthand accounts by white writers who experienced lynchings as children are nearly all stories of the authors' rejection of the racial violence exhibited in these rituals. The writers present their experiences of lynching as pivotal in their self-awareness and conversion from racism.

The silence surrounding the participation of children in lynchings might seem to suggest that white southerners did not encourage children's presence at the ritual; however, white adults requested and required children's attendance at mass mob lynchings, even dismissing students from school so that they could attend.[16] The pervasiveness of lynchings and literary treatments of them made racial violence seem commonplace, and therefore unremarkable, to many young southern whites.[17] In 1904, Mary Church Terrell noted that lynchings were so widespread as to hardly invite comment.[18] Such indifference remained evident in 1934 when Elizabeth S. Harrington of the National Student Council noted: "Lynching is something that the Southern student knows about; something that they have heard discussed since their childhood. There are few students in the South who have not lived in the vicinity where lynching has not been, and perhaps still is, a part of the town."[19] Many white youths accepted public racial violence as an unremarkable aspect of segregation. This is not surprising in light of the statistic that a southern white mob lynched an African American, on average, once a week between 1882 and 1930.[20]

The white parents of a few children actively discouraged their children from discussing the racial violence they witnessed. This occurred more often in the 1930s, as the antilynching movement gained strength and the government began to take punitive action against those participating in lynchings.[21] It was far more common in the black community, however, to repress discussion of racial violence. African Americans dared not tell the truth about racial violence for fear of making themselves a target of it. Across the South, African Americans suppressed discussions of their experiences of racial violence and altered their records to create a narrative acceptable to whites.[22] Additionally, the black community's recollections of racial violence are often lost, as many blacks fled their communities after a lynching.[23] A few African American men and communities resisted whites' attempts to lynch them or inflict other acts of violence. Sometimes accused men would "prefer suicide to the noose" or would seek protection within the black community. Occasionally, African Americans met white mobs with armed resistance. In Wiggins, Mississippi, in 1906, members of the African

American community exchanged more than five hundred shots with a white mob attempting to punish some blacks who had prevented the lynching of a "bad nigger."[24] Yet the more typical response of blacks to white lawlessness was to remain in the relative safety of the black community or to migrate.

The Audience

While the lynching ritual's primary social function may have been the teaching and reinforcing of a southern white view of masculinity, this celebration of white male domination would not have succeeded without an audience of women, girls, and young children. It is difficult to know the ages of those referenced in accounts as "young children," but children normally accompanied their mothers to lynchings, and the primary role of the children and women was to provide an audience for men and older boys. Their cheers offered the white men a visible sign of support, similar to applauding for a favorite team at a sporting event. At an 1899 lynching in Maysville, Kentucky, women shouted their approval during the torture of the victim, and their calls were accompanied by "the piping tones of children sounding high above the roar." In addition to offering encouragement, young children at times assisted women and girls with their roles in the mob, such as collecting tinder to build the fire. At the Maysville lynching, young children carried dried grass and kindling wood to "keep the fire burning all afternoon."[25] After the 1934 lynching of Claude Neal in Brewton, Alabama, the mob drove his mutilated body to his mother's home. As the car carrying the victim's corpse approached, "little children, some of them mere tots," waited "with sharpened sticks for the return of Neal's body." After the body was removed from the car, the "children drove their weapons deep into the flesh of the dead man."[26] The account fails to specify the ages of the white children participating. Both eyewitnesses and secondhand accounts may have described the children as "mere tots" in order to convey the horror of such savage behavior in the very young. Although it was uncommon for young children to maim a victim's body, Neal's lynching was one of the most brutal racial killings recorded, and adults, in the turmoil of the event, may have encouraged children to step outside their supporting role.

Frenzied mobs on occasion injured or killed those they sought to protect, including children in the audience. In 1919, the *Raleigh (N.C.) News & Observer* mentioned that five mob members had died during their efforts to remove an African American from jail, including Rachael Levi, a "young" female bystander.[27] Such injuries demonstrate the frequency and ordinariness of white youths' attendance at southern mass mob lynchings. In 1903, stray bullets killed twelve-year-old Peter Smith and another un-named youth. Smith had been watching a mob murder George White when a mob member near the back of the crowd accidently shot him in the back. The bullet critically wounded the boy, and the newspaper reported: "Smith is not expected to live. The other injured youth was shot in the nose and is expected to live."[28]

Occasionally, women and girls participated by lighting the pyre or scavenging for souvenirs. Although these behaviors illustrate that women sometimes engaged in roles in the lynching more active than providing the men with an audience, women rarely infringed on the male right to directly attack the victim during the ritual. In 1919, girls in a mob in Omaha distrib-uted rocks from tin buckets for men to throw. The young women, however, did not throw the rocks themselves.[29] Even though most females refrained from direct aggression against the victim, exceptions do exist.[30] In Atlanta, Georgia, in 1920, after a mob mutilated Philip Gathers, doused him with gasoline, and lit him on fire, four young women with guns pushed their way to the front of the crowd and shot him. Having done that, however, the women quickly stepped back and allowed the men to further disfigure and dismember Gathers's body.[31] Although this example offers a rare exception, women's direct participation in physical violence against a victim was usually constrained by the social expectation that southern women exhibit proper female behavior and respect men's dominant role in the ritual.

The "rape-lynch" complex further strengthened the ideal of female passivity and the need for white women to be sheltered from black men. With the defense of white womanhood offered as a primary justification of lynching, females' passive presence at lynchings proved their reliance on white males for protection and hid white males' fears that they could not maintain sexual control over white women, who might willingly seek out black sexual partners. As an audience, girls and young women served several purposes. Primarily, white males needed spectators to approve their exhibition of masculinity. Patriarchy required that white women maintain the communal hierarchy by being subordinate to and dependent on white males, demonstrated by their outward allegiance to a male-defined view of feminine virtue. The lynching rhetoric not only allowed white males to articulate their idealized conception of womanhood but it also excused the actions of males by furthering the idea that African Americans possessed an insatiable sexual desire for innocent white women. In torturing black men's bodies, white men attacked black sexuality.[32] In claiming to kill in defense of white women and their purity, white men not only sought to exhibit their masculinity but also to reinforce their social, political, economic, and sexual prerogative over both black men and white and black women.

Ironically, the vulnerability of women and children was used not only to justify mob actions, but also at times to protect male mob members. James Cameron's account of his attempted lynching in 1930 included a description of how several white men, one with a gun, entered his cell block followed by "a young white girl, very pretty still in her teens. . . . Her eyes were wide, like a frightened and startled doe."[33] Her presence justified the white mob's actions, which they cited as necessary for the protection of white womanhood. She also, however, acted as a shield, protecting the men from trigger-happy law-enforcement officers. Many authorities willingly surrendered African American prisoners, although, by the 1930s, fear of legal retribution and the increasingly violent behavior of mobs led some law-enforcement officials to defend themselves and their prisoners. Crowds often placed girls in the front of lynch mobs when storming jails or court-houses to make the police or militia "less inclined to use their firearms."[34] Having women and children present, however, did not always ensure that the establishment would not retaliate. In an extreme case in Sherman, Texas, the mob became so large and uncontrollable after destroying the courthouse that the governor called in the National Guard, which used tear gas against the throng, which included women and children.[35] Although boys' presence at lynchings always played a socially important role within the community, by the 1930s, boys' attendance also protected adult male mob members from criminal prosecution. Mobs used the knowledge that a court would not charge or sentence a child to circumvent punishment for adults. The NAACP report on the 1916 lynching of Jesse Washington in Waco, Texas, noted, "they got a little boy to light the fire (Legally you could not arrest a little boy)."[36]

Boys' Behaviors

While females learned that their part in upholding segregation was defen-sive, the charge of actively upholding white supremacy fell most heavily on males. In the Old South, male children had been "under special obligation to prove early virility," and attitudes toward boys emphasized the protection of white women, their families, and their honor.[37] If such guardianship required violence, society justified that action as necessary. Parenting guidebooks and fictional literature in the era of segregation encouraged creating a generation of physically strong and aggressive men. In Raleigh, North Carolina, in 1906, eleven-year-old Jack McClay, a white boy, and his white friend played "lynching." McClay tied a rope around the neck of his playmate, secured it to a nail in the wall, and left his friend hanging with just his toes touching the floor. The boy was severely hurt, and his parents brought the case to court. Jack's mother, however, proudly refused to reprimand her son for his rough yet masculine play.[38]

Members of the white community shielded boys who participated in mobs from outsiders' criticism and from legal prosecution. Frederick Van Nuys of Indiana presided over the 1934 U.S. Senate judiciary subcommittee considering "A Bill to Assure to Persons within the Jurisdiction of Every State the Equal Protection of the Laws and to Punish the Crime of Lynching," which explored the possibility of the federal government enacting an antilynching law. In questioning George W. Colburn, who was called as a witness regarding a lynching, Senator Van Nuys became increasingly frustrated that the community had not only condoned boys' behavior at lynchings but had also protected them from legal punishment.

> SENATOR VAN NUYS: Was your community depopulated that night or was the usual number of people on the streets?
>
> MR. COLBURN: I would say it was depopulated from a certain class; yes sir.
>
> SENATOR VAN NUYS: What class?
>
> MR. COLBURN: Youngsters.
>
> SENATOR VAN NUYS: Boys of what age, would you say?
>
> MR. COLBURN: Twelve to twenty-five years.
>
> SENATOR VAN NUYS: Nearly all the youngsters were out of town that evening?
>
> MR. COLBURN: They were not visible in our place of business; no, sir.
>
> SENATOR VAN NUYS: Did any of them pretend to have any first-hand knowledge about the mob and who led it or anything along that line?
>
> MR. COLBURN: Not that I could identify by name; no sir.
>
> SENATOR VAN NUYS: Were they boys of your town?
>
> MR. COLBURN: Yes, sir.

It is interesting that, throughout the exchange, Senator Van Nuys assumed that all participants were male. The senator then attempted to solicit information about the boys' activities. Colburn continued to deny knowledge of the boys' names or their activities in the mob. Van Nuys, clearly disbelieving Colburn, continued with his questioning: "Did some of them pretend to know who were leaders of the mob? Did some of them say that they were present at the mob?" Colburn responded, "I have heard some of them say they were present in Princess Anne, but I could not give any names now because it did not impress itself on my mind at the time."[39] Colburn confirmed the presence of boys from his town, yet his unwillingness to recall their names or their actions suggests that, in his judgment, his and the community's best interests lay in concealing the boys' identities.

Inquiries into the violent deaths of African Americans, even those that occurred with prominent local men and officials in attendance, usually resulted in the declaration that the death occurred at "the hands of persons unknown."[40] While Colburn protected his community's boys, they themselves often displayed less discretion. At the same hearing, Arthur Garfield Hays, a representative of the American Civil Liberties Union, noted that one boy "was unavoidably identified with the lynching through his own boastful statements made on the occasion to the newspapers under his own signature." After the boy was identified as a participant, however, community sentiment resulted in his release after only a fleeting attempt to punish him.[41]

A close examination of the roles that boys and adolescent males played within mass mobs exposes the methods through which white boys could exhibit their readiness to take on adult male responsibilities at spectacle lynchings. The lynching ritual offered several ways for young males to contribute. At first, a boy functioned in the mob as a helper to men, taking on minor aggressive roles and mimicking men but not participating directly in violent acts.[42] When males entered their early teens, they began to directly participate—with encouragement or instruction from men—in the violent behavior of the lynching ritual, thereby proving their virility and masculinity. To establish that they had entered manhood, adolescent males committed daring and brutal acts of a kind that only a man would be permitted. When white male youths performed such actions in front of the community, they signified their readiness for adulthood and independence from adult male supervision. The appropriate age at which the adult male community considered boys to be men remains undefined and variable, but generally appears to be after puberty.[43]

Boys contributed to the disorder of the lynch mob, shattering windows and helping men seize victims, emulating the men's violence rather than taking independent action themselves.[44] In 1930, the *Atlanta Constitution* informed its readers that a mob of men and boys, in an attempt to seize a victim, had overpowered the National Guard.[45] At a lynching in Omaha on September 28, 1919, a group of teenagers led the crowd to the courthouse to "get the Nigger." During the lynching, boys in the crowd broke lanterns, took the oil out of them, and ignited it on the street, probably in imitation of the fire started by adult men to burn the victim.[46] Older boys proved their readiness to take on the responsibilities of grown men through committing direct violence against African Americans. A 1933 article in the *New York Times* described the "frenzied mob of 3,000 men, women and children" who, "sneering at guns and teargas," overwhelmed state troopers to seize an African American prisoner accused of "assaulting" a white women. After the community procured the victim, "one boy, apparently about 18 years old, slashed the Negro's ear almost off with a knife."[47] By taking direct action against an African American charged with sexually attacking a white woman, this white adolescent proved himself to the community by showing his willingness to commit violence against an African American male. In Texarkana, Arkansas, an unknown number of boys, alongside men, in 1891 "amused themselves for some time sticking knives into [Ed] Coy's body and slicing off pieces of flesh."[48]

Young men also functioned as instigators of lynchings, being the first to encounter a violation and report it in order to initiate mob violence. In the Old South, male honor functioned as a mechanism of social control, ensuring that the community viewed male violence with approval.[49] Southern men promoted a view of the close relationship between violence and honor throughout the Jim Crow period as racialized violence ritualized antebellum codes of male behavior. In societies with clear notions of honor and shame, males build their personal reputation by their acts of physical bravery, including their response to insults.[50] White boys who had internalized this model instigated lynchings in response to real or perceived trespasses against southern honor. Instigating racial violence allowed young white males the chance to prove their courage and willingness to defend white supremacy and perpetuate white male honor through violence. On May 9, 1930, while the judge considered the verdict for the alleged rapist George Hughes in Sherman, Texas, a mob of boys gathered. One boy, impatient for the judgment, threw a can of gasoline through a courthouse window.

Another threw in a match. When the gasoline did not catch on fire, the second boy climbed in the window, struck another match, and remarked, "Now the damned courthouse is on fire." One of Sherman's older residents who witnessed the scene stated, "The rosters of the Sherman public schools would show the name of every boy in that group."[51] The schoolboys' actions helped incite a mob, which seized Hughes from the courtroom. The boys continued to provoke the mob as they tore an American flag from the walls of the courthouse, urging white men to take justified action against the "nigger who had raped a white woman."[52]

The mob's intended victim played a crucial role within the ritual and lynchings overwhelmingly targeted young African American males, the group most likely to challenge segregation. White southerners had countered this danger by figuratively emasculating black males in white culture, but lynchings offered them a chance to complete the act physically. Because African Americans were seen as capable of tainting whiteness through sexual relations with white women, southern white males perceived black male sexuality as the greatest threat to white supremacy. White men countered this threat by castrating African Americans; by unsexing black males, white males, in effect, raped them.[53] Castration became a central aspect of mass mob lynchings and was intended to assert white male control over the sexuality of both black men and white women.

In performing sexual violence, men and boys performed their masculinity by demonstrating their ability to safeguard the future of white supremacy. An October 13, 1917, headline in the *Chicago Defender* read, "Boy Unsexes Negro before Mob Lynches Him." When a dispute got out of hand between Bert Smith, an African American, and a white man in Houston, Texas, several oil drillers observing the argument attacked Smith. They "then forced a 10-year-old white lad who carried water around the camp to take a large butcher knife and unsex him."[54] The account does not make it clear whether the men had actually compelled the boy to participate or if his coercion by adults was the writer's embellishment, perhaps intended to soften the barbarity of the deed for northern readers. The boy may have participated freely in order to prove his masculinity, or the men may have required him to perform the castration as a test of manliness. Regardless, before the adult mob members murdered Smith, they denied him his masculinity by having a boy castrate him.

The removal of a black man's sexual organs during the lynching ritual, often while he was still alive, feminized his body before the audience and left white males as the uncontested representation of masculinity. An extreme example of sexual mutilation occurred at the lynching of Claude Neal, where white men cut off his penis and testicles and forced him to eat them, and then tortured him until he admitted he enjoyed consuming them.[55] While such behavior is even more brutal than that typically exhibited in other lynchings, it demonstrates the power relationship enacted through castration. The penis of a black man became a highly prized lynching souvenir for whites, perhaps because white men both feared and desired the power black men's sexuality represented to white society.[56] One investigator reported that after Jesse Washington's lynching, a mob member left the scene with the "proof" of the castration in his handkerchief.[57] Such sexual souvenirs symbolically transformed control, as white men forcibly seized the sexual prowess they desired for themselves.[58]

In collecting souvenirs, whites symbolically consumed the sacrificed body, which reinforced communal values and offered the community a way to remember the ritual and the (temporary) restoration of order that resulted after a lynching. Boys and young men figured prominently in the aftermath of lynchings by gathering "relics [such] as the teeth, nails, and bits of charred skin" from the victim.[59] A souvenir is a fragment meant to represent a larger experience, and the extralegal nature of lynchings added an illicit, even romanticized, aspect to the memento.[60] As a symbol of the lynching experience, the souvenir encouraged the repeated retelling of the events of the lynching. One report described a southern white man who carried the mummified right hand of a victim in his pants pocket, likely in order to relive his role within the ritual through repeated telling of the story to eager white audiences.[61] Immediately after Sam Hose died at his 1899 lynching in Atlanta, Georgia, men cut his heart and liver out of his body and removed his bones, crushing them into small bits for mementos. Souvenir seekers also destroyed the tree from which he hung, breaking it into pieces. Those not present at the lynching could purchase pieces of the man's remains: bits of bone for twenty-five cents and slivers of the liver for ten cents.[62] Hose's knuckles became a display in the front window of a grocery store for all to see, reminding the proud community of its actions.[63] Devouring the victim and the nearby scene may have functioned as a type of communion for the white community, allowing whites to embrace the dominant values of their society and to savor the perceived righteousness of their violent actions.[64]

Souvenirs of lynchings allowed whites, who commodified black bodies in popular culture, to transform the black physical body into an object. Boys often sought to profit from grisly mementos by selling them both to those who had observed the lynching as well as to those who wished they had witnessed the violence.[65] The *Chicago Record-Herald* reported on February 27, 1901, that after the burning of George Ward's body for several hours, his feet had remained intact. Someone in the crowd "called an offer of a dollar for one of the toes, and a boy quickly took out his knife and cut off a toe." Other offers followed, and "the horrible traffic continued, youths holding up toes and asking for bids."[66] Acts of castration and the physical carving up of African American bodies for white consumption demonstrate white males' anxieties about their own masculinity and their fear of the threat posed by black sexuality.[67]

Souvenir hunting after a lynching often signaled a return to peace for white southerners. On May 23, 1936, the *Norfolk (Va.) Journal and Guide* ran the front-page headline, "Souvenir Hunters Loot Ruins of Slain Pair's Home." The related story was accompanied by a picture of several boys digging through the remains of a home. The next day, another headline proclaimed, "Ominous Calm Pervades Gordonsville on Sabbath, Guide Reporter Discovers." The correspondent noted that many people, including a "school bus of children," had driven to view the spot where a mob of two thousand had lynched sixty-five-year-old William Wale.[68] A similar scene after a lynching was described in another article: "The bushes behind which the murder was committed have been cut down for a distance of several yards and carried away by relic hunters. Many of those who visited the scene today, among them a large number of young men, carried away a sprig or a branch of the bushes."[69] Although women, children, and men all scavenged for souvenirs, boys appear to have been the most active in this regard.

Outside the Ritual

At times, young white men tested their masculine roles outside of the lynching ritual. After World War I, white boys increasingly policed African Americans' behavior in response to white southerners' fear that black American soldiers returning from Europe might resist Jim Crow practices after having experienced more egalitarian treatment in the military and overseas. This fear led to an upsurge in attacks on young black men perceived by southern whites as having exhibited an "uppity" attitude or an expectation of social equality with whites. Charles Kelly, a black veteran of World War I, drove his father, the Reverend Ranse Kelly, to church one Sunday in 1919. On the way, his car met another car in the road, driven by a white youth. Apparently, Kelly "did not turn out of the road soon enough to suit the boy so he went home and got his father, two brothers and sister." They found Kelly, at which point, "the father of the white boy, Hugh Sams, drew his gun and asked Kelly why he did not turn out of the road. Kelly tried to run, whereupon he was shot in the back and killed."[70] As young men, white youths reported to adult men any behaviors from an African American that they perceived as inappropriate. As a black soldier viewed as a potential threat to white domination, Kelly offered an even more inviting target.

Some male youths went beyond simply exposing violations, instead taking matters into their own hands, with mixed results. Depending upon the circumstances, the community either praised the white youths' actions as commendable or censured the boys for overstepping their bounds. In June 1934, a group of white male youths interrupted a picnic of several African American teenagers and "made some improper advances to some of the colored girls. Of course, that was resented by the colored boys." When the black boys objected and sought to defend themselves and their girlfriends, a fight ensued. The white gang left for reinforcements, returned, and lynched Dick Blue, one of the African American youths who had stood up to them. On Sunday, others came to view Blue's body, showing apparent pride in the youths' actions and creating a sense of white unity through viewing the black body.[71] The tacit approval that teenagers sometimes received for acts of racial violence often encouraged them to take matters into their own hands. Henry Bedford, an African American, and Mr. Cawthorne, a white, argued over land Bedford had mortgaged to Cawthorne. During the argument, Cawthorne felt Bedford's attitude "rather 'sassy' for a 'nigger' to a white man" and ordered Bedford off his land. Cawthorne's son told a friend about the argument, and young Cawthorne "got two of his young friends to go after Bedford." They found Bedford, forced him into a car, drove him outside of town, and proceeded to beat him to death. The sheriff detained the boys, but the community responded by severely criticizing the sheriff for arresting and jailing the boys for several days just for "killing a nigger."[72] The community defended the youths, suggesting that at least some members considered their actions to be commendable.

As white boys assumed their adult male roles, they frequently attacked those who had committed a minor violation of segregation's mores or those who made easy, yet allowable, targets, such as older male African Americans. Boyd Cypert, the district attorney of Little Rock, Arkansas, told NAACP representatives investigating the lynching of John Carter that "two white boys went out one night with the definite and expressed intention of killing a Negro, for a lark." They shot an elderly black man and "left him beside the road." Cypert admitted that the community "felt that this was going too far." Still, many in the town expressed the view that jail was too harsh a punishment for the boys, and when the case went to trial, the "jury brought a verdict of not guilty, and afterwards expressed the opinion that the scare and expense of the trial remained punishment enough."[73] In response to an account of four white youths who broke into the house of a sixty-year-old black fisherman and shot him, an observer noted that the white male youths had "learned only too well" the lessons taught in the "lynching school in which all boys of the state are being educated."[74] Some white boys tested the boundaries of Jim Crow by instigating fights with African Americans, knowing that if the blacks responded by fighting back, they would violate Jim Crow codes and provoke vigilante punishment. In Laurens, South Carolina, African American George Robertson observed several white boys attacking a black boy, whom he rushed to aid. For defending the boys' victim, the town accused Robertson of assault, and a mob subsequently removed him from jail. Claiming to interpret Robertson's response as an attack on the larger white male community, the mob hung him from a railroad bridge outside the city.[75]

White southerners distinguished between justified violence, which they considered necessary to uphold white patriarchy, and uncontrolled aggression for dishonorable reasons. The socialization of white males occurred in a steady progression from boyhood to manhood. Adult white men determined what actions were appropriate for boys and young men to undertake, and on a few occasions, when the men thought the boys had overstepped their roles, they attempted to rein in the boys. The *Richmond Daily Enquirer* on March 30, 1900, reported, "the boys of the East End of Richmond who had been having trouble with the Negroes of the section, became so enraged last Tuesday they decided to take the matter at once in hand and lynch the offenders." A gang of white boys, all less than thirteen years old, chased a twelve-year-old black boy, throwing stones at him until the boy, fearing for his life, ran into the house of a white woman. The white boys outside the house yelled that "they would get him if they had to die." The white woman sent for the police, who arrested four of the boys, fined them, and warned them against more violence.[76] Adult males disciplined the boys, who had infringed on white men's social prerogatives.

African American boys were well aware of the violent capabilities of white adolescents, and many lived in fear of a white accusing them of a crime against segregation. On January 26, 1921, under the headline "Details of the Crime," the *Memphis (Tenn.) News Scimitar,* reported the death of Frank Daily, the five-year-old son of a white farmer. Searchers discovered Daily's "hacked and slashed" body a quarter mile from his family's farm. In a rather rare occurrence, the newspaper published the perpetrator's confession. In the account, sixteen-year-old Matthew Houston, portrayed as a "half-witted negro," described how Frank had visited their house to play with him and his twin brother. For amusement, Frank had climbed out the window of the house and onto the roof, lost his balance, and fallen onto a plank on the ground. His brother told Houston: "You better kill him. Better kill him and hide him, or they'll get you." Houston then "got scared of the white folks" and apparently murdered Frank to keep the young white boy from blaming Houston or his brother for his injuries. That five-year-old Frank would accuse Houston of harming him appears to have been a foregone conclusion to the black teenagers.[77]

Southern whites sought to teach and exhibit proper white male behavior to future generations through lessons in racial violence. Boys mimicked adult males under the watchful eyes of their parents and community members, supporting and observing the roles that they would someday fill. White adults might reprimand boys who took matters into their own hands without an adult's legitimizing presence, for white adult males maintained the responsibility of policing racial violence in a patriarchal society. For white male adolescents, however, the lynching ritual offered a public venue in which to prove their readiness for manhood through acts intended to be understood as the aggressive protection of white female sexuality. Public displays of masculinity at lynching rituals offered white men a space in which to demonstrate their ability to uphold the tenets of white southern masculinity, as well as to perpetuate white supremacy to southern youth. The actions of white southern males reveal how white southerners conceptualized, taught, and perpetuated white male masculinity in an attempt to preserve racial segregation and patriarchy. Young men also practiced their masculine roles outside of lynchings, carrying out gang violence against African Americans whom the teenagers considered easy, and socially sanctioned, targets. White communities often condoned such acts as examples of young men attempting to perform what they viewed as their honorable and masculine role of defending white supremacy.

For the white community, racial violence functioned to restore social order and publicly reasserted the community's commitment to white patriarchy. Eventually, however, a person or event would contest (or appear to contest) segregation, and white supremacy would again appear unstable. Public violence offered an opportunity to celebrate, if only for a short time, a version of white male masculinity that could vanquish all threats. White men maintained control of the ritualized violence in order to preserve their supremacy, which was acknowledged by those below them in the social hierarchy. Interestingly, every aspect of ritualistic lynching focused on displaying a strong white male masculinity, from the cheering women and children, to the mutilation of a black male body, to the conclusion and collection of souvenirs. Thus, this public ritual of racial violence, intended to demonstrate male power, also suggests that white males were, indeed, losing their ability to control white women and African Americans.

6

"Is This the Man?"

White Girls' Participation in Southern Lynchings

> He [John Hartfield] was nervous and broke down, and his cries as he
> perished were pitiful, while he was being taken by the angry mob to the
> trestle to pay the penalty for the crime he committed against Mississippi's
> young womanhood.
>
> —*New Orleans States-Item,* June 26, 1919

In 1919, teenager Mattie Hudson of Vicksburg, Mississippi, claimed that
at five o'clock in the morning a black man had entered her bedroom and
attempted to rape her. Hudson, who lived with her parents, asserted that
after her attacker forced his way through a screened window, she "shrieked
for help and fought him." She was "unharmed except to suffer a severe ner-
vous shock as the result of her harrowing experience."[1] The town quickly
began a search with bloodhounds for the culprit and brought Hudson to
the jail to view a lineup. Among the men presented to her was Lloyd Clay,
a twenty-two-year-old African American. Hudson was "not certain" in
her identification of him.[2] Despite her doubt, the mob became convinced
of Clay's guilt and removed him from jail. The crowd brought Clay before
Hudson again. "'Is this the man?' they asked, 'Say the word,' shouted others."
Hudson acquiesced, now claiming to recognize his clothes, and upon seeing Clay's profile, identified him as her attacker.[3] The mob hung Clay from
a tree, and men began to jerk his legs in order to break his neck. Members
of the crowd prepared a bonfire, and men, women, and children watched
Clay's body burn.[4]

A little over a month later, the newspaper revealed that Hudson's late-
night visitor had been her white boyfriend. When her parents had asked
who was in her room, Hudson began to scream and conjured up a black

assailant to explain the window screen torn by her partner as he escaped outside. Her white lover's chauffeur corroborated this story.[5] Hudson had deflected attention from her own sexual indiscretion with an accusation she knew would incite the community. Her conscience may have caused her to hesitate in naming Clay as her attacker, but ultimately Hudson realized that the community required a black body as a sacrifice. In front of a mob urging her to give her blessing to the lynching, she identified Clay and created an excuse for her earlier failure to recognize him. Mattie Hudson's false accusation cost Clay his life, but her life remained unaffected; she suffered neither social stigma nor criminal prosecution.

What is most striking in accounts of lynchings based on rape accusations in the Jim Crow South is the number of girls and teenagers who accused black men of sexual assault. Adolescent girls leveled more than half of all accusations of rape, and their motivations differed from those of adult white women.[6] Lynchings such as Lloyd Clay's raise larger questions as to why so many young and teenage girls charged African American men with rape and why the community believed them, often despite evidence to the contrary. Within the white community, girls' and young women's accusation and identification of a black male as their assailant justified the lynching as necessary for the protection of white womanhood. The white community utilized this rhetoric even when the girl inaccurately identified the victim or when no rape occurred, for the murder of an African American reinforced white supremacy and induced black fear. Additionally, the white community at times used the excuse of sexual assault to mask white crimes and conceal political, economic, or other motives for lynchings.

The assumption that white womanhood needed safeguarding was based on the belief that white women never desired to engage in sexual relationships with black men. The view of southern females as victims in need of protection also reinforced white men's exclusive sexual access to white women.[7] The white community had to believe, unwaveringly, in the accusations of white females. Communities cultivate a mimetic desire to retain social order, and when a society fears social breakdown, as in the segregated South, it responds violently. An expendable victim who embodies the social threat is accused. Most important, the community cannot doubt the scapegoat's guilt if they wish to reap the social benefits of white unity.[8] Thus, in order for the lynching to function properly for southern whites, the community always had to regard the perpetrator as guilty and the accuser as an innocent victim. In this way, young girls could charge African American men with sexual crimes knowing that the community would regard their accounts as the solemn truth. Trapped by their own rhetoric and their application of the rape-lynch mythology, the white community could not afford to question a white girl's claim of sexual violation, no matter how dubious, as it undermined the entire justification of white patriarchy. Thus, the white community supported all white females who instigated the lynching ritual in the Jim Crow South. This offered some white females the opportunity to circumvent traditional feminine roles as long as their accounts of their own actions plausibly portrayed them as maintaining the proper racial boundaries and preserving an ideal of white feminine virtue.

There is a definite difference in the social roles prescribed for white women born before and after the Civil War.[9] Those who remembered slavery socialized their daughters, as they had been socialized, to prize their racial privilege, which resulted in the idealization of antebellum racial roles and the perception of white supremacy as a natural inheritance. Some white girls in the New South, however, interpreted and adapted the lessons taught by their mothers and the larger white community in unexpected ways, employing the accusation of rape with varying levels of sophistication to further their personal agendas. It is often difficult to evaluate the veracity of girls' allegations of rape; some claims were later found to be false or, at the very least, questionable. It appears that white girls, at times, made effective use of the knowledge that when they were caught in a compromising situation, mentioning a black male attacker would deflect questions about their own actions.

Historians of the antebellum South have found that accusations of rape prior to the Civil War did not always result in the white community seeking immediate violent retribution.[10] Instead, the white community often failed to support the alleged assault victim and doubted her innocence. Whites often would release without punishment black men whom they considered falsely accused; indeed, some whites believed their black slaves to be more trustworthy than a lower-class white woman.[11] In the antebellum South, class often trumped race in the white community's response to rape charges against blacks, and slave owners were inclined to protect, rather than to punish, their male slaves, whom whites viewed as valuable property.[12]

There was also a stark contrast in how the southern white community responded to a white woman who accused a black man of rape before and after the Civil War.[13] Before the war, the community sometimes shunned the female victim, such as the white, poverty-stricken Bertha Ferguson, whose behavior the townspeople deemed too inconsistent to make her rape charge plausible.[14] After the Civil War, when the system of slavery no longer supported the traditional social and racial hierarchy, a decisive social shift occurred. In the postbellum South, the rape of a white woman by a black man represented the central racial fear of white southerners, for in order to maintain white supremacy, white women and black men must remain separate. This meant that white females, regardless of class, symbolized the future of the white race, and as such, white males must defend them against black men at all costs.

Although the truth of the rape charges that led to lynching in the segregated South is nearly impossible to determine, the veracity of the charges was not a primary concern. Regardless of a charge's legitimacy, the allegation and its prescribed response from the community offered white southerners a way to unite along racial lines, strengthening white supremacy. The depiction of black males published across the South by newspapers and reports vividly described them as savages who would revert to brutality without the chains of slavery to control them. This representation of black males included them having an uncontrollable sexual desire for young white women, fortifying the idea that sexual attack could occur at any time. In Georgia, thirty-year-old Ruby Hurst and sixteen-year-old Rita Mae Richards disappeared one Wednesday in 1937. On Saturday, the newspaper reported that searchers had found Mrs. Hurst's body on the outskirts of town. "She had been killed apparently by a hatchet and ice pick." After a renewed hunt, citizens discovered Miss Richards's mutilated body near the spot where Hurst's had been found. The newspaper concluded, "Miss Richards had been subjected to criminal assault; Mrs. Hurst had not been." Thus, the assumed black rapist allegedly sexually violated the younger white girl, while brutally murdering but not raping the older white woman. In reporting this detail, the paper not only highlighted the vulnerability of adolescent white females, but also reinforced the rhetoric of black males' sexual desire for young white females. Authorities arrested twenty-four year-old Willie Reed, the African American deemed responsible for the crimes, but Reed died while in police custody. Denied a lynching, a mob broke into the mortuary, hauled Reed's body to the town's ballpark, and burned it.[15]

Newspaper accounts of lynchings for assault portrayed the victim in specific ways. Southern society considered unmarried females "girls" regardless of their age, and newspaper articles identified an alleged victim as a girl and used "Miss" before her name. Usually a brief description was given of what the white girl was doing when the alleged attack occurred. Most often she was described as going to or returning from church or school, furthering the image of vulnerable, innocent, and chaste young white women. In June 1900, a mob in New Orleans hanged and burned an African American man, later believed to be innocent, for the murder of thirteen-year-old Christina Winterstein, a "schoolgirl" raped and killed on her way home from a commencement exercise. The paper contrasted her youth and scholastic achievement with her "unusually atrocious" murder, which "naturally" pointed to an African American perpetuator.[16]

In 1901, the *Chicago Record-Herald* reported the lynching of African Americans Will Godley and Eugene Carter in Missouri for assaulting and murdering Miss Casselle Wilds as she returned home from Sunday school. Her brother, who had stayed longer at church, discovered her body a mile from town in a culvert with her throat cut. The newspaper helpfully reported their interpretation of what had occurred, noting that "evidence of a terrible struggle was shown" and that, near the site of the crime, "a copper-colored negro" had been seen. The paper "supposed that the negro sprang upon her when she was passing and attempted to force her beneath the bridge." Miss Wilds, however, "fought with such desperation that he could not accomplish his purpose," forcing the black man to "cut her throat in the struggle." After the lynching of Godley and Carter, white men and boys meted out further retribution against the African American community that night as they carried out a raid in the black quarters of Pierce City. This resulted in the death of French Godley (Will Godley's grandfather), as well as that of a white boy hit by a stray bullet. The next day the paper proudly proclaimed that while yesterday's story had implied that her assailant had raped her, Miss Wilds's body, in fact, "was not violated."[17]

Although the rhetoric of the rape-lynch complex suggested that dying to keep one's virtue was better than surviving an assault by an African American man, in the Jim Crow South there appeared to be few, if any, negative social consequences for white girls who reported a rape, truthfully or not.[18] If assaulted, the community members blamed the black man, for they believed a white girl would never tolerate a black man's advances. Even if the girl was discovered to have lied, whites appear to have responded with relief, dismissing the false allegation without any social or legal repercussions for the white girl. Regardless of its veracity, her accusation functioned as a preemptive strike against any would-be rapist, sent a lesson to the black community, and reinforced white social values.

Identification and Reporting

Young white females were central in instigating the lynching ritual and elevating it to sacramental murder. The process often began with white girls reporting to white male authorities their need for protection.[19] In 1920, three girls informed the local Alabama police that an African American man had attempted to violate them sexually. Despite being "thrown to the ground" by their alleged assailant, who was brandishing a gun, the girls escaped. The white males of the community, in response to the girls' account, formed a posse, which captured and murdered African American George Davis.[20]

One of the staples of the lynching ritual, primarily in cases of assault or attempted rape, became the identification of the perpetrator by the white female victim. The media's accounts reported the ritualized practice of having a female victim confirm for the mob the identity of her attacker. This act authorized and justified the white mob's actions. The white girl who identified her alleged aggressor was an essential player in a religious trial of sacrifice, as the black beast rapist must die for his sins and the salvation of white supremacy.[21] Like white males engaged in the lynching ritual, the white female accuser functioned as an actor at the center of the performance, and through her indictment and identification, she became, if only for a short time, a symbol of white female chastity and racial purity.

If authorities arrested a suspect, the identification could occur at the jail. Generally, however, confirmation occurred at the location chosen by the mob, often near the site of the alleged crime, where with great fanfare the crowd waited for the girl to verify the man as her attacker. A positive identification sealed the guilt of the accused. In 1921, at Beaumont, Texas, the eight-year-old daughter of Mr. and Mrs. N. C. Colter identified her alleged attacker. The girl claimed that, on her walk home from the store, a black man had raped her. "She returned to her home and told her mother what had happened. [Henry] Cade was immediately arrested." He protested his innocence while the crowd erected a gallows and sent for the girl. Then, "with the negro standing on the gallows, the girl pointed her chubby hand at the negro and said: 'He is the man.' The trap was then sprung and the negro's neck was broken by the drop."[22] In 1900, in Huntsville, Alabama, the mob brought African American Elijah Clark before his alleged thirteen-year-old white female victim, who "positively identified" him near the crime scene. "The identification complete," the mob, led by the white girl's brother, hung Clark from a tree.[23]

At times, the girls' identifications appeared tenuous. In 1924, two white girls, thirteen and sixteen years old, from Fort Meyers, Florida, reported having been sexually violated. A search party of hundreds of men formed, and the sheriff captured one African American suspect, Milton Williams, whom the mob promptly removed from prison and shot. The crowd captured a second African American, "Bubber" Wilson, the next morning on a train as he attempted to leave the city. The *New York Journal* concluded, "Both men were said to have been identified by the girls before they were killed." It would seem difficult for this to occur in both cases considering that the mob dragged the second victim off a train and quickly murdered him.[24] Although it is doubtful that identification took place in both cases, the newspaper's claim that the girls had identified the victims assured readers of the legitimacy of lynching justice and assured mob members that the community had acted righteously. Headlines such as "Mob Member Laughs at Probe—Officers Won't Act He Says, Declaring Negro Positively Identified" suggest that when an alleged rape victim publicly acknowledged her attacker, due process for the identified attacker was not considered necessary.[25]

While the lynching ritual ideally included a face-to-face identification, the community often accepted less reliable testimony from alleged victims in order to justify the lynching.[26] In 1919, Ellisville, Mississippi, residents lynched R. D. McGee because his accuser, an eleven-year-old white girl, "identified him by his clothing." Confident in the accuracy of her recollection, the growing mob paraded McGee through town to the place of the alleged offense and lynched him.[27] The *Jackson (Miss.) Daily News* reported that all the sawmills "throughout this territory, have closed down in order to permit employees to attend the lynching, and there is hardly an industry within a radius of fifty miles of here that is in operation."[28] In November 1919, another Mississippi lynching occurred based on a white girl's claim that while she was returning home from school, a black man chased her into the woods. She escaped by outrunning him, and she claimed to recognize a local African American man, Amen Neville Foxworth, as her attempted rapist. Based on a verbal, rather than a face-to-face, identification, law enforcement arrested Foxworth, after which a mob overpowered the officers and lynched him.[29]

Occasionally, if the crime resulted in a white girl's injury or death, a third party might identify her attacker. In 1925, the authorities arrested a black man for assaulting a young white girl in Tennessee. "Sheriff Roberts, acting on a writ issued in a justice court," took the suspect to her home, where Bob Gaines, her father, made the identification. The girl herself did not identify the man face to face due to her "grave condition."[30] On a rare occasion, the trauma of the alleged attack offered an excuse for whites to lynch without a positive identification from the female victim. In 1919, a white mob in Omaha, Nebraska, lynched Joe Code, charged with assaulting five-year-old Lizzie Yates, despite the fact the girl could "not be induced to look at the negro, so nothing could be obtained from her in the way of identifying her assailant."[31] In many cases, the mob erroneously murdered an innocent black man for the alleged crime of sexual assault upon a white girl. The process, within the lynching ritual, of the female victim identifying her assailant was intended to prevent the execution of the wrong person. Yet many African Americans innocent of the alleged charges were murdered, even in cases where young white girls identified them as the perpetrators. This occurred for various reasons, including misinterpreted circumstances, mistaken identity, or community pressure.

Misunderstandings and Misidentifications

The white media's accounts of the rape-lynch cycle became formulaic in the New South. The story began with the accusation leveled by the white girl, followed by a description of the punishment meted out by the mob, and concluded with acknowledgment of the relief of the white female accuser that justice had been carried out. One journalist from the *Little Rock Daily News* described his attendance at a 1927 lynching. The correspondent remained with the alleged victim, nineteen-year-old Glennie Stewart, as the mob brought the supposed rapist before Stewart, who shouted, "That's him!" While the crowd proceeded to hang and shoot the man, the reporter remained focused on Stewart, whose "eyes never left the body of the negro." When the violence was over and the crowd, having avenged the assault, calmed, Stewart softly exclaimed, "Thank God."[32]

The publication of various accounts of assault heightened white southerners' fears and produced an increasing concern over any contact between a white girl and a black male. Any perceived crossing over the boundaries of segregation by blacks, no matter how minor, could result in deadly retribution. African American Jeff Brown of Cedar Bluff, Mississippi, rushed to catch his train as it prepared to leave the station. In his hurry, Brown accidentally brushed against the daughter of a white farmer. She screamed at this violation, and nearby white males acted quickly, running after Brown and "jerking him off the moving train." The white men proceeded to beat

Brown before hanging him from a nearby tree.[33] This heightened concern about African American males resulted in white girls accusing African Americans of assault for attempting to help them. In Bastrop, Louisiana, a mob killed Andrew McCloud in 1934 for attempted rape. On a date to a dance, an unnamed white girl's escort became drunk and drove the car into a ditch. "He was too intoxicated to go for help and the girl started out for a gasoline station on foot. A Negro stepped out of the night, she said, and started to drag her into the woods. Before he could get her off the road, a car approached frightening him away." Perhaps McCloud had been trying to offer assistance or remove the girl from the path of an oncoming car. The girl, however, perceived his approach as licentious, reported it, and a mob of three thousand lynched twenty-six-year-old McCloud.[34]

Even without a white girl's accusation, whites often assumed that any black men near any white girl intended to abduct and ravish her. The community misinterpreted the circumstances when thirty-five-year-old John Griggs of Newton, Texas, assisted an ill white girl. One evening, a white girl and boy attended "a wild party near a box factory." Her white male companion apparently left the girl lying "dazed and apparently drugged in a ditch," where Griggs found her and took her into his house, which was seen by one of the neighbors. The news of this spread until a posse arrived at Griggs's house and found the unconscious white girl on his bed. The authorities immediately arrested Griggs. On the way to the jail, a mob met the officers, who turned Griggs over to the crowd, which hung him and riddled his body with bullets. The girl and her male companion, both members of prominent white families, spent the night in jail, but were released without censure.[35]

Two accounts of an incident in McGhee, Arkansas—one from a white newspaper and another from an African American one—help differentiate the rhetoric from reality. In 1921, the white newspaper reported, "Miss Arbella Bond and her escort, J. Simms, were attacked by a Negro who stationed himself in the road and commanded them to stop their car." They did not halt, and shots were "exchanged between Mr. Simms and the Negro" without injury. The couple reported the incident to the police, who captured and jailed a young black man. He allegedly confessed, and a mob formed and "in some manner got possession of the prisoner." His body "was found hanging to a tree east of town . . . riddled with bullets." The local African American paper countered, "The white folks' paper published here doesn't seem to try to present any facts in so grave an affair." The alternative account identified the victim as fourteen-year-old Leroy Smith, whose stepfather worked for the Good Roads Company. In jail, before the mob arrived, Smith told authorities he had been frog hunting with two other boys. They separated, and Smith spotted a car "which he thought was the car of the foreman at the camp, and that he tried to stop the car in order that he could get a ride to the camp." Instead, the white man in the car shot at him.[36] The African American account suggests a misunderstanding that escalated out of control. The white paper's record, however, exacerbated fear about African American men and their violent tendencies, reinforcing the view that white men must physically control them.

White girls' inability to distinguish between African American men also resulted in mobs lynching the wrong black man. Authorities arrested twenty-four-year-old Ed Roach on July 7, 1920, for allegedly attacking fourteen-year-old Annie Lou Chambers of Roxboro, North Carolina. Brought to the jail, Chambers "positively identified" Roach as her assailant. A mob of two hundred people gathered, and hung and shot Roach. A week later, Mr. Teer, Roach's employer, verified that Roach had worked for the contractor all day, while the alleged rape had occurred between two and three in the afternoon. Several people remembered Roach working until he asked permission to catch a train to Roxboro at five thirty for a doctor's appointment. On his way to the train station, two white men noticed him, followed him onto the train, and arrested him when they reached town. Mr. Teer noted that a man of Roach's size and wearing similar clothing had traveled earlier in the direction of the crime scene. This was the man, Mr. Teer hypothesized, who had committed the offense.[37]

In 1903, Suzie Johnson of Eastman, Georgia, faced a black man whom the posse captured in response to her reported assault. When the mob brought him to her family's house for identification, she confirmed that he was the man who had raped her, Ed Clause. When asked what she wanted done to him, she replied, "He ought to be killed." The mob then took the man to a nearby tree and repeatedly shot his body until he "was literally cut to pieces." Twelve days later, however, the *Chicago Record-Herald* proclaimed, "Wrong Man Lynched as Rapist." The account noted that the man lynched was not Clause. Perhaps Johnson gave the posse a name that she knew belonged to a black man without knowing the man well enough to identify him. Alternatively, Johnson, perhaps all too familiar with Clause, may have identified another as the assailant in order to protect him. According to newspaper reports, after Johnson positively identified her rapist, the man protested to the mob that he had never seen Johnson before. Johnson's giving the posse a name and the mob a positive identification allowed the culminating act of the rape-lynch cycle to occur. While the unknown man's death did serve the intended purpose of spreading terror, the community still believed in Clause's guilt and attempted to carry out their own form of justice, tracking him to a nearby town and sending officers to arrest him. The paper noted, however, that unless he was brought back by a lynch mob, Clause was unlikely to return.[38] The indifference such accounts exhibited to the execution of several African Americans, even those later proven to be innocent of the charges made against them, illustrates the widely held belief among southern whites that the death of a black man, even for a crime he did not commit, remained an essential mechanism of social control. Reports of lynching the wrong man published by most white newspapers were not attempts to set the record straight, but rather served to exhibit the white community's lack of concern about punishing the appropriate individual.

Another death, in Thomasville, Georgia, based upon a nine-year-old schoolgirl's claim of sexual attack, also resulted in a deadly misidentification. The girl's screams brought her mother, who found her daughter alone. Men with bloodhounds trailed the alleged perpetrator to a stockade. The nine-year-old schoolgirl then twice identified Willie Kirkland, in the prison camp for horse stealing, "as the man who had attempted to attack her."[39] His arrest occurred after the first identification, his lynching after the second. Afterward, the mob tied his body to the back of a truck and dragged it around the public square before placing his corpse on the lawn of the courthouse. The warden expressed doubt about Kirkland's guilt, noting that he "did not leave the stockade . . . the day of the attack."[40] The symbolic display of Kirkland's body on the steps of the courthouse represented the desire of the community to justify its fulfillment of the rape-lynch complex as protecting the white girl, regardless of the lynch victim's guilt. As William Fitzhugh Brundage notes, "It is no more possible to determine the number of instance[s] in which mob victims actually had committed rape than to know how many innocent black men were executed because of mistaken identity."[41]

Communal Motives

In their zeal to find and punish a black male body for an alleged sexual crime, southern white men often overlooked the possibility that a white had committed the violent offense. The automatic assumption that sexual attacks were committed by blacks also concealed whites' agenda of political or social control. In 1919, a man assaulted a sixteen-year-old white girl on her way to school in Dade City, Florida. The actual culprit was Luther Wilson, a white man who had blackened his face and hands. When he tied the girl up, some black paint rubbed off, and she recognized him as a relative through marriage. In an interview, the girl recalled that Wilson told her "if she said anything about it, he would swear his innocence and put the blame on a black man. Everyone would believe him, he said."[42] In 1920, Bessie Revere, the "daughter of one of the most prominent" families in Quitman, Georgia, lay unconscious following a suspected rape. Despite Revere's inability to identify the person responsible for her condition, the paper described him as a "big, black brute." As a posse formed to search the countryside for her assailant, Revere regained consciousness in time to prevent the town from dispatching the search party, instead identifying her attacker as James Harvey, a successful and highly regarded white man.[43]

It is unknown how many white men committed crimes for which mobs lynched African American men, but occasionally the community caught the white culprit. In Raleigh, North Carolina, Charles E. Davis, a "prominent Wake county farmer," claimed in 1920 that an unidentified black man had murdered his wife. After authorities began to doubt his story that a "lecherous looking black" had killed her, they arrested Davis for killing his wife, and he hung himself in the county jail.[44] A similar incident occurred near Charlestown, South Carolina, in 1902, when a white man confessed on his deathbed to murdering his wife. After he had reported his wife's death at the hands of an unknown African American, white mobs had lynched three innocent black men for her murder.[45]

White girls who instigated lynchings by identifying their attackers had different motives for doing so than did other members of the white community who leveled such accusations. White townspeople used the claim of rape by white girls to justify their own violent actions, and accusations of sexual impropriety leveled by males often became a smokescreen used to punish African Americans for a lesser or different crime.[46] In 1925, authorities arrested Jack West of Orlando, Florida, for breaking into a white man's house. When the court acquitted West, he tried to leave town, but a white man accused West of "assaulting his 3-year-old daughter." White southerners, who could allow a thief to leave the area, could not permit the departure of a ravager of a young white girl. A mob removed him from a train and lynched him.[47] In the 1930s, the white community employed accusations of blacks' rape of young white girls in order to thwart black radicalism. In

Camp Hill, Alabama, in 1931, a group of white men violently broke up a Communist meeting of African Americans, resulting in the death of one and injuries to seven others. Authorities claimed two of the African American men at the meeting had sexually attacked two white girls on a freight train. The International Labor Defense, a Communist organization, coordinated a worldwide protest against the violence because the charges were a "frame-up; and without factual basis."[48] It seems likely white men violently broke up the meeting for political reasons and justified their aggression with the accusation of rape.[49]

Only a few cases offer hints at the motives behind a community's accusation of rape. The NAACP's investigation into Bud Johnson's lynching uncovered an eyewitness account that illustrated the mob's invocation of the rape-lynch mythology to defend a murder provoked by economic and social motives. On July 31, 1919, the Reverend H. A. Bryan swore out a deposition, retelling as a witness the events leading to the death of Bud Johnson. Johnson, a soldier, had received permission to return home from World War I to care for his ill father. Upon his arrival in Florida, Johnson learned of his father's death and his debt from the funeral expenses. "Whites" wanted Johnson to pay off his debt by giving up his father's farm, but he refused. While the Reverend Bryan visited Johnson at the family farm, a mob of 250 people gathered. Bryan heard the mob shout, "get ropes, get coal oil and gasoline and let us burn this Negro up. . . . He is saucy. He thinks he is a soldier." The mob took Johnson across the Florida border to Alabama in an effort to avoid legal punishment. Once they crossed the state line, the mob tied Johnson to a stump and "poured kerosene over the uniform, on his head." Then a young woman "lit a newspaper with a match and set it to the body." Afterward, the mob feared legal retribution because Johnson had been in active military service. The mob leaders decided, "we will say 'rape' and make some woman say 'yes.'" When a Birmingham judge called for an investigation into the lynching, the jury returned a verdict of manslaughter for several mob members. The testimony reveals that the mob leaders found the girl who lit the fire and "threatened to kill her if she did not say that Bud Johnson assaulted her." If the girl testified to rape, the members believed, then the court would pardon them. The defense, however, never called her as a witness.[50]

A correlation appears between community accusations of rape and times of financial or political stress. At the close of World War I, as black veterans returned home to the South, the number of lynchings rose as whites attempted to control real and perceived resistance to segregation. In the early twentieth century, labor issues remained a concern in the South, resulting in an increasing number of lynchings of employees and sharecroppers. An unsigned letter sent to the NAACP in 1919 from Waycross, Georgia, discussed an incident of a false rape accusation brought by a mother on behalf of her child. Sandy Ray, a seventeen-year-old African American sharecropper, finished his work and retrieved his coat from his employer's house. He then picked some grapes from an arbor near the house while the white farmer's three-year-old daughter played nearby. A five-cent piece fell out of Ray's pocket, and the girl sprinted over, grabbing the coin. He asked for his money back, and the little girl refused, so Ray forcibly seized the money from her hand and returned home. The girl threw herself on the ground in a tantrum, screaming and flailing. Her mother arrived, discovered Ray's presence shortly before the incident, and promptly assumed her child's behavior to be the result of a sexual assault. Convinced that a rape had occurred, the mother called a doctor, who "carefully examined the child, with particular pains expended to see whether or not any attempt to assault the child had been made." The doctor concluded that "the child's body bore no bruises or any mark of rough handling." Despite this, the mother insisted that a sexual violation occurred. The story that Ray had raped the girl made the rounds in Waycross, and the police took him into custody for "safekeeping," but a mob gathered, broke into the jail, removed Ray, and lynched him.[51] This incident demonstrates the effectiveness of the rhetoric of the black beast rapist, for despite the lack of evidence supporting the charge of sexual assault, the mother insisted that the girl had been raped simply because Ray was near her and she was having an angry fit. It is also possible that the girl's outburst may have offered the needed excuse to exact violent retribution in a labor dispute or to send a message to other African Americans in the area.

A similar incident occurred in 1919, in Scott, Georgia, leading to the lynching of Jim Walters for allegedly assaulting the eleven-year-old daughter of his employer, Mr. Haywood, behind the barn. This account, which was anonymously sent to the NAACP as an unsigned letter from "a colored man of good standing in his community," reported, "They caught the negro and his [Haywood's] little 11 Year old girl behind the barn" and "they claim that he raped her." However, "the general opinion is that it was not no rape." Regardless, "just about all the white mens in town was out there hardly no clerks in the stores" as a mob formed.[52] The letter's author suggested that both the black and white community likely understood the accusation of rape to be false, yet whites utilized it as a convenient excuse to attack a black man, probably for political or economic reasons.

Active Girls and Young Women

Adults' motivations for participating in lynchings were often different from those of the girls and young women who personally instigated the lynch ritual. Historians have found that the activities of adult women in lynch mobs were at times acts of resistance against white patriarchy.[53] Although both teenage white girls and adult white women may have used the lynching ritual to gain a presence in the public sphere, their goals in doing so differed. It appears that most adolescents and girls utilized the power to accuse and identify for a measure of personal gain rather than for political power; the benefits the girls sought ranged from monetary compensation and communal attention to hiding misbehaviors or sexual promiscuity.

White girls occasionally received praise for assisting in punishing a would-be ravager or helping to catch violators of segregation's mores. In Little Rock, Arkansas, white men lynched twenty-five-year-old African American Robert Hicks for writing a note to a white girl. The girl, who remained unidentified, apparently told some of her male relatives about the correspondence. When "the negro came to the girl's home Wednesday evening and asked if she received his note," a band of men seized him.[54] In Columbus, Mississippi, a white girl facilitated the lynching of an unidentified black man, who, she alleged, had come to her house and made improper advances. Although the girl agreed to meet him later for a liaison, she instead reported his overtures. When the African American man arrived in the place of assignation, a band of white men lay in wait for him.[55] Other girls obtained rewards beyond praise and attention. In Athens, Georgia, a fourteen-year-old girl turned in Obe Cox after discovering him crouched under a fig tree. Her reporting the whereabouts of this black man accused of murdering a white farmer's wife earned her a five-hundred-dollar reward.[56]

The violations of racial conventions were often alleged to have occurred away from the community, suggesting that white girls had learned the code of conduct that regulated behavior between whites and blacks and knew that their brief moments of being alone were the times their charges of sexual assaults would seem most plausible. As the historian Leon Litwack notes, white women "often fed the obsession with black sexuality by depicting themselves as virtually under siege" in order to force white men to prove their manhood by removing the threat of a black beast rapist."[57] Additionally, most alleged offenders were described as being unknown to the victims, increasing the fear that allegations of sexual assault provoked in the white community. The white girls who reported such attacks erased their own personal identities, including any social stigma attached to them or their class, and became romanticized by the community and media as a victim—white, female, and blameless.

This especially appears to have been the case along roadways, where numerous white girls described alleged assaults that share similarities across geography and time. Often, in roadway rape stories, the girls emerge as heroes, describing how they managed to struggle with their assailant and escape, frequently with their virtue intact. These accounts are difficult to prove or disprove, but the format of the charge allowed white girls the freedom to describe the perpetrator and offered a convenient explanation for an extended absence or tardy return home. In Royston, Georgia, a mob lynched Lint Shaw at the scene where two white girls reported his attempt to rape them after their car broke down in April 1936. Shaw, identified by the girls as the man who had pursued them with a knife, allegedly abandoned his intentions when one of the girls screamed and frightened him away.[58] The *Montgomery Advertiser* reported on two incidents within a single year in which young African American males allegedly approached young white women in their buggies in an illicit manner. One encounter occurred in August 1913, when an African American man purportedly approached a young white woman driving along a "lonely road." The newspaper article noted that the man attempted to drag the girl from her cart with assault in mind. He fled, however, "when she called to her two brothers who were following her in another buggy." The girl failed to identify her aggressor, and men with bloodhounds set out to track him. They arrested Richard Puckett, whom a mob removed from jail and lynched.[59]

White girls learned from their mothers that their own sexuality needed to be repressed, but the discovery that the white community would believe any accusation made against a black male offered some girls a way to circumvent regulations for female behavior, allowing them to hide misbehaviors ranging from skipping school to sexual affairs.[60] In 1926, three girls sneaked away on their school field trip to a nearby recreational area, where Albert Blades, who was visiting Osceola, Arkansas, from St. Louis, Missouri, came upon the girls. Startled in their illicit playing, the girls screamed and ran away.

One of the eleven-year-old girls fell as she fled, and when Blades reached out to help her up, she screamed louder. The girls hurried to the authorities and reported that a strange black man had assaulted them. Bloodhounds tracked Blades and brought him before the girls. After one of the girls identified Blades, an estimated crowd of 1,200, mutilated, hung, and burned him, despite his repeated pleas that he was innocent. After the lynching, "doctors who examined the child said that she had not been [sexually] attacked." The girls used their accusation against Blades to deflect punishment for their misbehavior in leaving their school group, and they appear to have received no reprimand for their seemingly false accusation.[61]

For white females, physical aggression did not fit into the gender mores of the segregated South, but indirect hurtful behavior offered girls an alternative way to participate in social aggression.[62] Despite the socially approved image of white women as passive and in need of protection, at times they likely did engage in social aggression, but there is no way to know exactly why this occurred. Only limited research exists on female social aggression, but preliminary studies find early adolescence to be the stage at which girls most often engage in manipulative behavior and attempt to defy cultural conventions.[63] Although social aggression is less direct than physical aggression, girls are most likely to develop the capacity for violent social behavior in relationships with romantic partners.[64]

In 1919, Ruth Meeks, an eighteen-year-old girl from Ellisville, Mississippi, accused an African American man of rape, probably to cover up her consensual sexual relationship with another man. Meeks told authorities that while she was walking along a secluded road, a young black man approached her. In her account, she recalled that she screamed, and he "drew a large gun and thrusting it into her face, commanded quiet under penalty of death." At gunpoint she was "subjected to indignities worse than death" and "forced to remain until four o'clock the following morning, when by a subterfuge she persuaded him to don her clothing and make his escape."[65] That he raped her, remained in her company, and then escaped by disguising himself in her clothes at her suggestion seems highly suspect. If he had assaulted her and then permitted her to return home, he would have essentially sealed his death warrant since she could then report the assault and identify him. The undertones of Meeks's account suggest that she fabricated her story to hide a voluntary liaison and to explain her failure to return home until four in the morning without her clothing.

Accusing a black man of assault allowed white females to extract themselves from uncomfortable situations and prevented punishment for the girls' suspicious behavior while publicly maintaining their pose of moral virtue.[66] Fourteen-year-old Ruby Anderson, from Paris, Kentucky, in 1920 claimed rape as an alibi for multiple absences. Anderson accused forty-year-old Grant Smith of "having assaulted her on several occasions." A mob seized Smith and hung him from a telephone pole.[67] Anderson's claim that Smith had "assaulted" her several times before she told authorities suggests either that she had been extremely afraid of Smith or that she was engaging in social manipulation. Her concern about admitting to the white community that an involuntary sexual liaison had occurred seems inconsistent with the quick and decisive nature of her accusation of rape. Anderson, in singling out Smith, followed the pattern of giving the name of a black man the community could punish for violating her purity. Perhaps she gave the name in response to community pressure to identify her attacker. Like Maddie Hudson, she may have accused a man who was completely innocent of the charge. Nevertheless, her allegation provided an excuse for her absence on "several occasions." Perhaps Anderson had engaged in voluntary sexual relations with Grant Smith and identified him in an effort either to punish him for ending their affair or to distance herself from her own violation of a social taboo. Regardless, blaming a black man allowed young females to deflect attention away from their whereabouts and actions.

The later exposure of a woman's accusation of sexual assault as false demonstrably failed to negatively impact the woman's status or the social position of her family within the white community. After James Scott, an African American, served in World War I, he and his wife moved from Chicago to Columbus, Missouri; it was their first experience living in a segregated town. They lived in relative affluence, he working as a janitor at the University of Missouri and she as an elementary school teacher.[68] On April 21, 1923, the police arrested Scott for the assault of Regina Almstedt, a white high school student. The mob took Scott and several other suspects to the Almstedt home and paraded them outside while Regina watched from inside. She identified Scott as her rapist and provided a positive identification a second time at the police station, with her mother at her side, saying, "I never want to see his face again." Regina Almstedt also claimed Scott's voice resembled her attacker's and that the perpetrator "had a strange smell, like one might pick up working with and disposing of dead animals." The removal of dead university lab animals was part of Scott's job.[69] Such a detail implies that Almstedt knew Scott; however, it is unclear whether she had contact with Scott before accusing him. Perhaps she gleaned this information about his job after she identified Scott the first time.

That night, a mob gathered and requested that the sheriff turn Scott over to them. He refused, but an hour later, the mob regrouped and began to strike the entrance of jail with hammers and chisels. The crowd, which included prominent businessmen, the chief of police, and a former city councilman, swelled to nearly a thousand. Men crammed the corridors of the jail trying to reach Scott, grabbed him, and dragged him to a nearby bridge, where mob members threw a rope around his neck and forced him off the bridge.[70] Bringing the charge of rape against Scott did not tarnish Regina's reputation within the community. She married, raised a family, and kept her social position, illustrating that, unlike in the antebellum South, society did not shun white girls as corrupted by black influence; instead, the alleged assault functioned to bind the white community together.

Beulah Davis's white family celebrated Scott's lynching, and her mother talked about it openly "because she wanted her children to learn from it." Davis remembers walking through the streets of Columbia as a young girl after the lynching, observing "more smiles on the white faces they passed on the street."[71] No one in the Almstedt family spoke of the event until her grandson read his grandmother's diary fifty years later.[72] Her grandson reported that James Scott did not rape Regina Almstedt, a knowledge that, in a newspaper interview, he said, "greatly relieved" him.[73] Almstedt's grandson expresses no shame or guilt about his grandmother's false accusation, which cost Scott his life. Indeed, his reaction shows that the idolization of the purity of white southern women continues even today.

Like young white men, young white women sometimes faced punishment for their involvement in violence against African Americans outside of the lynching ritual. In 1927, a superior court jury in Thomasville, Georgia, convicted an eight-year-old girl for her participation in a racial flogging. Ruth Foster allegedly accompanied several males into the home of Frank Gill and his wife and witnessed their whipping.[74] The girl, however, claimed she had watched the violence from a car. While it was not explicitly stated, the group of men, among them her brother, apparently wanted her to come with them since her presence validated their actions on behalf of white womanhood. The court found the group guilty of rioting, and the judge sentenced them to twelve months in the state penitentiary.[75] Although the court later suspended Foster's year-long sentence, that her actions (or lack thereof) merited punishment suggests another reason for the reprimand. As this violence had occurred outside of a lynching ritual, the community could punish white transgressors if they acted inappropriately. In this instance, the white men claimed the Gills had stolen liquor, a crime neither violent nor directly harming a white. With the economic depression occurring in the South, perhaps the community feared that this rough treatment of blacks would upset local race relations.

Although the rhetoric of Jim Crow focused primarily on controlling African American men, black women occasionally became the targets of a lynch mob if they injured a white girl. In Shreveport, Louisiana, a white mob lynched Jennie Steers, a black woman, in 1903, for giving sixteen-year-old Elizabeth Dolan "a glass of poisoned lemonade, causing her death." A mob gathered, "took her to a tree, placed a rope around her neck, and demanded a confession. The woman refused and was hanged."[76] In South Carolina, a mob in Orangeburg removed from jail and lynched an African American woman in 1914 after she confessed to beating a twelve-year-old girl to death with a stick of wood.[77]

During Jim Crow, white females' allegations of assault united the white community along race and class lines by initiating a violent and public celebration of whiteness. After the Civil War, the white community had to defend, without question, its construction of white girls' sexuality in order to preserve the larger system of segregation. Whites insisted on the innocence of white girls even in cases where the girls had instigated consensual sexual relations. In Mississippi, in 1929, two white girls enticed two African American bellboys into their hotel room. When the bellboys were discovered with two "scantily clad" white girls, a mob formed and took the boys into a nearby wooded area, where they sexually mutilated and hung them.[78] By castrating their victims, the white men showed their willingness to protect white womanhood by removing black manhood; yet the white mob ignored the sexual aggressiveness of the two white girls.

The accusations of rape that white girls and adolescents leveled against black men during Jim Crow do not fit into the historical frameworks used to explain how white men and adult women utilized the rape-lynch rhetoric. The large number of young girls who accused black men of sexual assault demonstrates white southerners' fears that white females' increasing independence could disrupt white supremacy. Although the white adult community clearly employed the ideology of the black beast rapist for its own motives, young white females' charges of black sexual assault demonstrate how thoroughly girls had learned the lessons of segregation. At times, white girls interpreted and utilized the white community's ideas about white female sexuality for personal gain, without suffering social or legal consequences for their part in instigating the lynching ritual. Their accusations pinpointed the cracks developing in Jim Crow's façade.

Conclusion

I have seen very small white children hang their black dolls. It is not the child's fault; he is simply an apt pupil.

—African American housekeeper

Despite elite white male southerners' success in reconstituting white supremacy legally and socially during the 1870s and 1880s, they struggled to maintain cultural, political, and economic control throughout the late nineteenth and first half of the twentieth centuries. White southerners vigilantly worked toward white supremacy's survival while African Americans and reformers fought for its demise.[1] White adults, fearful that each generation that came of age without experiencing slavery would violate the racial dictates of segregation, focused on socializing generations of white youth into adults' racial beliefs. The social roles created by white adults for their children during segregation were intended to replicate and perpetuate the ideology and practices of white supremacy. Thus, the racially segregated Jim Crow South is an ideal site in which to examine the historical process of the formation of social identity. As white southerners attempted to adapt to a modernizing economy that undermined white male privilege, they created experiences for their white youth that endeavored to reenact, in every possible way, white triumph over black bodies. During segregation, white southerners successfully indoctrinated their children into this view of society, producing only a few whites who, as adults, published narratives that described in negative terms their childhood socialization in racial mores. The ideological consistency between southern whites' private and public lives made white supremacy appear as the natural order of things to many white youth.

The decades between 1890 and World War II were not without challenges to white supremacy, yet white southerners remained focused on preserving segregation throughout World War I, economic depressions, and early black migration.[2] Their attempts to preserve white supremacy would have been unnecessary if the social order had been stable, but segregation required constant reinforcement from each generation. White adults utilized multiple spaces to socialize their children into their future roles. These lessons began in the home, within the private sphere of the white southern family. In order to prevent intimate contact between blacks and whites, white parents told their children stories intended to teach them to view white space as separate from black, thus perpetuating the idea of racial separation similar to a caste system.[3] However, these lessons also demonstrated the fragility of white supremacy. Unlike a permanent caste system, the racial system of Jim Crow was inherently unstable, and with African Americans living and working in close quarters with whites, it was nearly impossible to completely enforce segregation in daily life.

The white community strengthened the race-related lessons learned at home as white youth attended segregated public schools and their newly published southern texts presented an idealized image of race relations and gender roles carefully crafted to reflect the concepts that white adults deemed appropriate for their children. The fictional readings used in the curriculum of white southern schools displayed social behaviors modeled on a historical fantasy of antebellum society. The theme of African Americans' racial inferiority found in southern textbooks and fiction also appeared in stories set outside the South. These materials reinforced to the youthful white reader that a black, in any context, could never equal a white. The process of reducing African Americans to inhuman caricatures in texts offered both adults and children a safe way to control black bodies.

These lessons spilled into the larger space of the public sphere through the emerging mass culture of youth. Advertising campaigns reinforced an idealized image of white power by perpetuating racial caricatures of black bodies and suggesting to white children that African Americans enjoyed their subservient roles. Mass-produced toys based on these racialized images allowed white youth to interact with representations of African Americans and confirmed their prerogative to control black bodies. In order to keep alive a historical nostalgia for an imagined time of unquestioned white power, southern adults also encouraged young whites to perform white adults' teachings about the South's past in plays and social rituals. The children's auxiliary of the Ku Klux Klan and the Children of the Confederacy both allowed older children to role-play what whites perceived as ideal historical race and gender roles while advocating for their restoration.

White youth implemented what they had learned in these lessons in white southern ideology through their responses to and participation in the public and violent enforcement of segregation. Opponents of lynching often focused on white children as members of the mob, expressing concern over the impact of racial violence on the next generation of whites. While Congress debated antilynching laws and northern newspapers condemned lynching as barbaric, black antilynching advocates recognized the didactic purpose served by the lynching ritual and argued that the vivid lessons of racial brutality effectively functioned to maintain segregation.

Ideological conflict could occur in young southern whites when the community's nostalgia for passive, deferential, and controllable African Americans clashed with the reality of whites committing public acts of racial violence. Most southern white children reacted to racial violence in one of two ways. Some, horrified by the brutality of the violence, became aware of and rejected their socialization, often forsaking southern cultural institutions in later life and participating in social activism. Those youths remained a minority. Most young white southerners, when confronted with their community's cruelty toward African Americans, accepted this violence as consistent with their earlier lessons in race relations. White southern children's acceptance of racial violence demonstrated their successful indoctrination into the mores of segregation and the ideology of white supremacy.

Mass mob lynchings offered one of the most visible forms of violent socialization, as the ritual served the dual purpose of suppressing African American resistance and reasserting to whites their own conceptions of race and gender. The entire white community participated in southern race-based lynchings, which reflected the gender tensions underlying white patriarchy. In the post-Reconstruction South, the lynching ceremony, a public act of physical brutality, offered white southern males a public forum in which to act out their idealized masculine role as protectors while exhibiting to the women and children in the audience their ability to assert control over the bodies of both white women and African Americans.

Lynchings reflected the belief of southern white men that the primary danger to the future of southern society was black male sexuality; consequently, the primary victims of whites' racial violence were young African American men. Contemporary observers and the white media justified these targets of the rape-lynch cycle by utilizing rhetoric that portrayed African American males as black beasts that lusted after young white females. The ideology of the New South offered little room for uncertainty about white women's morality, and the narrative of the black beast rapist required a white female heroine who resisted the black man's assault, sometimes at the cost of her own life. White southern society and white men justified attacking and mutilating black male bodies as necessary in order to protect white females from the perceived sexual threat posed by black men. As they matured, white male youths often participated directly in mob violence, including castrating their male African American victims, which allowed whites to consume, and therefore dominate, black male bodies and the threat they had come to represent.

As white adolescents took up the reins of white supremacy, girls made use of the ideology of passive, protected females in ways that allowed them to expand and shift their own roles. White society employed idealized images of white females that encouraged white girls and women to see themselves as virtuous, domestic, and dependent upon men to protect and provide for them. As part of these lessons, white girls also learned that the slightest overstepping of Jim Crow's racial boundaries by a black deserved swift punishment. Any accusation of a black man's impropriety toward a white female required the violent white male punishment of at least one African American male, which was witnessed and justified by the larger white community. As the identifiers of black offenders and as the instigators of the white community's violent reprisals for the alleged offense, white girls validated the lynching ritual as necessary to protect white womanhood, offering a convenient rebuff to those who questioned the motives behind racial violence. The numerous accounts of sexual attack reported by young white females, many of which were later proved false, suggest that some white girls instigated the ritual in order to exercise a measure of social power. These southern white girls learned the lessons of segregation so well that they exploited the rhetoric of white supremacy to advance and conceal their own agendas.

For decades, white southerners' efforts to create a seamlessly racist society for their children were resoundingly successful. In the early twentieth century, however, social movements as well as increased African American resistance brought national scrutiny and a decline in the violent enforcement of segregation.[4] During the 1930s, lynchings decreased, due in part to shifting cultural attitudes, urbanization, pressure for economic handouts from the New Deal, and the efforts of antilynching organizations.[5] The support of many whites for segregation began to decline during and after World War II. Previously, southern whites could enumerate many reasons for sustaining segregation, primary among them ensuring their own economic and political superiority. After 1939, the world began to focus on the global conflict and the consequences of the domination of one race by another. Many in the United States, including white southerners, came to believe that it was hypocritical for Americans to fight a war abroad against tyranny while violently oppressing blacks in the South. Challenges to segregation had already begun in the 1930s. The mobilization of the black community was evidenced in an increase in the NAACP's membership and in the publicizing of racial incidents by the black press and black churches.[6] The long civil rights movement, which began in the early 1940s, gained momentum in the following decades with the pivotal 1954 Supreme Court decision *Brown v. Board of Education,* which declared segregated schools illegal.[7] With the passage of the Voting Rights Act of 1965, Jim Crow appeared legally dead.

White southerners did stop believing in and attempting to enforce white supremacy after 1939.[8] Instead, those who sought to perpetuate white supremacy publicly surrendered to the demands of the civil rights movement while privately seeking alternative methods to maintain their ideology. After the legal end of segregation, whites no longer had unchallenged exclusive access to southern institutions, and society became increasingly intolerant of open examples of extralegal violence. Unable to use their former methods to express racial dominance, white supremacists were forced to shift the process of socialization away from the public sphere and into the home. Although daily acts of racial injustice still occurred in southern communities as some whites sought to maintain a semblance of their former racial domination, for the most part whites could no longer engage in the social practices that, during Jim Crow, had reflected the widespread white acceptance of the ideology of white supremacy.

Children remained at the center of the debate over racial separation after World War II, but their direct participation waned as a reversal in race-related rhetoric occurred. White southerners began echoing what African Americans had been saying for decades, that subjecting white children to overt racial messages harmed both whites and blacks. White southerners now argued for the protection of white youth from racialized images and products in order to minimize white youth's exposure to African Americans. This, whites reasoned, would preserve racial separation. In 1958, white southerners mobilized against Garth Williams's children's book *The Rabbits' Wedding,* in which a black and a white rabbit fall in love and marry.[9] Fearful that the two romantic rabbits represented a larger attempt to "brainwash" white children into accepting integration, white southerners across the South banned the book. One Alabama senator encouraged white southerners to remove the book from libraries and burn it.[10] Despite both protests that the color of the fur on rabbits hardly reflected human racial characteristics and northern editorials mocking southerners for overreacting, many southern whites viewed the book as subversive and dangerous to the white South's youth. This public outcry shows a definite shift away from the approaches and methodologies from fifty years earlier, when lynching photographs appeared in newspapers depicting smiling children posing alongside black mutilated corpses. That white southerners began articulating this position in the mid-twentieth century demonstrates two key points. First, white southerners acknowledged the power of images, products, and texts to influence the racial consciousness of white youth. Ironically, whites had employed such methods themselves for decades in order to perpetuate white supremacy. In the last half of the twentieth century, as whites were forced to share public spaces and could exert less control over southern culture, they sought to stop these racial messages from entering public spaces where white children could encounter them. Second, this reveals a shift in the role of children within white-supremacist ideology. Instead of active agents of racial change, children became the passive site for political and social rhetoric against racial integration.

Their overarching goal of dominating African Americans led southern whites during the Jim Crow era to create a common language with which to discuss and control race relations. Whites' use of this rhetoric in their communities and in the socialization of their children was so widespread across the South that it became part of a collective consciousness. The roles that southern white children were taught to play during segregation illustrate how southern whites understood their own culture. The shifts in how whites expressed the ideology of white supremacy demonstrate their awareness that segregation was a contested social system, and required white southerners to instruct their children in their ideals and their fears if they were to succeed in preserving their way of life.

NOTES

Introduction

Epigraph from Lillian Smith, *Killers of the Dream* (New York: Anchor Books, 1963), 16.

1. I first encountered this image at the exhibit Without Sanctuary: Lynching Photography in America, a collection of more than one hundred lynching postcards and related material from the South in the late nineteenth and early twentieth centuries. The collection was later published as a book (James Allen, *Without Sanctuary: Lynching Photography in America* [Santa Fe: Twin Palms, 2000]), description of picture 57. This image also appeared in a National Association for the Advancement of Colored People 1935 antilynching pamphlet (National Association for the Advancement of Colored People Collection, Library of Congress, Washington, D.C. [hereafter cited as NAACP Collection], Group I, Series C, Box 352, Subject File: Marianna, Fla., 1935).

2. The accusation against Stacy was that he frightened a white woman when he approached her to ask for food. Before the lynching, the police escorted Stacy to the home of Mrs. Jones for a positive identification (Walter T. Howard, *Lynchings: Extralegal Violence in Florida during the 1930s* [Selinsgrove, Pa.: Susquehanna University Press, 1995], 75, 77).

3. NAACP Collection, Group I, Series C, Box 352, Subject File: Marianna, Fla., 1935.

4. Walter White, *Rope & Faggot: A Biography of Judge Lynch* (Notre Dame, Ind.: University of Notre Dame Press, 2002), 3.

5. Gail Bederman, *Manliness & Civilization: A Cultural History of Gender and Race in the United States, 1880–1917* (Chicago: University of Chicago Press, 1995), 11–12. See also Michael Kimmel, *Manhood in America: A Cultural History* (New York: Free Press, 1996), chap. 4.

6. This whiteness united whites along class lines, allowing lower-class whites to commit acts of violence that would go unpunished, creating an illusion of their own power (William Fitzhugh Brundage, *Lynching in the New South: Georgia and Virginia, 1880–1930* [Urbana: University of Illinois Press, 1993], 15). Grace Hale argues that lynchings functioned for white adults to strengthen segregation by helping to create "a collective, all-powerful whiteness." In addition, communal lynchings would not have been possible without the consent and often the participation of the social elite (Hale, *Making Whiteness: The Culture of Segregation in the South, 1890–1940* [New York: Pantheon, 1998], 237).

7. Listen Pope, *Millhands and Preachers: A Study of Gastonia* (New Haven: Yale University Press, 1946), 49–68; Hale, *Making Whiteness,* 34.

8. See Diane Miller Sommerville, "The Rape Myth in the Old South Reconsidered," *Journal of Southern History* 61 (August 1995): 481–518; or her book *Rape and Race in the Nineteenth-Century South* (Chapel Hill: University of North Carolina Press, 2004); and Peter Bardaglio, "Rape and Law in the Old South: 'Calculated to Excite Indignation in Every Heart,'" *Journal of Southern History* 60 (1994): 749–72.

9. For a discussion of the black beast rapist, see Joel Williamson, *The Crucible of Race: Black/White Relations in the American South since Emancipation* (New York: Oxford University Press, 1984).

10. Ruth Frankenberg, *White Women/Race Matters: The Social Construction of Whiteness* (Minneapolis: University of Minnesota Press, 1993), is a well-known study that argues for the invisibility of race.

11. Southern historians have debated segregation's beginnings and stability for decades. W. J. Cash, in *The Mind of the South,* argues that except for a few "quaint sentimentalities," the New South was indeed a continuation of the Old South. Cash maintains that any difference between the New and Old South was exaggerated since, for the "Man at the center," life had changed little since the Civil War (Cash, *The Mind of the South* [New York: Houghton Mifflin, 1941], chap. 2). C. Vann Woodward, in his 1951 *Origins of the New South,* responds to Cash by arguing that the fall of the Confederacy, the end of slavery, and the reorganization brought by Radical Reconstruction had wrought drastic changes in the South (Woodward, *Origins of the New South, 1877–1913* [Baton Rouge: Louisiana State University Press, 1951]). In 1955, in *The Strange Career of Jim Crow,* Woodward puts forth the thesis that racial segregation did not begin during, or even immediately after, slavery. Instead, he argues, Reconstruction was a period of flux for black and white racial roles. Segregation, he maintains, began in the 1890s, when racial tensions resulted in de jure segregation. The goal of this new system centered on keeping political and economic power from African Americans (Woodward, *The Strange Career of Jim Crow* [New York: Oxford University Press, 1955]). Howard N. Rabinowitz argues that there was less fluidity in race relations before the 1890s than Woodward suggests (Rabinowitz, *Race Relations in the Urban South, 1865–1890* [New York: Oxford University Press, 1978]). John W. Cell argues that racial caste systems such as those found in the United States South and South Africa are, in part, the result of struggles for modernization (Cell, *The Highest Stage of White Supremacy: The Origins of Segregation in South Africa and the American South* [Cambridge: Cambridge University Press, 1982]). Barbara Fields examines the fluidity in race relations that Woodward found after the Civil War in her study of the meanings of "free" labor after emancipation in the Border State of Maryland (Fields, *Slavery and Freedom on the Middle Ground: Maryland during the Nineteenth Century* [New Haven: Yale University Press, 1985]). Edward Ayers furthers Woodward's thesis but from the perspective of daily life, finding that segregation became a form of modernization for the South as Democrats gradually took over and sanctioned

segregation. Ayers also argues that this modernization caused African Americans and whites to work though new situations such as the rise of a black middle class (Ayers, *Promise of the New South: Life after Reconstruction* [New York: Oxford University Press, 1993]). See also Orville Vernon Burton, "Race and Reconstruction: Edgefield County, South Carolina," *Journal of Social History* 12, no. 1 (1978): 31–56.

12. Eric Foner, *Reconstruction: America's Unfinished Revolution, 1863–1877* (New York: HarperCollins, 1988), 198.

13. Historians of southern white women note the shift that occurred during and after the Civil War. Drew Gilpin Faust focuses on elite plantation women and finds that these women were eager to return to the antebellum system of patriarchy in return for the economic, racial, and social protection it offered (Faust, *Mothers of Invention: Women of the Slaveholding South in the American Civil War* [Chapel Hill: University of North Carolina Press, 1996]). Elizabeth Fox-Genovese argues that white women after the Civil War desired to retain their place in society, choosing and supporting a repressive patriarchy because it gave them power over black women (Fox-Genovese, *Within the Plantation Household: Black and White Woman of the Old South* [Chapel Hill: University of North Carolina Press, 1988]). Lee Ann Whites finds the Civil War a time of crisis for both men and women. Whites maintains that the Civil War was an experience that emasculated southern men as they had lost the war and failed to protect their property or their women. During Reconstruction, however, white women stepped down from their new social roles. With the restoration of their manhood, white men returned to their place at the top of the racial and social hierarchy (Whites, *The Civil War as a Crisis in Gender: Augusta, Georgia, 1860–1890* [Athens: University of Georgia Press, 2000]). See also Laura Edwards's consideration of gender relations during the Civil War and Reconstruction in *Gendered Strife and Confusion: The Political Culture of Reconstruction* (Urbana: University of Illinois Press, 1997). For a discussion of white women and religion, consider Jean E. Friedman, *The Enclosed Garden: Women and Community in the Evangelical South, 1830–1900* (Chapel Hill: University of North Carolina Press, 1985).

14. The boundary between childhood and adulthood can be difficult to define, but broadly, "youth" is the time before adulthood, and what constitutes "adulthood" is socially constructed and contextually variable. In the post–Civil War South, it appears that marriage signified the end of childhood; sources invariably refer to an unmarried female, regardless of age, as a girl, and to a married one, regardless of age, as a woman. For boys, the distinction is less clear but appears to occur when they publicly perform their adult responsibilities. The scholarship on the historical construction of childhood often begins with the much-debated work of Philippe Aries, who argues that until the Industrial Age, when human resources were more readily available, there was no sentimental attachment to children. He finds that it was not until the Victorian era that the "myth" of children's innocence was born and parents began to shelter their children from the harsh realities of life and give each child love and attention (Aries, *Centuries of Childhood: A Social History of Family Life* [London: Cape, 1962]). Edward Shorter and

Lawrence Stone investigate the effect of industrialization on families. Shorter examines the evolution of the family in eighteenth- and nineteenth-century France, arguing that industrialization was the catalyst for the transition from what he terms the "traditional family" of the eighteenth century to the "modern," nuclear family of the nineteenth century (Shorter, *The Making of the Modern Family* [New York: Basic Books, 1975]). Lawrence Stone argues that economic, political, and societal changes are reflected in changes in the parent-child relationship (Stone, *The Family, Sex, and Marriage in England, 1500–1800* [New York: Harper and Row, 1977]). Linda A. Pollock argues that childhood in the past was more humane and loving, going against the previous teleology that children were once cruelly treated and only recently showered with affection (Pollock, *Forgotten Children: Parent-Child Relations from 1500 to 1900* [New York: Cambridge University Press, 1983]).

15. Aries, *Centuries of Childhood*, chap. 2.

16. Howard P. Chudacoff, *Children at Play: An American History* (New York: New York University Press, 2007), 101. The concept of childhood is culturally constructed, and some historians find that a protective childhood only became a reality for some families after World War II (Steven Mintz, *Huck's Raft: A History of American Childhood* [Cambridge: Harvard University Press, 2004]), preface, 2, 8; Hugh Cunningham, *Children and Childhood in Western Society since 1500* [New York: Longman, 1995], 72–78).

17. Geographically defining the segregated South is difficult; however, the social system of segregation occurred in spaces where slavery and racial boundaries had previously been in place. For this study, I have included states that seceded from the Union to protect their white supremacy, as well as Border States that maintained a segregated society.

18. Many scholars have demonstrated how the lives of African Americans in the South, especially women, altered dramatically with the end of slavery. Jacqueline Jones examines the experiences of Freedwomen after the Civil War and finds Reconstruction and Jim Crow a time of contestation between black and white women over who controlled their labor. Black women ultimately worked in white establishments in order to ensure the survival of their household and a better future for their children (Jones, *Labor of Love, Labor of Sorrow: Black Women, Work, and the Family, from Slavery to the Present* [New York: Vintage Books, 1985]). James Anderson argues that Freedmen and Freedwomen had their own agendas, including education, which they saw as an opportunity for upward mobility. Despite their political disenfranchisement, Anderson shows how black families and communities went to great lengths to create and maintain schools, and to institute their own curriculums and teaching formats (Anderson, *The Education of Blacks in the South, 1860–1935* [Urbana: University of Illinois Press, 1988]). Glenda Gilmore explores how African American middle-class women were able to challenge and work within the system of white supremacy, filling the gap created by black men's disenfranchisement and becoming ambassadors to the white community (Gilmore, *Gender and Jim Crow: Women and the Politics of White Supremacy in North Carolina,*

1896–1920 [Chapel Hill: University of North Carolina Press, 1996]). Leslie A. Schwalm argues that Freedwomen resisted and attempted to control their own labor (Schwalm, *A Hard Fight for We: Women's Transition from Slavery to Freedom in South Carolina* [Urbana: University of Illinois Press, 1997]). Tera Hunter's examination of black women after the Civil War also found that black women celebrated their freedom. Although they tried to avoid it, black women engaged in household work, and by 1880, 98 percent of black female wage earners were domestics (Hunter, *To 'Joy My Freedom: Southern Black Women's Lives and Labors after the Civil War* [Cambridge: Harvard University Press, 1997], 50). As Vernon Burton has pointed out, free blacks did not disregard the values of white institutions but rather set up their own independent versions of social, political, religious, and educational institutions (Burton, *In My Father's House Are Many Mansions: Family and Community in Edgefield, South Carolina* [Chapel Hill: University of North Carolina Press, 1987]).

19. See Allison Davis, Burleigh B. Gardner, and Mary R. Gardner, *Deep South: A Social Anthropological Study of Caste and Class* (Chicago: University of Chicago Press, 1941; repr., Columbia: University of South Carolina, 2009), 91. See also Allison Davis and John Dollard, *Children of Bondage: The Personality Development of Negro Youth in the Urban South* (Washington, D.C.: American Council on Education, 1940); and Charles S. Johnson, *Growing up in the Black Belt: Negro Youth in the Rural South* (Washington, D.C.: American Council on Education, 1941). Kenneth B. Clark studied both white and black children in an effort to improve race relations (see Clark and Mamie K. Clark, "Skin Color as a Factor in Racial Identification of Negro Preschool Children," *Journal of Social Psychology*, Bulletin 11 [1940]: 159–69). The U.S. Supreme Court case *Brown v. Board of Education* used their work during the 1954 trial.

20. See Holland Thompson, *From the Cotton Field to the Cotton Mill: A Study of the Industrial Transition in North Carolina* (New York: Macmillan, 1906); and Glen H. Elder Jr., *Children of the Great Depression*, twenty-fifth anniversary edition (1974; Boulder, Colo.: Westview Press, 1999). See also David Carlton, *Mill and Town in South Carolina, 1880–1920* (Baton Rouge: Louisiana State University Press, 1982); and Shelley Sallee, *The Whiteness of Child Labor Reform in the New South* (Athens: University of Georgia Press, 2004). More recently, white children workers received their own examination from Jacqueline Dowd Hall, which explored children mill workers as being reflective of the South's industrialization and the creation of a working-class identity (Hall, *Like a Family: The Making of a Southern Cotton Mill World* [Chapel Hill: University of North Carolina Press, 2000]).

21. Jennifer Lynn Ritterhouse, *Growing up Jim Crow: How Black and White Southern Children Learned Race* (Chapel Hill: University of North Carolina Press, 2006).

22. Ibid., 73.

23. Although children do not categorize the world in the same way adults do, children are capable of highlighting the differences between themselves and others.

Sociological, psychological, anthropological, and child development studies examine childhood as an integral site for identity formation. This makes childhood an ideal site to understand the creation of conceptions of individuality and difference. Empirical studies agree that by the age of four children have developed racial prejudices. Research demonstrates that these prejudices are unique to the child; they are not simply a reflection of adult beliefs (Frances Aboud, *Children & Prejudice* [Oxford: Blackwell, 1998], 43). Judith D. R. Porter found that differences in perceptions between sex and social class are subordinate to race in determining prejudice, concluding that social class and sex affected prejudice to a lesser degree then race (Porter, *Black Child, White Child: The Development of Racial Attitudes* [Cambridge: Harvard University Press, 1971]). No single theory successfully accounts for understanding how children acquire their beliefs, but the most common theory is the social reflection theory, which holds that a child's beliefs reflect those of the existing social order. Researchers do agree that parental, peer, communal, and cultural contexts all affect the development of prejudice. The anthropologist Robyn M. Holme finds that children's beliefs result from their adaptation to their environments (Holme, *How Young Children Perceive Race* [London: Sage, 1995]). In their article "Parental and Peer Influences on Children's Racial Attitudes," Frances E. Aboud and Anna-Beth Doyle found that children in environments where parents are explicit in their racial beliefs tend to reflect those beliefs (Aboud and Doyle, "Parental and Peer Influences on Children's Racial Attitudes," *International Journal of Intercultural Religion* 20 [1996]: 371–83).

1. "My Mother Had Warned Me about This"

Title quote and epigraph: Sarah-Patton Boyle, *The Desegregated Heart: A Virginian's Stand in Time of Transition* (New York: Morrow, 1962), 39–40; Clifton Johnson, *Highways and Byways of the South* (New York: Macmillan, 1905), 352.

1. Boyle, *The Desegregated Heart,* 39–40. See Jennifer Lynn Ritterhouse, *Growing up Jim Crow: How Black and White Southern Children Learned Race* (Chapel Hill: University of North Carolina Press, 2006), chap. 1.

2. Howard P. Chudacoff, *Children at Play: An American History* (New York: New York University Press, 2007), 99.

3. Ellen Herman, "The Paradoxical Rationalization of Modern Adoption," *Journal of Social History* 36, no. 2 (Winter 2002): 346.

4. This rhetoric echoed the observation of the philosopher John Locke that children would grow up to be future citizens, discussed in Barbra Arneil, "Becoming versus Being: A Critical Analysis of the Child in Liberal Theory," in *The Moral and Political Status of Children,* ed. David Archard and Colin Murray MacLeod (Oxford: Oxford University Press, 2002), 75.

5. United States, William L. Chenery, and Ella Arvilla Merritt, *Standards of Child Welfare: Children and Youth: Social Problems and Social Policy* (New York: Arno Press, 1974), 11.

6. Ibid., 15.

7. Shirley Wajda, "A Room with a Viewer: The Parlor Stereoscope, Comic Stereographs, and the Psychic Role of Play in Victorian America," in *Hard at Play: Leisure in America, 1840–1940,* ed. Kathryn Grover (Amherst: University of Massachusetts Press, 1992), 113.

8. Isaac Lockhart Peebles, *The Duty of Parents or The Training of Children* (Nashville: M. E. Church South, 1919), 34.

9. Bernard Mergen, "Children's Play in American Autobiographies, 1820–1914," in *Hard at Play: Leisure in America, 1840–1940,* 171.

10. Geo Gilman Smith, *Childhood and Conversion* (Nashville: Publishing House of the Methodist Episcopal Church, 1891), 75.

11. *Parental Responsibility: A Sermon Preached before West Hanover Presbyterian, August 8, 1889* (Richmond: Presbyterian Committee of Publication, 1889), 12.

12. Ibid., 28.

13. Thomas W. Shannon and Emory Adams Allen, *Personal Help for Parents: Vital Knowledge for Parents, Including a Talk to Fathers and a Talk to Mothers about the Responsibilities of Parenthood and a Specific and Comprehensive Guide for the Instruction of Children in the Delicate Matters of Sex,* Personal Help series, vol. 2 (Marietta, Ga.: Mullikin, 1918), 3.

14. Frances Duke Wynne, *Preparing for Parenthood* (Miami: Hefty Press, 1935), 4.

15. Shannon and Allen, *Personal Help for Parents,* 163–66.

16. Wynne, *Preparing for Parenthood,* 57. Such lessons also include how boys needed to learn "to stand up for the other fellow, to be square with the gang, to be loyal to the gang and the gang's ideals." This encouragement of gang behavior often allowed adolescent boys to engage in testing the boundaries of segregation, as I discuss in chapter 5.

17. Shannon and Allen, *Personal Help for Parents,* 166.

18. Sam P. Jones, *Quit Your Meanness: Sermons and Sayings of Rev. Sam P. Jones* (Chicago: Cranston and Stowe, 1886), 406.

19. William Cooke Boone, *What God Hath Joined Together: Sermons on Courtship, Marriage, and the Home* (Nashville: Broadman Press, 1935), 107–9.

20. Ibid., 107.

21. Shannon and Allen, *Personal Help for Parents,* 72, 143–45.

22. Mary Jo Maynes, "Age as a Category of Historical Analysis: History, Agency, and Narratives of Childhood," *Journal of the History of Childhood and Youth,* 1, no. 1 (Winter 2008): 116.

23. Steven Mintz, *Huck's Raft: A History of American Childhood* (Cambridge: Harvard University Press, 2004), preface. E. Anthony Rotundo, in his review of Priscilla Ferguson Clement's *Growing Pains: Children in the Industrial Age, 1850–1890, Journal of Social History* 98 (Spring 1999): 671–76, discusses how the ideology of childhood is crucial to studying the experiences of youth.

24. For examinations of southern autobiography, see *Located Lives: Place and Idea*

in Southern Autobiography, ed. Bill J. Berry (Athens: University of Georgia Press, 1990). James Olney explores how authors throughout time have used memory to create narratives (Olney, *Memory and Narrative: The Weave of Life Writing* [Chicago: University of Chicago Press, 2001]). Paul John Eakin argues that the act of living affects one's identity, and that the self and the life story are symbiotic in their connection (Eakin, *How Our Lives Become Stories: Making Selves* [New York: Cornell University Press, 2001]). Linda Anderson uses feminist, psychoanalytic, and poststructuralist approaches to understand life stories (Anderson, *Autobiography* [New York: Routledge, 2001]). Sidonie Smith and Julia Watson examine the components of autobiographical texts, including memory, experience, and identity. In doing so, they argue that the authors use the autobiography as a means to establish their identity and find their voice (Smith and Julia Watson, *Reading Autobiography: A Guide for Interpreting Life Narratives* [Minneapolis: University of Minnesota Press, 2002]).

25. John Edgerton, *Speak Now Against the Day* (New York: Knopf, 1994), 11.

26. Jennifer Jensen Wallach, *"Closer to the Truth Than Any Fact": Memoir, Memory, and Jim Crow* (Athens: University of Georgia Press, 2008), 4.

27. Ibid., 112–14.

28. Jacquelyn Dowd Hall established in her examination of *The Making of a Southerner* that Katharine Du Pre Lumpkin exploited her reformer status to "re-remember her childhood, resituating her memories in a new perspective derived both from research and from left-wing politics of her time" (Hall, "'You Must Remember This': Autobiography as Social Critique," *Journal of American History* 85 [September 1998]: 439–65).

29. Olney, *Memory and Narrative,* chap. 1. See also James Olney "Autobiographical Traditions Black and White," in *Located Lives: Place and Idea in Southern Autobiography,* ed. Bill J. Berry (Athens: University of Georgia Press, 1990).

30. Richard Wright, *Black Boy* (New York: Harper and Row, 1946); Anne Moody *Coming of Age in Mississippi* (New York: Dial, 1968); Benjamin Mays, *Born to Rebel: An Autobiography* (New York: Scribner, 1971).

31. In general, southern autobiographies are preoccupied with attempts to understand what is distinctive about the South, as southern writers seek to understand their distinctive culture and its place within the national consciousness and in doing so attempt to define and redefine the South (see Jacquelyn Dowd Hall, "'You Must Remember This,'" 439–65; Lynn Z. Bloom, "Coming of Age in the Segregated South: Autobiographies of Twentieth-Century Childhoods, Black and White," in *Home Ground: Southern Autobiography,* ed. Bill J. Berry [Columbia: University of Missouri Press, 1991]; and Darlene O'Dell, *Sites of Southern Memory: The Autobiographies of Katharine Du Pre Lumpkin, Lillian Smith, and Pauli Murray* [Charlottesville: University Press of Virginia, 2001]).

32. Bloom, "Coming of Age in the Segregated South," 110–11.

33. A racial awakening is distinct from a religious conversion, although they share similarities. Writers describe both conversion and racial awakenings as marked by a sudden "change of heart," accompanied by an abrupt change in attitudes and concep-

tions of self. Racial awakening stories differ from religious conversions in that they lack visions, conversations with God, or the physical illnesses generally associated with religious rebirth. Both experiences, however, provide individuals with a way to express emotional struggle. This includes conveying the conflicting demands of a segregated system (Clifton H. Johnson, ed., *God Struck Me Dead: Religious Conversion Experiences and Autobiographies of Ex-Slave* [Boston: Pilgrim Press, 1969], xvii). In *But Now I See: The White Southern Racial Conversion Narrative*, Fred Hobson examines conversions to antiracism. Hobson treats these authors as willing participants in a segregated society, who through revelation of their racial wrongdoings attempt to liberate themselves from their racial guilt and offer justice and compassion to African Americans. Hobson believes that racial guilt can occur only in adulthood, and he places these stories within a religiously tinged cycle of confession, repentance, and redemption. Hobson's framework overlooks youth as the site where these authors actively learned, recognized, and rejected their racism (Hobson, *But Now I See: The White Southern Racial Conversion Narrative* [Baton Rouge: Louisiana State University Press, 1999], 2).

34. Alvin Morrill, Christine Yalda, Madelaine Adelman, Michael Musheno, and Cindy Bejarano, "Telling Tales in School: Youth Culture and Conflict Narratives," *Law & Society Review* 34, no. 3 (2000): 523.

35. Katharine Du Pre Lumpkin, *The Making of a Southerner* (Athens: University of Georgia Press, 1991), 130.

36. Anne Braden, *The Wall Between* (New York: Monthly Review Press, 1958), 19.

37. Boyle, *The Desegregated Heart*, 5, 11.

38. Ibid., 1.

39. Ibid., 14.

40. Braden, *The Wall Between*, 21.

41. Boyle, *The Desegregated Heart*, 26.

42. Elizabeth Fox-Genovese, "Between Individualism and Community: Autobiographies of Southern Women," in *Located Lives: Place and Idea in Southern Autobiography*, ed. Bill J. Berry (Athens: University of Georgia Press, 1990), 87.

43. Katharine Du Pre Lumpkin's parents also enrolled her in the children's Ku Klux Klan. There, with help from her mother, she made robes from old sheets with cheesecloth crosses (see chap. 3 of this volume). The children held secret meetings and planned imaginary violence against African Americans (Lumpkin, *The Making of a Southerner*, 136).

44. John Dollard, *Caste and Class in a Southern Town* (New York: Doubleday Anchor, 1937), 64.

45. Lumpkin, *The Making of a Southerner*, 91.

46. I discuss memories of racial violence in chapter 4.

47. Lumpkin, *The Making of a Southerner*, 86.

48. Ibid., 134.

49. Dollard, *Caste and Class in a Southern Town*, 62–68.

50. Lillian Smith, *Killers of the Dream* (New York: Anchor, 1963), 25–27.

51. H. L. Mitchell, *Mean Things Happening in This Land: The Life and Times of H. L. Mitchell, Co-Founder of the Southern Tenant Farmers Union* (Montclair: Allanheld, Osmun, 1979), 3.

52. Marion Wright, interview by Jacquelyn Hall, March 8, 1978, 9, Southern Oral History Program Collection, Southern Historical Collection, University of North Carolina at Chapel Hill.

53. Ibid., 8.

54. Boyle, *The Desegregated Heart,* 21–22. This lesson led to new feelings: "When no racial conventions were violated, I loved Negroes," but "when a Negro didn't 'keep his place' I felt outraged." Since her parents had forced Boyle to uphold the racial rules of segregation, she became irate when she noticed the regulations of Jim Crow violated (ibid., 30–31).

55. Junius Irving Scales and Richard Nickson, *Cause at Heart: A Former Communist Remembers* (Athens: University of Georgia Press, 1987), 47–48.

56. Will D. Campbell, *Brother to a Dragonfly* (New York: Continuum, 2000), 61–64.

57. Melton McLaurin, *Separate Pasts: Growing up White in the Segregated South* (Athens: University of Georgia Press, 1998), 37–40.

58. L. Smith, *Killers of the Dream,* 28.

59. Jay Watson, "Uncovering the Body, Discovering Ideology: Segregation and Sexual Anxiety in Lillian Smith's *Killers of the Dream,*" *American Quarterly* 49, no. 3 (September 1997): 481.

60. Darlene O'Dell discusses Smith's writings and the importance of the body as a site for repression and memory (O'Dell, *Sites of Southern Memory,* 90–92).

61. L. Smith, *Killers of the Dream,* 90.

62. Ibid., 74.

63. For example, Lillian Smith's father taught her "the steel-like" decorum that she must demand of all males, especially African American men (Anne C. Loveland, *Lillian Smith: A Southerner Confronting the South, A Biography* [Baton Rouge: Louisiana State University Press, 1986], 5, 7).

64. Alice Spearman Wright, interview by Jacquelyn Hall, February 28, 1976, 27, Southern Oral History Program Collection, Southern Historical Collection, University of North Carolina at Chapel Hill.

65. Ibid., 49.

66. Pamela R. Matthews, "Between Ellen and Louise: Female Friendship, Glasgow's Letters to Louise Chandler Moulton, and *The Wheel of Life,*" in *Ellen Glasgow: New Perspectives,* ed. Dorothy M. Scura (Knoxville: University of Tennessee Press, 1995), 112–15.

67. Anne Goodwyn Jones, *Tomorrow Is Another Day: The Woman Writer in the South, 1859–1936* (Baton Rouge: Louisiana State University Press, 1982), 54.

68. Ibid., 4–9.

69. Jacqueline Dowd Hall, "'To Widen the Reach of Our Love': Autobiography,

History, and Desire," *Feminist Studies* 26, no. 1 (Spring 2000): 231–47.

70. Watson, "Uncovering the Body, Discovering Ideology," 471.

71. Lumpkin, *The Making of a Southerner*, 189–90.

72. Ibid., 200.

73. Ibid., 135.

74. Boyle, *The Desegregated Heart*, 22, 25.

75. Larry L. King, *Confession of a White Racist* (New York: Viking Press, 1971), 3–4.

76. Alice Kester and Clark Foreman are also examples of those who found redemption through sharing a meal. In 1926, Howard Kester enrolled at the Vanderbilt University School of Religion, a racially liberal campus. His wife, Alice, confronted one of the southern "sins," at a Negro Baptist Publishing House lunch. She tried to eat at the same table as African Americans, but could not keep her food down, running home in tears. After this failed attempt, however, Alice "fraternized naturally with blacks" (Anthony P. Dunbar, *Against the Grain: Southern Radicals and Prophets, 1929–1959* [Charlottesville: University Press of Virginia, 1981], 23). Clark Foreman was to attend a talk by W. E. B. Du Bois, "but did not know that a dinner was involved." He refused to go at first because he had never shared a meal with an African American and felt that he could not do so. He was eventually convinced to go (Patricia Sullivan, *Days of Hope: Race and Democracy in the New Deal Era* [Chapel Hill: University of North Carolina Press, 1996], 28).

77. Lumpkin, *The Making of a Southerner*, 207.

78. Braden, *The Wall Between*, 27. It is important to note that Braden, Lumpkin, Smith, and Spearman Wright were all highly educated women who attended college, often in the North, where they encountered African Americans as equals.

79. Wright interview, 46.

80. Mitchell, *Mean Things Happening in This Land*, 22–23.

81. Lumpkin, *The Making of a Southerner*, 133.

82. Chambliss's unapologetic story is ironic due to its place in the introduction of his 1934 master's thesis (Chambliss, "What Negro Newspapers of Georgia Say about Some Social Problems" [master's thesis, University of Georgia, 1934], 5–8).

83. Boyle, *The Desegregated Heart*, 28.

2. "We Learned Our Lessons Well"

Title quote and epigraph: Lillian Smith, *Killers of the Dream* (New York: Anchor, 1963), 17; William Faulkner, *Requiem for a Nun* (New York: Random House, 1951), 92.

1. National Museum of American History, Warshaw Collection #60, Ku Klux Klan, Box 1.

2. Ibid.

3. Ibid. In 1916, Rose also published "The Ku Klux Klan and *The Birth of a Nation*," which appeared in the *Confederate Veteran*, 157–59. The author's note explained that Mrs. S. E. F. Rose was the historian of the Mississippi Chapter of United Daughters of

the Confederacy (Nancy B. Brown, "The Ku Klux Klan and *The Birth of a Nation*," Tennessee Genealogy Web Project. www.tngenweb.org/giles/afro-amer/history/birth.html).

4. The South's disregard for northern books had colonial roots (Edgar W. Knight, "An Early Case of Opposition in the South to Northern Textbooks," *Journal of Southern History* 13, no. 2 [May 1947]: 245–64).

5. John S. Ezell, "A Southern Education for Southrons," *Journal of Southern History* 17, no. 3 (August 1951): 306.

6. Ibid., 315.

7. Ibid., 305.

8. Anya Jabour, "'Grown Girls, Highly Cultivated': Female Education in an Antebellum Southern Family," *Journal of Southern History* 64, no. 1 (February 1998): 26.

9. Ibid., 34.

10. Carolyn Slasinski-Griem, "State Control of Education," *American Journal of Comparative Law* 38 (1990): 477.

11. For white southerners in the New South, schools emerged as the site from which to offer suggestions for reform of the South's problems, such as providing public-health education to combat hookworm infestation. William Link notes that reformers assisted public schools in order to hide their "real motives of social and racial control" (Link, *The Social Context of Southern Progressivism, 1880–1930* [Chapel Hill: University of North Carolina Press, 1993], 125).

12. Louis R. Harlan, "The Southern Education Board and the Race Issue in Public Education," *Journal of Southern History* 23, no. 2 (May 1957): 189.

13. William A. Link, "Privies, Progressivism, and Public Schools: Health Reform and Education in the Rural South, 1909–1920," *Journal of Southern History* 54, no. 4 (November 1988): 629.

14. Harlan, "The Southern Education Board and the Race Issue in Public Education," 200.

15. Ibid., 201.

16. Gail Murray, *American Children's Literature and the Construction of Childhood* (London: Twayne, 1998), 143.

17. Katharine Du Pre Lumpkin, *The Making of a Southerner* (Athens: University of Georgia Press, 1991), 127.

18. Ibid.

19. Lester J. Cappon, "The Provincial South," *Journal of Southern History* 16, no. 1 (February 1950): 23.

20. Darlene O'Dell, *Sites of Southern Memory: The Autobiographies of Katharine Du Pre Lumpkin, Lillian Smith, and Pauli Murray* (Charlottesville: University Press of Virginia. 2001), x.

21. R. S. Bigler, C. Spears Brown, and M. Markell, "When Groups Are Not Created Equal: Effects of Group Status on the Formation of Intergroup Attitudes in Children," *Child Development* 72, no. 4 (2001): 1151–62.

22. Lumpkin, *The Making of a Southerner,* 127.

23. Donnarae MacCann, *White Supremacy in Children's Literature: Characterizations of African Americans, 1830–1900* (New York: Routledge, 2001), 1.

24. Francis B. Simkins, "Tolerating the South's Past," *Journal of Southern History* 21, no. 1 (February 1955): 14.

25. Larry L. King, *Confession of a White Racist* (New York: Viking Press, 1971), 14–15.

26. Ibid., 17.

27. Robert Burns Eleazer, *School Books and Racial Antagonism: A Study of Omissions and Inclusions That Make for Misunderstanding* (Atlanta: Executive Committee Conference on Education and Race Relations, 1937), 6.

28. Marie Elizabeth Carpenter, *The Treatment of the Negro in American History School Textbooks: A Comparison of Changing Textbook Content, 1826 to 1939, with Developing Scholarship in the History of the Negro in the United States* (Menasha, Wis.: Banta, 1941), 13.

29. Ibid., 16, 59.

30. Ibid., 74.

31. National Association for the Advancement of Colored People, *Anti-Negro Propaganda in School Textbooks* (New York: National Association for the Advancement of Colored People, 1939), 7.

32. Arkansas, *List of Approved Library Books for Classified Elementary Schools* (Little Rock: Arkansas State Board of Education, 1935), 9.

33. Tennessee and Pearl Williams Kelley, *Tennessee School Library List: Books for High Schools* (Nashville: State Department of Education, 1914), 188.

34. For example, Katharine Du Pre Lumpkin remembered how her father chose the books she and her siblings read. Her mother reinforced at home the awe for white men learned at school, as her mother had the daily task of guiding her through the literature (Lumpkin, *The Making of a Southerner,* 123).

35. Eleazer, *School Books and Racial Antagonism,* 6.

36. Lawrence D. Reddick, "Racial Attitudes in American History Textbooks of the South," *Journal of Negro History* 19, no. 3 (July 1934): 237.

37. Eleazer, *School Books and Racial Antagonism,* 13.

38. *Anti-Negro Propaganda in School Textbooks,* 11.

39. Reddick, "Racial Attitudes in American History Textbooks of the South," 231–33.

40. Carpenter, *The Treatment of the Negro in American History School Textbooks,* 79, 81.

41. *Anti-Negro Propaganda in School Textbooks,* 11.

42. Reddick, "Racial Attitudes in American History Textbooks of the South," 233.

43. This image was originally published in Mary G. Kelty's *Growth of the American People and Nation* (Boston: Ginn, 1931), reprinted in Carpenter, *The Treatment of the Negro in American History School Textbooks,* 108.

44. Carpenter, *The Treatment of the Negro in American History School Textbooks,* 122.

45. Mark M. Krug, "On Rewriting of the Story of Reconstruction in the U.S. History Textbooks," *Journal of Negro History* 46, no. 3 (April 1961): 135.

46. Reddick, "Racial Attitudes in American History Textbooks of the South," 248–49.

47. Ibid., 255.

48. Ibid., 264.

49. National Association for the Advancement of Colored People, *Anti-Negro Propaganda in School Textbooks,* 8.

50. Simkins, "Tolerating the South's Past," 11.

51. Murray, *American Children's Literature and the Construction of Childhood,* xv.

52. William Fitzhugh Brundage, *The Southern Past: A Clash of Race and Memory* (Cambridge: Belknap Press of Harvard University Press, 2005), 3–4.

53. Ibid. 233.

54. Murray, *American Children's Literature and the Construction of Childhood,* 117. During the 1920s, children's stories, which previously followed characters from childhood to adulthood, begin to focus exclusively on childhood (Anne Scott MacLeod, *American Childhood: Essays on Children's Literature of the Nineteenth and Twentieth Centuries* [Athens: University of Georgia Press, 1994], 166).

55. Murray, *American Children's Literature and the Construction of Childhood,* 106.

56. The persistence and longevity of the "Aunt Jemima" advertisements demonstrate the commercial success of the "Mammy" stereotype. Such imagery continued the violation of black women's bodies by whites, especially white males, which began under slavery (O'Dell, *Sites of Southern Memory,* 20).

57. Lizzetta LeFalle-Collins, "Memories of Mammy," in *Art and the Performance of Memory,* ed. Richard Cándida Smith (New York: Routledge, 2002), 234–35, 241, 243; David Pilgrim, "The Mammy Caricature," Ferris State University Jim Crow Museum of Racist Memorabilia, www.ferris.edu/news/jimcrow/mammies/.

58. See Micki McElya, *Clinging to Mammy: The Faithful Slave in Twentieth-Century America* (Cambridge: Harvard University Press, 2007).

59. David Pilgrim, "The Tom Caricature," Ferris State University Jim Crow Museum of Racist Memorabilia, www.ferris.edu/news/jimcrow/tom/.

60. David Pilgrim, "The Coon Caricature," Ferris State University Jim Crow Museum of Racist Memorabilia, www.ferris.edu/news/jimcrow/coon/. See also Joseph Boskin, *Sambo: The Rise & Demise of an American Jester* (New York: Oxford University Press, 1986).

61. Washington State University, "Origin of the Pickaninny," http://salc.wsu.edu/Fair_S02/FS13/Entertainment/Pickaninny%20Origin.htm.

62. David Pilgrim, "The Picaninny Caricature," Ferris State University Jim Crow Museum of Racist Memorabilia. www.ferris.edu/news/jimcrow/picaninny/.

63. David Pilgrim, "The Brute Caricature," Ferris State University Jim Crow Museum of Racist Memorabilia. www.ferris.edu/news/jimcrow/brute/.

64. Some novels reinforced class ideas, such as Horatio Alger's *Ragged Dick* (1868), in which, after hard work and sacrifice, the hero attains a higher-class station in life (MacLeod, *American Childhood,* 87).

65. Murray, *American Children's Literature and the Construction of Childhood,* 96.

66. Donnarae MacCann and Gloria Woodard, *The Black American in Books for Children: Readings in Racism* (Metuchen, N.J.: Scarecrow Press, 1972), 1. See also David Nasaw, *Schooled to Order: A Social History of Public Schooling in the United States* (New York: Harper and Row, 1988), for a revisionist examination of the public schools.

67. Ruth L. Theobald, *Library Books for Elementary Schools, Kentucky* (Frankfort: Kentucky Department of Education, 1937), 155, 184.

68. Virginia, *List of Books Suggested for First Purchase for Virginia Elementary Schools* (Richmond: Virginia State Board of Education, 1937), 6.

69. Ellis Credel, *Little Jeemes Henry* (New York: Thomas Nelson and Sons, 1936), 38.

70. Augusta Baker, "Guidelines for Black Books: An Open Letter to Juvenile Editors," in *The Black American in Books for Children: Readings in Racism,* ed. Donnarae MacCann and Gloria Woodard (Metuchen, N.J.: Scarecrow Press, 1972), 51.

71. O'Dell, *Sites of Southern Memory,* 26.

72. Murray, *American Children's Literature and the Construction of Childhood,* 125.

73. Maud Lindsay's other highly recommended book, *Silverfoot,* contains anti-northern sentiment as well as happy, loyal, and comedic slave characters who help to care for the sons of the master. Louisiana's book list summarizes this book, which it calls "a pleasant picture of home life on a Southern plantation," as follows: "Three little cousins were entrusted with the protection of the pony Silverfoot when their uncle went off to join the Confederate army" (Louisiana, *Library List for the Elementary Schools of Louisiana* [Baton Rouge: State Department of Education of Louisiana, 1934], 82).

74. Lumpkin, *The Making of a Southerner,* 123.

75. Louise-Clarke Prynelle, *Diddie, Dumps, and Tot* (New York: Grosset and Dunlap, 1882), preface.

76. Dorothy Broderick, *Image of the Black in Children's Fiction* (New York: Bowker, 1973), 45.

77. South Carolina, *Elementary Library Catalog, 1938: Recommendations of Committee on Selection of Books for Elementary Schools, Including Delivered Prices When Purchased through Textbook Commission* (Columbia: State Department of Education, 1938), 20.

78. Virginia, *List of Books Suggested for First Purchase for Virginia Elementary Schools,* 24.

79. Thomas Nelson Page also wrote *Among the Camps, or Young People's Stories of the War* (New York: Scribner's Sons, 1891). This novel describes slave children as filthy, and they all speak in heavy dialect. The plantation owner's son Jack receives a slave (Jake) from his grandfather. Jack is envious of Jake, who lounges around all day. The two engage in shenanigans when they go to a Yankee camp where Jack repeatedly shows his

intellectual and moral superiority, his bravery, and his own manly self-worth (Murray, *American Children's Literature and the Construction of Childhood,* 115).

80. Thomas Nelson Page, *Two Little Confederates* (New York: Scribner's Sons, 1932), 65.

81. Ibid., 39–42.

82. Ibid., 189.

83. Dorothy Leetch, *Tommy Tucker on a Plantation* (Boston: Lothrop, Lee and Shepard, 1925), 9.

84. Louisiana, *Library List for the Elementary Schools of Louisiana,* 82.

85. Leetch, *Tommy Tucker on a Plantation,* 122–25.

86. Maud Lindsay, *Little Missy* (Boston: Lothrop, Lee and Shepard, 1922), 7–8. Rose B. Knox's *Boys and Sally down on a Plantation* is another example of this genre. Touted in Kentucky's book list as "a lively story of a large cotton plantation in Alabama," this book "gives a splendid description of all of the actives typical of plantation life" (Theobald, *Library Books for Elementary Schools, Kentucky,* 164).

87. Ibid., 98.

88. Joel Chandler Harris, as I discuss shortly, used this technique in the "Uncle Remus" stories.

89. Louise Clarke Pyrnelle, "Diddie, Dumps, and Tot," Electronic Text Center, University of Virginia Library, http://wyllie.lib.virginia.edu:8086/perl/toccer-new?id=PyrDidi.sgm&images=images/modeng&data=/texts/english/modeng/parsed&tag=public&part=16&division=div1.

90. Broderick, *Image of the Black in Children's Fiction,* 13. Another incident revolving around religion has Uncle Bob setting up a Sunday school for "the little darkies." Later, in his sermon, the plantation's black preacher identifies "sassin' uv white folks," and the "slightin' uv yer wuck!" as sins leading to damnation (ibid., 121).

91. Rose B. Knox, *Gray Caps* (New York: Doubleday, Doran, 1932), 11–12.

92. Ibid., 48.

93. Ibid., 14.

94. Louisiana, *Library List for the Elementary Schools of Louisiana,* 88.

95. Virginia, *List of Books Suggested for First Purchase for Virginia Elementary Schools,* 5. This is another example of the genre recommended for North Carolina rural schools as "a story of the Civil War, in which the daring and bravery of Robert E. Lee, Stonewall Jackson and other Confederate generals are graphically told. It is a most attractive story of the War Between the States" (North Carolina, James Yadkin Joyner, and Minnie Wells Leatherman, *Approved Lists of Books for Rural Libraries* [Raleigh: Edwards and Broughton, 1916], 19).

96. Lindsay, *Little Missy,* 16.

97. Ibid., 17–18.

98. Ibid., 61–62.

99. Shelley Fisher Fishkin, "Teaching Mark Twain's Adventures of Huckleberry

Finn," PBS Online, www.pbs.org/wgbh/cultureshock/teachers/huck/essay.html.

100. For an examination of the responses the novels received, see Stuart Hutchinson, ed., *Mark Twain: Tom Sawyer and Huckleberry Finn* (New York: Columbia University Press, 1998).

101. South Carolina, *Elementary Library Catalog, 1938,* 77.

102. Louisiana, *Library List for the Elementary Schools of Louisiana,* 94.

103. Mark Twain, *The Adventures of Huckleberry Finn* (New York: Harper and Brothers, 1912), 142.

104. Mark Twain, "The Adventures of Huckleberry Finn." University of Virginia Library, http://etext.lib.virginia.edu/images/modeng/public/Twa2Huc/twahuc11.jpg.

105. Jocelyn Chadwick-Joshua, *The Jim Dilemma: Reading Race in Huckleberry Finn* (Jackson: University Press of Mississippi, 1998), 70.

106. South Carolina, *Elementary Library Catalog,* 77.

107. Louisiana, *Library List for the Elementary Schools of Louisiana,* 94.

108. Chadwick-Joshua, *The Jim Dilemma,* 9.

109. Twain first introduces Jim as a superstitious slave (Twain, *The Adventures of Huckleberry Finn,* 8).

110. Ibid., 207.

111. Elaine Mensh and Harry Mensh argue that Huck's pranks, which continue throughout the book and range from pretending to drown to the more serious offense of withholding information about Jim's freedom, are Huck's efforts to reconcile his beliefs with his actions of helping a black man escape slavery (Mensh and Mensh, *Black, White, & Huckleberry Finn: Re-imagining the American Dream* [Tuscaloosa: University of Alabama Press, 2000]).

112. Twain, *Adventures of Huckleberry Finn,* 71–72.

113. Ibid., 365.

114. Fishkin, www.pbs.org/wgbh/cultureshock/teachers/huck/essay.html.

115. North Carolina, James Yadkin Joyner, and Minnie Wells Leatherman, *Approved Lists of Books for Rural Libraries,* 24.

116. Lawrence W. Levine, *Black Culture and Black Consciousness: Afro-American Folk Thought from Slavery to Freedom* (New York: Oxford University Press, 1978).

117. Joel Chandler Harris, *Nights with Uncle Remus: Myths and Legends of the Old Plantation* (New York: Appleton, 1881).

118. Murray, *American Children's Literature and the Construction of Childhood,* 133–34.

119. See also Jennifer Ritterhouse, "Reading, Intimacy, and the Role of Uncle Remus in White Southern Social Memory," *Journal of Southern History* 69 (August 2003): 585–622.

120. Bertram Wyatt-Brown, *Hearts of Darkness: Wellsprings of a Southern Literary Tradition* (Baton Rouge: Louisiana State University Press, 2003), chap. 4, "The Trickster Motif and Disillusion: Uncle Remus and Mark Twain."

121. Bannerman wrote an entire series of *Little Black Sambo* books, many appeared

on southern reading lists for public elementary schools. Those titles include *The Story of Little Black Mingo* (New York: Stokes, 1902); *The Story of the Teasing Monkey* (New York: Stokes, 1907); *The Story of Little Black Quasha* (New York: Stokes, 1908); *The Story of Little Black Bobtail* (New York: Stokes, 1909); and *The Story of Sambo and the Twins* (New York: Stokes, 1936). These stories had similar illustrations as those described in *The Story of Little Black Sambo.*

122. David Gast, "The Dawning of the Age of Aquarius for Multi-Ethnic Children's Literature," in *The Black American in Books for Children: Readings in Racism* (Metuchen, N.J.: Scarecrow Press, 1972), 171.

123. Phyllis J. Yuill, *Little Black Sambo: A Closer Look* (New York: Racism and Sexism Resource Center for Educators, 1976), 3.

124. Helen Bannerman, *The Story of Little Black Sambo* (Chicago: Reilly and Britton, 1908), 31; also in Yuill, *Little Black Sambo: A Closer Look.* 3. The image of blackface Sambo was published in 1917 (ibid., 14).

125. Helen Bannerman, *The Story of Little Black Sambo* (New York: Blue Ribbon Press, 1934), 41.

126. Theobald, *Library Books for Elementary Schools, Kentucky,* 13.

127. North Carolina, *Book List for the Elementary School Library, 1940–1941* (Raleigh: State Textbook Commission, 1940), 7.

128. Florida, *A Suggested Library Book List for Florida Schools* (Tallahassee: State Department of Education, 1939), 9.

129. Mary Clemens, *Our Little Child Faces Life* (Nashville: Cokesbury Press, 1939), 9.

130. Ibid., 16.

131. *The Story of Dr. Dolittle* was only one of many children's books that taught such lessons. Annie Vaughan's books *Frawg* and *Boochy's Wings* talk about a black boy and animals that mimic his behavior, connecting African American behavior to that of primitive animals. The Louisiana list described the book *Frawg* as an "Amusing story of a five-year-old negro boy who lives with his six brothers and sisters in a little cabin on an Alabama plantation" (Louisiana, *Library List for the Elementary Schools of Louisiana,* 95). *Frawg* also appeared on state-generated recommended-reading lists for elementary grades in Florida, Georgia, Kentucky, Louisiana, and Virginia.

132. Theobald, *Library Books for Elementary Schools, Kentucky,* 166.

133. Louisiana, *Library List for the Elementary Schools of Louisiana,* 83.

134. Hugh Lofting, *The Story of Doctor Dolittle* (New York: Stokes, 1920), 19.

135. Ibid., 22–23.

136. Ibid., 48.

137. Ibid., 50.

138. Ibid., 72.

139. Several passing references also imply inferiority; for example, one passage discusses how the black men of Africa hunt most of their animals by sneaking up behind them while they are not looking, i.e. in a cowardly way (ibid., 81).

140. Ibid., 97.

141. Ibid., 100.

142. Ibid., 101.

143. Ibid., 130.

144. Broderick, *Image of the Black in Children's Fiction,* 108–19, also explores Bumpo's desire to be white and Lofting's portrayals of black characters (Lofting, *The Story of Doctor Dolittle,* 105–6).

145. Hugh Lofting, *The Voyages of Doctor Dolittle* (New York: Lippincott, 1950), 80.

146. Ibid., 325–26.

147. MacLeod, *American Childhood,* 183. Many famous series books such as the Nancy Drew series, the Hardy Boys series, and the Bobbsey Twins series contained stereotypical black characters (Murray, *American Children's Literature and the Construction of Childhood,* 135). For the evolution of the portrayal of black characters in children's literature, see John Scott Wilson, "Race and Manners for Southern Girls and Boys: The 'Miss Minerva' Books and Race Relations in a Southern Children's Series," *Journal of American Culture* 17, no. 3 (Fall 1994): 69–74, which shows the changes in the black southern characters in "Miss Minerva" books between 1918 and 1939.

148. Murray, *American Children's Literature and the Construction of Childhood,* 137. The circulation records for this publication are largely lost.

149. National Conference on the Christian Way of Life, *And Who Is My Neighbor? An Outline for the Study of Race Relations in America,* pt. 1 (New York: Association Press, 1924), 7–8.

3. Consumerism Meets Jim Crow's Children

1. For the rise of advertising and the creation of consumer markets, see Susan Strasser, *Satisfaction Guaranteed: The Making of the American Mass Market* (New York: Pantheon, 1989); and Roland Marchand, *Advertising the American Dream: Making Way for Modernity, 1920–1940* (Berkeley and Los Angeles: University of California Press, 1986).

2. Grace Hale, *Making Whiteness: The Culture of Segregation in the South, 1890–1940* (New York: Pantheon, 1998), 121–68.

3. M. M. Manring, *Slave in a Box: The Strange Career of Aunt Jemima* (Charlottesville: University Press of Virginia, 1998); Marilyn Kern-Foxworth, *Aunt Jemima, Uncle Ben, and Rastus: Blacks in Advertising, Yesterday, Today, and Tomorrow* (Westport, Conn.: Praeger, 1994); Micki McElya, *Clinging to Mammy: The Faithful Slave in Twentieth-Century America* (Cambridge: Harvard University Press, 2007).

4. See Hale, *Making Whiteness,* chap. 1; and Donnarae MacCann, *White Supremacy in Children's Literature: Characterizations of African Americans, 1830–1900* (New York: Routledge, 2001), 1–5.

5. The historian Eric Lott argues that minstrel shows allowed northern white male

laborers to appropriate black culture for their own entertainment. In doing so, Lott observes, white men expressed and controlled the fear they felt for the black body. Lott finds that alongside this contempt was a fascination and longing for the transgression that minstrelsy offered. This co-optation worked to reduce black males to bodies that held representations of sexuality, labor, and the anxiety that white men felt about black men (Lott, *Love and Theft: Blackface Minstrelsy and the American Working Class* [New York: Oxford University Press, 1993]).

6. William Fitzhugh Brundage, *The Southern Past: A Clash of Race and Memory* (Cambridge: Belknap Press of Harvard University Press, 2005), 105–7.

7. Katharine Du Pre Lumpkin, *The Making of a Southerner* (Athens: University of Georgia Press, 1991), 200.

8. Ralph McGill, *The South and the Southerner* (Boston: Little, Brown, 1959), unpaginated; quote is on the first page of chapter 10.

9. David Pilgrim, "The Tom Caricature," Ferris State University Jim Crow Museum of Racist Memorabilia, www.ferris.edu/news/jimcrow/tom/.

10. The image was originally published in 1914 (Smithsonian Institute, National Museum of American History Archives, Warshaw Collection, Foods, General, Folder: Cream of Wheat Oversized, Drawer 17, Folder 18, 1914).

11. Anne McClintock, *Imperial Leather: Race, Gender, and Sexuality in the Colonial Contest* (New York: Routledge, 1995).

12. Smithsonian Institute, National Museum of American History Archives, Ayers Collection, Subject: Cereal, Box 7, Book 49–51, Folder: Cereal and Food 1902–3.

13. Smithsonian Institute, National Museum of American History Archives, Warshaw Collection, Cereals, Box 1, Folder: Cream of Wheat, 1907.

14. Smithsonian Institute, National Museum of American History Archives, Ayers Collection, Subject: Cereal, Box 7, Book 49–50, Folder: Cereal and Food, 1902–3.

15. Mary Louise Roberts discusses Richard Thomas and Anne McClintock's arguments about ideals of cleanliness and filth by establishing social hierarchies to justify segregation and control of population (Roberts, "Gender, Consumption, and Commodity Culture," *American Historical Review* 103, no. 3 [January 1998]: 834).

16. Jan Nederveen Pietrese, *White on Black: Images of Africa and Blacks in Western Popular Culture* (New Haven: Yale University Press, 1992); Timothy Burke, *Lifebuoy Men, Lux Women: Commodification, Consumption, and Cleanliness in Modern Zimbabwe* (Durham: Duke University Press, 1996), 10. See also Frantz Fanon, *Black Skin, White Masks* (New York: Grove, 1967).

17. Steven Hahn, *Roots of Southern Populism: Yeoman Farmers and the Transformation of the Georgia Upcountry, 1850–90* (New York: Oxford University Press, 1983); Steven Hahn, *A Nation under Our Feet: Black Political Struggles in the Rural South from Slavery to the Great Migration* (Cambridge: Harvard University Press, 2004).

18. *Ladies' Home Journal,* December 1899, back cover.

19. McClintock, *Imperial Leather,* 13. Anne McClintock's examination of the signifi-

cance of soap in Victorian culture does not explore how other sites imported and used these meanings. Her analysis, however, does provide a useful framework for exploring issues of race and gender in the American South's advertisements for toiletries (image from BBC online collection "Black Representations in Advertising," http://news.bbc .co.uk/2/shared/spl/hi/pop_ups/02/uk_black_representation_in_advertising/html/3 .stm).

20. Vincent Vinikas, *Soft Soap, Hard Sell: American Hygiene in an Age of Advertisement* (Ames: Iowa State University Press, 1992), xi.

21. Juliann Sivulka, *Stronger Than Dirt: A Cultural History of Advertising Personal Hygiene in America, 1875 to 1940* (Amherst, N.Y.: Humanity Books, 2001), chaps. 5 and 6. See also Suellen Hoy, *Chasing Dirt: The American Pursuit of Cleanliness* (New York: Oxford University Press, 1996).

22. Smithsonian Institute, National Museum of American History Archives, Warshaw Collection, Box 2, Folder 21, Fairbanks, N. K., Co.

23. Procter & Gamble Company, "I'll meet you at 9 in my Beauty Parlor," Ivory Soap Advertising Collection, 1883–1998, http://americanhistory.si.edu/archives/Ivory/ detail.asp?index=0207910021.jpg&startCount=20&skipNo=yes&skip_num=4&key =African,Americans&subject=&output=text&dates=1880–1939&coll=Ivory_Soap_ Advertising_Collection,_1883–1998&form_genre=. Originally published in *Scribner's Magazine* in 1932.

24. E. O. Hardin, *Phunology: A Collection of Tried and Proved Plans for Play, Fellowship, and Profit* (New York: Abingdon-Cokesbury Press, 1923), 429.

25. McClintock, *Imperial Leather*, 184.

26. Saidiya Hartman, *Scenes of Subjection: Terror, Slavery, and Self-Making in Nineteenth Century America* (New York: Oxford University Press, 1997), 7, see also chap. 1.

27. McElya, *Clinging to Mammy*, 224–28.

28. David Pilgrim, "The Picaninny Caricature," Ferris State University Jim Crow Museum of Racist Memorabilia, www.ferris.edu/news/jimcrow/picaninny/.

29. Smithsonian Institute, National Museum of American History Archives, Warshaw Collection, Baking Powders, Advertising Card Folder 2, Box 1, Folder 3.

30. Ibid.

31. Image from National Museum of American History Archives, Warshaw Collection, Baking Powders, Box 2, Folder 2125, no date.

32. David Pilgrim, "The Picaninny Caricature," Ferris State University Jim Crow Museum of Racist Memorabilia. www.ferris.edu/news/jimcrow/picaninny/.

33. Image from National Museum of American History Archives, Warshaw Collection, Cutlery, Box 2, Sears and Co.

34. McClintock, *Imperial Leather*, 223–25.

35. Arthur A. Krentz, "Play and Education in Plato's *Republic*," paper presented at the Twentieth World Congress of Philosophy, Boston, 1998, www.bu.edu/wcp/Papers/ Educ/EducKren.htm.

36. John Locke, *Some Thoughts Concerning Education* (Sioux Falls: NuVision, 2007), 104.

37. Ibid., 105–6.

38. Donald J. Mrozek, "The Natural Limits of Unstructured Play, 1880–1914," in *Hard at Play: Leisure in America, 1840–1940,* ed. Kathryn Grover (Amherst: University of Massachusetts Press, 1992), 223; Julie Rivkin and Michael Ryan, eds., *Literary Theory: An Anthology* (Oxford: Blackwell, 2004), 431–36. In the early twentieth century, the emerging theorist Sigmund Freud discussed the gratification play provides, introducing the pleasure principle as a motive behind children's actions, teaching them to avoid unpleasant behaviors and repeat favorable ones, translating their instincts into reason. Another theorist, Jean Piaget, found play to be the primary mode of learning in children, noting that playing allowed children to learn about themselves and others. His peer Lev Vygotsky also perceived play to be an important aspect of child development and viewed children as active agents who used play to imagine the world beyond them (Jennie Lindon, *Understanding Children's Play* [Cheltenham, UK: Nelson Thornes, 2001], 28–32).

39. Gary Cross, *Kids' Stuff: Toys and the Changing World of American Childhood* (Cambridge: Harvard University Press, 1997), 60.

40. Ibid., 18, 26.

41. Ibid., 23.

42. Bernard Mergen, "Made, Bought, and Stolen: Toys and the Culture of Childhood," in *Small Worlds: Children and Adolescents in America, 1850–1950,* ed. Elliott West and Paula Petrik (Lawrence: University Press of Kansas, 1992), 94; Miriam Formanek-Brunell, *Made to Play House: Dolls and the Commercialization of American Girlhood, 1830–1930* (New Haven: Yale University Press, 1993), 27; Mergen, "Made, Bought, and Stolen," 89. See also Carroll W. Pursell Jr., "Toys, Technology, and Sex Roles in America, 1920–1940," in *Dynamos and Virgins Revisited: Women and Technological Change in History* (Metuchen, N.J.: Scarecrow Press, 1979): 252–67.

43. James Spero, ed., *Collectible Toys and Games of the Twenties and Thirties from Sears, Roebuck and Co. Catalogs* (New York: Dover, 1988), 8.

44. Ibid., 29.

45. Pamela Nelson, "Toys as History: Ethnic Images and Cultural Change," in *Ethnic Images in Toys and Games Balch Institute,* www.balchInstitute.org/museum/toys/history.html.

46. Spero, *Collectible Toys and Games of the Twenties and Thirties,* 97. The description also noted that the dancer is "All dressed up in bright colors on a darky-cabin base."

47. Ibid., 59.

48. Patricia A. Turner, *Ceramic Uncles and Celluloid Mammies: Black Images and Their Influence on Culture* (New York: Anchor, 1994), 11.

49. Nelson, "Toys as History."

50. Spero, *Collectible Toys and Games of the Twenties and Thirties,* 55.

51. Denis Mercier, "From Hostility to Reverence: 100 Years of African-American

Imagery in Game," Jim Crow Museum of Racist Memorabilia. www.ferris.edu/news/ jimcrow/links/games.

52. Spero, *Collectible Toys and Games of the Twenties and Thirties,* 66.

53. Mercier, "From Hostility to Reverence," 2.

54. Cross, *Kids' Stuff,* 50–51; see also Pursell, "Toys, Technology, and Sex Roles in America, 1920–1940," 252–67.

55. Miriam Formanek-Brunell, "Sugar and Spite: The Politics of Doll Play in Nineteenth-Century America," in *Small Worlds: Children and Adolescents in America, 1850–1950,* ed. Elliott West and Paula Petrik (Lawrence: University Press of Kansas, 1992), 108.

56. Cross, *Kids' Stuff,* 50–51. It is important to note that while some authors argue that while adults used dolls for feminine socialization, daughters often used dolls for their own purposes (Formanek-Brunell, "Sugar and Spite," 108).

57. Howard P. Chudacoff, *Children at Play: An American History* (New York: New York University Press, 2007), 47.

58. Cross, *Kids' Stuff,* 80.

59. Margaret Adams, ed., *Collectible Dolls and Accessories of the Twenties and Thirties from Sears, Roebuck and Co. Catalogs* (New York: Dover, 1986), 36. "Topsy" was another "colored" baby doll with three curls of yarn hair that also was dressed in a brightly colored dress (Adams, *Collectible Dolls and Accessories of the Twenties and Thirties,* 104).

60. Bill Schroeder, *The Standard Antique Doll Identification and Value Guide, 1700–1935* (Paducah: Collector Books, 1976), 87.

61. Cross, *Kids' Stuff,* 100.

62. Henry Carrington Bolton, *The Counting-Out Rhymes of Children: Their Antiquity, Origin, and Wide Distribution, A Study in Folk-lore* (Detroit: Singing Tree Press, 1969), 52.

63. Ibid., 24.

64. This racist rhyme can be traced back to the 1850s (Roger D. Abrahams, ed., *Jump Rope Rhymes: A Dictionary* [Austin: University of Texas Press, 1969], 61).

65. Ibid., 55, 53.

66. Confirmed in Mississippi in 1909 (ibid., 61). A taunt from Mississippi: "I know something I ain't gonna tell, Three little niggers in a coconut shell; One could read, and one could write, And one could smoke his daddy's pipe" (Marcie C. Brown, *Amen, Brother Ben: A Mississippi Collection of Children's Rhymes* [Jackson: University Press of Mississippi, 1979], 93).

67. Abrahams, *Jump Rope Rhymes,* 36.

68. Ibid., 156.

69. Ibid., 161.

70. Ibid., 115, 208.

71. Ibid., 26.

72. Ibid., 144–45.

73. Ellen Booth Church, "Performing Plays in Preschool," *Scholastic Parents,* www2 .scholastic.com/browse/article.jsp?id=983.

74. Ethel Theodora Rockwell, *Children of Old Carolina: A Historical Pageant of North Carolina for Children* (Chapel Hill: University of North Carolina Extension Bulletin, 1925), 34.

75. Ibid., 35.

76. Marie Bankhead Owen, *How Alabama Became A State: Third of a Series of Children's Plays in Commemoration of the Close of a Century of Statehood* (Montgomery: Paragon Press, 1919), 4.

77. Ibid., 8.

78. S. Sylvan Simon, ed., *Easily Staged Plays for Boys, Nine New Non-Royalty Plays* (New York: Samuel French, 1936), 28. This book was recommended for southern schools even though it was published in the North.

79. Ibid., 40.

80. During segregation, the literature produced for a general churchgoing audience, regardless of denomination, spoke with a remarkably singular voice throughout the late nineteenth and early twentieth centuries. The Confederacy's downfall signaled to many the abandonment by a God who had deserted their cause. As southerners attempted to reconstruct their lives, they also tried to re-create the social order of the antebellum South through Jim Crow segregation, producing their own catechism and hymn books that reflected their religious, racial, and gender beliefs (Gail Murray, *American Children's Literature and the Construction of Childhood* [London: Twayne, 1998], 143). Religion is often the site through which daily struggles are resolved as spiritual crises, and an examination of sermons, Sunday school lessons, and church literature makes apparent that many white southerners did use the Bible and religious rhetoric to sanction segregation and white supremacy. As Evelyn Brooks Higginbotham's examination of the southern black Baptist churches notes, organized religions offer a unifying space for social discourses (Higginbotham, *Righteous Discontent: The Women's Movement in the Black Baptist Church, 1880–1920* [Cambridge: Harvard University Press, 1993]). See also Paul Harvey, "Sweet Homes, Sacred Blues, Regional Identities: Studying Religion, Race, and Culture in the American South," *Religious Studies Review* 23 (July 1997): 231–38.

81. E. O. Harbin, *Phunology: A Collection of Tried and Proved Plans for Play, Fellowship, and Profit, for the Use of Epworth Leagues, Sunday School Classes, and Other Young People's Societies* (Nashville: Dept. of Sunday School Supplies, 1920).

82. For more on minstrel shows, see Robert Toll, *Blacking Up: The Minstrel Show in Nineteenth-Century America* (New York: Oxford University Press, 1974); and Robert Cantwell, *When We Were Good: The Folk Revival* (Cambridge: Harvard University Press, 1996).

83. Eric Lott notes that whites first divided their culture from blacks and then transgressed this divide by watching representations of African Americans that allowed whites to dominate them (Lott, *Love and Theft*, 484). Robert Cantwell noted that minstrelsy allowed whites to indulge in their fetish for black culture and black bodies (Cantwell, *When We Were Good*, 60).

84. Adelaide H. Wyeth, *Hunkers' Corners: An Entertainment in Three Scenes* (Chicago: Dramatic Publishing, 1908), 5.

85. Lindsey Barbee, *The Thread of Destiny* (Chicago: Denison, 1914), 6.

86. Ibid., 9.

87. Sophie Huth Perkins, *Mirandy's Minstrels* (Chicago: Denison, 1906), 19.

88. Hartman, *Scenes of Subjection,* chap. 1.

89. For a history on the second rise of the Klan, see Nancy MacLean, *Behind the Mask of Chivalry: The Making of the Second Ku Klux Klan* (New York: Oxford University Press, 1994).

90. Jackie Hill, "Progressive Values in the Women's Ku Klux Klan," *Constructing the Past* 9, no. 1 (2008): 24.

91. Ibid., 22.

92. See also Kelli R. Kerbawy, "Knights in White Satin: Women of the Ku Klux Klan" (master's thesis, Marshall University, 2007).

93. Kathleen M. Blee, *Women of the Klan: Racism and Gender in the 1920s* (Berkeley and Los Angeles: University of California Press, 1991), 164.

94. Lumpkin, *The Making of a Southerner,* 136.

95. D. W. Griffith and Walter Huston, "Prelude" to *Birth of a Nation* (Ideal Pictures, 1930).

96. Blee, *Women of the Klan,* 162.

97. Lumpkin, *The Making of a Southerner,* 136.

98. Tri-K-Klub, *Races: Trust, RACES, Influence: Knowledge: Kindling, Leadership, Unity, Brains-Brawn-Breadth,* Tri-K-Klub series no. 3 (Little Rock: Tri-K-Klub, A Department of Women of the Ku Klux Klan, 1915), 3.

99. Ibid., 4.

100. Ibid., 6.

101. Ibid., 10.

102. Ibid., 9.

103. Ibid., 14.

104. Blee, *Women of the Klan,* 161.

105. Tri-K-Klub, *Influence: Trust, Races, INFLUENCE: Knowledge: Kindling, Leadership, Unity, Brains-Brawn-Breadth,* Tri-K-Klub series no. 4. (Little Rock: Tri-K-Klub, A Department of Women of the Ku Klux Klan, 1915), 5–10.

106. Ibid., 12–13.

107. Ibid., 15.

108. Ku Klux Klan and Junior Klan, *Constitution and By-laws Junior Ku Klux Klan* (n.p.: Junior Klan Publications, 1924), 5–6.

109. Blee, *Women of the Klan,* 161.

110. Ku Klux Klan and Junior Klan, *Kloran: Junior Order Ku Klux Klan* (n.p.: Junior Klan Publications. 1924), 6.

111. Ku Klux Klan and Junior Klan, *Constitution and By-laws Junior Ku Klux,* 39–40.

112. Ku Klux Klan and Junior Klan, *Kloran: Junior Order Ku Klux Klan,* 42–43.

113. Ibid., 4–12.

114. Ibid., 46–47.

115. Ku Klux Klan and Junior Klan, *Constitution and By-laws Junior Ku Klux,* 44.

116. United Daughters of the Confederacy, "Founder and Co-Founder," www.hqudc .org/about/founder.html.

117. Amy L. Heyse, "Teachers of the Lost Cause: The United Daughters of the Confederacy and the Rhetoric of Their Catechisms" (Ph.D. diss., University of Maryland, 2006), 3.

118. Ibid., 83.

119. Ibid., 84.

120. United Daughters of the Confederacy, "United Daughters of the Confederacy Homepage," www.hqudc.org/.

121. Barbara Jean Emert, *The Georgia Division, Children of the Confederacy History, 1912–1987* (Georgia: Children of the Confederacy, Georgia Division, 1988), 1.

122. Mary B. Poppenheim, Maude Blake Merchant, and Ruth Jennings Lawton, *The History of the United Daughters of the Confederacy* (Richmond: Garrett and Massie, 1938), 182.

123. Children of the Confederacy, "Children of the Confederacy Homepage," www .hqudc.org/CofC/.

124. Poppenheim, Merchant, and Lawton, *The History of the United Daughters of the Confederacy,* 183.

125. Ibid., 188; Heyes, "Teachers of the Lost Cause," 95.

126. Karen L. Cox, *Dixie's Daughters: The United Daughters of the Confederacy and the Preservation of Confederate Culture* (Gainesville: University Press of Florida, 2003), 145.

127. Heyse, "Teachers of the Lost Cause," 1–13.

128. James M. McPherson, T*his Mighty Scourge: Perspectives on the Civil War* (Oxford: Oxford University Press, 2007), 96–98.

129. Heyes, "Teachers of the Lost Cause," 172.

130. Mildred Lewis Rutherford, *Monthly Programs for the Children of the Confederacy* (Athens: no publisher or date, but the program is for 1915), 1.

131. American Civil War.com, "Confederate Civil War Song Lyrics: The Bonnie Blue Flag Confederate Civil War Song," http://americancivilwar.com/Civil_War_Music/ song_lyrics/bonnie_blue_confederate_song.html.

132. Rutherford, *Monthly Programs for the Children of the Confederacy,* 4.

133. Cornelia Branch Stone, *U.D.C. Catechism for Children* (Staunton: J. E. B. Stuart Chapter no. 10, U. D.C., 1900), quoted in Heyes, "Teachers of the Lost Cause," 311.

134. Rutherford, *Monthly Programs for the Children of the Confederacy,* 9. Chapter 2 discusses the children's book *Diddie, Dumps, and Tot.*

135. Heyes, "Teachers of the Lost Cause," 275–76.

136. Children of the Confederacy of the United Daughters of the Confederacy,

Minutes of the Fourteenth General Convention (Augusta: United Daughters of the Confederacy, 1968), 7. The instructions for an essay contest remind the children to only use the phrase the "War Between the States."

137. Catherine Fosl, *Subversive Southerner: Anne Braden and the Struggle for Racial Justice in the Cold War South* (New York: Palgrave Macmillan, 2002), 19. Braden does not discuss this in her autobiography, and there is only one passing mention of it in a biography. Braden has constructed her childhood without discussing such clubs, perhaps for personal or political reasons.

138. Emert, *The Georgia Division, Children of the Confederacy History, 1912–1987*, 3.

139. Ibid., 17.

140. Ibid., 19.

141. United Daughters of the Confederacy, Thomas K. Spencer Chapter #947 Children of the Confederacy, "From Our Director," www.florida-scv.org/Camp556/augustajane/cofc.htm.

142. Lumpkin, *The Making of a Southerner*, 155.

4. "The Course My Life Was to Take"

Title quote and epigraph: H. L. Mitchell, *Mean Things Happening in This Land: The Life and Times of H. L. Mitchell, Co-Founder of the Southern Tenant Farmers Union* (Montclair, N.J.: Allanheld, Osmun, 1979), 2; United States, *Antilynching: Report (to accompany H.R. 2251), House of Representatives* (Washington, D.C.: U.S. Government Printing Office, 1937), 2.

1. Ibid.

2. Bernard Mergen, "Children's Play in American Autobiographies, 1820–1914," in *Hard at Play: Leisure in America, 1840–1940*, ed. Kathryn Grover (Amherst: University of Massachusetts Press, 1992), 169.

3. James L. McGaugh, *Memory and Emotion: The Making of Lasting Memories* (New York: Columbia University Press, 2003), 3, 89–90.

4. Darlene O'Dell, *Sites of Southern Memory: The Autobiographies of Katharine Du Pre Lumpkin, Lillian Smith, and Pauli Murray* (Charlottesville: University Press of Virginia, 2001), 65.

5. Mitchell, *Mean Things Happening in This Land*, 2.

6. Katharine Du Pre Lumpkin, *The Making of a Southerner* (Athens: University of Georgia Press, 1991), 130–32.

7. Ibid., 132; Elizabeth Fox-Genovese, "Between Individualism and Community: Autobiographies of Southern Women," in *Located Lives: Place and Idea in Southern Autobiography*, ed. Bill J. Berry (Athens: University of Georgia Press, 1990), 32.

8. Lumpkin, *The Making of a Southerner*, 133.

9. Marion Wright, interview by Jacquelyn Hall, March 8, 1978, 8, Southern Oral History Program Collection, Southern Historical Collection, University of North Carolina at Chapel Hill.

10. Marion Wright, interview by Arnold Shankman, March 11, 1976, 7, Southern Oral History Program Collection, Southern Historical Collection, University of North Carolina at Chapel Hill.

11. Catherine Fosl, *Subversive Southerner: Anne Braden and the Struggle for Racial Justice in the Cold War South* (New York: Palgrave Macmillan, 2002), 72.

12. Ibid., 79.

13. Mitchell, *Mean Things Happening in This Land,* 1.

14. Nancy MacLean, *Behind the Mask of Chivalry: The Making of the Second Ku Klux Klan* (New York: Oxford University Press, 1994), 150–51.

15. Donald E. Wilkes Jr., "The Last Lynching in Athens," *Flagpole,* September 1997, 8–9.

16. Patricia Sullivan, *Days of Hope: Race and Democracy in the New Deal Era* (Chapel Hill: University of North Carolina Press, 1996), 26–27.

17. Wilkes, "The Last Lynching in Athens," 8–9.

18. John Herbert Roper, *C. Vann Woodward: Southerner* (Athens: University of Georgia Press, 1987), 16.

19. Ibid., 17.

20. Thomas F. Gossett, *Race: The History of an Idea in America* (New York: Oxford University Press, 1997), 269.

21. Mary Jane Brown, *Eradicating This Evil: Women in the American Anti-Lynching Movement, 1892–1940* (New York: Garland, 2000), 28.

22. Michel Foucault, *Discipline and Punish: The Birth of the Prison,* 2nd ed. (New York: Vintage Books, 1995), 9.

23. Amy Louise Wood, *Lynching and Spectacle: Witnessing Racial Violence in America, 1890–1940* (Chapel Hill: University of North Carolina Press, 2009).

24. The term "spectacle lynching" emphasizes both the crowd and the camera gazing at the ritual (Grace Hale, *Making Whiteness: The Culture of Segregation in the South, 1890–1940* [New York: Pantheon, 1998], 202–3).

25. Ibid., 203–10. Local and regional newspapers were also responsible for the publicity and promotion of a lynching, as well as playing a key role in the creation of a genre of lynching narratives (Stanley J. Tambiah, "A Performance Approach to Ritual," in *Readings in Ritual Studies,* ed. Ronald Grimes [Upper Saddle River, N.J.: Prentice Hall, 1996], 497). The mob's actions were, as William Fitzhugh Brundage notes, "a highly ritualized choreography" (Brundage, *Lynching in the New South: Georgia and Virginia, 1880–1930* [Urbana: University of Illinois Press, 1993], 39).

26. Christopher Waldrep, "War of Words: The Controversy of the Definition of Lynching, 1899–1940," *Journal of Southern History* 66, no. 1 (2000): 75–100. See also Christopher Waldrep, *The Many Faces of Judge Lynch: Extralegal Violence and Punishment in America* (New York: Palgrave Macmillan, 2002). Brundage defines the southern lynch mob in this way (Brundage, *Lynching in the New South,* 292).

27. Michael J. Pfeifer, *Rough Justice: Lynching and American Society, 1874–1947* (Urbana: University of Illinois Press, 2004), 4–12.

28. Between 1882 and 1930, eight out of every ten victims of white mobs were African American (Brundage, *Lynching in the New South,* 8; E. M. Beck and Stewart E. Tolnay, "When Race Didn't Matter: Black and White Mob Violence against Their Own Color," in *Under Sentence of Death: Lynching in the South,* ed. William Fitzhugh Brundage [Chapel Hill: University of North Carolina Press, 1997], 149).

29. Stewart E. Tolnay and E. M. Beck, *A Festival of Violence: An Analysis of Southern Lynchings, 1882–1930* (Urbana: University of Illinois Press, 1992), 49. From 1882 to 1889, the percentage of lynchings for accusations of rape was 38.1; between 1900 and 1930, it was 24.8, with the entire South averaging 31.1.

30. Brundage, *Lynching in the New South,* 18–45.

31. Hale, *Making Whiteness,* 237.

32. Other early studies of lynching argue that this violence was the work of lower-class whites (see James Cutler, *Lynch-Law: An Investigation into the History of Lynching in the United States* [New York: Negro Universities Press, 1969]; and Arthur Franklin Raper, *The Tragedy of Lynching* [Baltimore: Black Classic Press, 1933]). Recent scholarship has complicated these views, noting that lynching united whites and oppressed blacks psychologically, economically, socially, and politically.

33. Gail Bederman, *Manliness & Civilization: A Cultural History of Gender and Race in the United States, 1880–1917* (Chicago: University of Chicago Press, 1995), 11–12, 49–51. See also Michael Kimmel, *Manhood in America: A Cultural History* (New York: Free Press, 1996), chap. 4.

34. David R Roediger, *Wages of Whiteness: Race and the Making of the American Working Class,* Haymarket series (London: Verso, 1999), 186. The sociologist Stanley J. Tambiah notes that rituals are highly dramatic cultural forms of communication in "A Performance Approach to Ritual," in *Readings in Ritual Studies,* ed. Ronald Grimes (New Jersey: Prentice Hall, 1996), 49. Catherine M. Bell argues that within dramatic rituals, a performance communicates social realities (Bell, *Ritual Theory, Ritual Practice* [New York: Oxford University Press, 1992], 37–39). The lynching ritual was thus a public performance that allowed whites to perform their beliefs and exhibit white culture to children.

35. Tambiah, "A Performance Approach to Ritual," 497.

36. Ida B. Wells-Barnett and Jacqueline Jones Royster, *Southern Horrors and Other Writings: The Anti-Lynching Campaign of Ida B. Wells, 1892–1900* (Boston: Bedford, 1997), 92. Hale describes Myrtle Vance as being three years old (Hale, *Making Whiteness,* 207).

37. Donald G. Mathews, "The Southern Rite of Human Sacrifice," *Journal of Southern Religion,* August 2002, http://jsr.as.wvu.edu/mathews.htm. See also Donald G. Mathews, *Religion in the Old South* (Chicago: University of Chicago Press, 1977).

38. Orlando Patterson, *Rituals of Blood: Consequences of Slavery in Two American Centuries* (Washington, D.C.: Counterpoint, 1998), 204. The site of lynchings also often contained a secular symbolic meaning, for common sites included churchyards, bridges,

and trees, all of which held religious and historic connotations of punishment.

39. Matthews finds a connection existed between "the South's most dramatic act of brutality and the pervasive drama of salvation preached from pulpits throughout the region" (http://jsr.as.wvu.edu/mathews3.htm).

40. Foucault, *Discipline and Punish,* 33–34.

41. Donald G. Mathews finds in the case of the black victim, punishment may be a "sublimation of people's self-assertive instincts and hostilities" (http://jsr.as.wvu.edu/mathews3.htm).

42. Michael Hatt, "Race, Ritual, and Responsibility: Performativity and the Southern Lynching," in *Performing the Body/Performing the Text,* ed. Amelia Jones and Andrew Stephenson (New York: Routledge Press, 1999), 77. Mob violence against African Americans often took on the veneer of a Sunday outing, or a celebration, with hundreds of men, women, and children in attendance (National Association for the Advancement of Colored People, *Burning at Stake in the United States: A Record of the Public Burning by Mobs of Five Men, during the First Five Months of 1919, in the States of Arkansas, Florida, Georgia, Mississippi, and Texas* [Baltimore: Black Classic Press, 1986], 21). A letter to James Weldon Johnson of the NAACP began, "My dear Mr. Johnson: Yesterday, here at Magnolia, Ark, at 11 A.M., on the public sq., the children, women and men burned alive a colored man." These people, the author continued, did so to celebrate Armistice Day (William G. Grover to Mr. James Weldon Johnson of NAACP, NAACP Collection, Group I, Series C, Box 350, Subject File: Lynching, Magnolia, Ark., 1919).

43. Elizabeth Freeman posed as a women's rights activist campaigning for women's suffrage, and her account, in combination with newspaper accounts, was used in an NAACP report that circulated to try to raise money for the antilynching cause. Freeman refers to seventeen-year-old Jesse Washington as a boy throughout her narrative. By referring to him as a boy, Freeman invokes the sympathy of a reader that a "child" would be subjected to such brutality. It is also a reflection of the cultural belief that boys and girls remained children until marriage (NAACP Collection, Group I, Series C, Box 370, Subject File: Lynching, Waco, Tex., 1916, Elizabeth Freeman report, 24, NAACP report, 4).

44. Tim Madigan, "Lynching on Northeast 12th," *Star Telegram,* October 6–13, 2002, 17, www.poynter.org/resource/13229/ColorHatemain.pdf.

45. James Allen, *Without Sanctuary: Lynching Photography in America* (Santa Fe: Twin Palms, 2000), afterword.

46. United States, *To Prevent and Punish the Crime of Lynching: Hearing before a Subcommittee of the Committee on the Judiciary, United States Senate, Sixty-ninth Congress, First Session on S. 121: A Bill to Assure to Persons within the Jurisdiction of Every State the Equal Protection of the Laws, and to Punish the Crime of Lynching, February 16, 1926* (Washington, D.C.: U.S. Government Printing Office, 1926), 28.

47. Leon F. Litwack, *Trouble in Mind: Black Southerners in the Age of Jim Crow* (New York: Knopf, 1998), 287–88; Hatt, "Race, Ritual, and Responsibility: Performativity and the Southern Lynching," 77.

48. Litwack, *Trouble in Mind,* 286–87.

49. A description of a girl attending appears in Wells-Barnett and Royster, *Southern Horrors and Other Writings,* 115–16, but without the year mentioned. The same lynching is described with the year in Litwack, *Trouble in Mind,* 289–90.

50. Ida B. Wells-Barnett and Frederick Douglass, *The Red Record: Tabulated Statistics and Alleged Causes of Lynching in the United States* (Cirencester, U.K.: Echo Library, 2005), 38–42.

51. Southern Commission on the Study of Lynching and George Fort Milton, *Lynchings and What They Mean: General Findings of the Southern Commission on the Study of Lynching* (Atlanta: Southern Commission, 1931), 38.

52. Hughes allegedly inquired to a white woman about money owed him by her husband. Hearing her husband was away, Hughes purportedly left and returned shortly with a shotgun, which he used to subdue the wife before sexually assaulting her (Helen J. Louge, "Angry Mob Rules in May 30, 1930," *Sherman Democrat Grayson County Sesquicentennial,* March 17, 1996, sec 2, p. 11).

53. NAACP Collection, Group I, Series C, Box 363, Subject File: Lynching: Bailey, N.C., 1927, *Chicago Whip,* August 20, 1927.

54. Wells-Barnett and Royster, *Southern Horrors and Other Writings,* 3. See also Pamela Newkirk, "Ida B. Wells-Barnett; Journalism as a Weapon against Racial Bigotry," *Media Studies Journal* 14, no. 2 (Spring/Summer 2000), www.hartford-hwp.com/archives/45a/317.html; and Patricia A. Schechter, *Ida B. Wells-Barnett and American Reform, 1880–1930* (Chapel Hill: University of North Carolina Press, 2001).

55. Donald Lee Grant, *The Way It Was in the South: The Black Experience in Georgia* (Athens: University of Georgia Press, 2001), 269–70.

56. Library of Congress, Rare Book and Special Collections Division, Daniel A. P. Murray Pamphlets Collection, "A Sermon on Lynch Law and Raping," preached by Rev. E. K. Love at the First African Baptist Church, Savannah, Georgia, November 5, 1893.

57. *New York World,* July 29, 1916, quoted in Ralph Ginzburg, *100 Years of Lynchings* (Baltimore: Black Classic Press, 1988), 104–5.

58. George C. Rable, "The South and the Politics of Antilynching Legislation, 1920–1940," *Journal of Southern History* 51, no. 2 (May 1985): 203.

59. Ibid., 208.

60. NAACP Collection, Group I, Section C, Box 360, Subject File: Lynching, Ellisville, Miss., 1919, Newsclippings.

61. Jacquelyn Dowd Hall examines the connection between lynching and social roles in *Revolt against Chivalry: Jessie Daniel Ames and the Women's Campaign against Lynching* (New York: Columbia University Press, 1993). Dowd Hall notes that Jessie Daniel Ames argued that the fear of rape "regulated white women's behavior" and rested upon the idea of white male protection. This chivalrous code dictated the relationships between white men and women and African Americans (xxi). See also Crystal Nicole Feimster, *Southern Horrors: Women and the Politics of Rape and Lynching* (Cambridge: Harvard University Press, 2009).

62. United States, *To Prevent and Punish the Crime of Lynching* (1926), 42–43.

63. Opponents of mob violence saw the presence of white women, whom they considered the primary socializing force for future generations, as reflecting the women's endorsement of the violence and expressed concern that they were passing this onto "the next generation by taking their children to lynching scenes" (Mary Jane Brown, *Eradicating This Evil: Women in the American Anti-Lynching Movement, 1892–1940* [New York: Garland, 2000], 30).

64. United States, "Statement of Rev. John T. Gillard," *Punishment for the Crime of Lynching: Hearings before a Subcommittee of the Committee on the Judiciary, United States Senate, Seventy-third Congress, Second Session on S. 1978: A Bill to Assure to Persons within the Jurisdiction of Every State the Equal Protection of the Laws and to Punish the Crime of Lynching, Part I, February 20 and 21, 1934* (Washington, D.C.: U.S. Government Printing Office, 1934), 70.

65. James Cameron, *A Time of Terror: A Survivor's Story* (Baltimore: Black Classic Press, 1994), 72. Cameron escaped from a Marion, Indiana, lynch mob in 1930.

66. Erskine Caldwell, introduction to *An Art Commentary on Lynching,* exhibition catalog (New York: Arthur U. Newton Galleries, 1935), unpaginated.

67. *The New Georgia Encyclopedia,* "Erskine Caldwell," www.georgiaencyclopedia .org/nge/Article.jsp?id=h-497.

68. *An Art Commentary on Lynching,* unpaginated. The tone of the image is discussed in Richard N. Masteller, "Caricatures in Crisis: The Satiric Vision of Reginald Marsh and John Dos Passos," *Smithsonian Studies in American Art* 3, no. 2 (Spring 1989): 23–45.

69. Karla F. C. Holloway, *Passed On: African American Mourning Stories: A Memorial* (Durham, N.C.: Duke University Press, 2003), 66.

70. Dora Apel, *Imagery of Lynching: Black Men, White Women, and the Mob* (New Brunswick, N.J.: Rutgers University Press, 2004), 89.

71. Amy MacKenzie, "Walter White on Lynching," *Interracial Review,* September 1946; 30–46. The interview can also be found in The Papers of the NAACP: Part 7: The Anti-Lynching Campaign, 1912–1955, Group I, Series C, Reel 5 (microfilm).

72. Arthur U. Newton Galleries, unpaginated.

73. Ibid.

74. Margaret Rose Vendryes, "Hanging on Their Walls: An Art Commentary on Lynching, the Forgotten 1935 Art Exhibition," in *Race Consciousness: African-American Studies for the New Century,* ed. Judith Jackson Fossett and Jeffrey A. Tucker (New York: New York University Press, 1997), 163.

75. A collection of souvenir lynching postcards can be found in the exhibit-turned-book *Without Sanctuary.* There is, unfortunately, no statistical evidence attesting to the number of children who attended or participated in racial violence.

76. Litwack, *Trouble in Mind,* 286–87.

77. In Bardwell, Kentucky, photographs of C. J. Miller's body, "dangling at the

end of a chain," were developed (*Birmingham [Ala.] Post,* October 27, 1934, quoted in Ginzburg, *100 Years of Lynchings,* 223).

78. Wood, *Lynching and Spectacle,* 75–76.

79. Mike Cox, "Ghost of 1916 Lynching Still Haunts Texas City," *Austin American–Statesman,* July 3, 2005, Life and Arts, K5.

80. Hatt, "Race, Ritual, and Responsibility," 83. See also Harvey Young, "The Black Body as Souvenir in American Lynching," *Theatre Journal* 57, no. 4 (December 2005): 639–57.

81. Fred A. Gildersleeve, "Large Crowd Looking at the Burned Body of Jesse Washington, 18 year-old-African American, Lynched in Waco, Texas, May 15, 1916," in Visual Materials from the National Association for the Advancement of Colored People Records, Library of Congress Prints and Photographs Division, Washington, D.C.

82. Awareness of the camera helped not only to enact whiteness, but also to exhibit it to a larger, national audience (Mary Esteve, *The Aesthetics and Politics of the Crowd in American Literature* [Oxford: Cambridge University Press, 2003], 141).

83. *Without Sanctuary,* image 41.

84. United States, *Punishment for the Crime of Lynching* (1934), 87.

85. Phillip Dray, *At the Hands of Persons Unknown: The Lynching of Black America* (New York: Random House, 2002), 136. The postcard image is in Wells-Barnett and Royster, *Southern Horrors and Other Writings,* 118.

86. NAACP Collection, Group 1, Series C, Box 350, Subject File: Lynching, Magnolia, Ark., 1919, *Chattanooga Daily Times,* February 13, 1918, 9.

87. National Association for the Advancement of Colored People, *An Appeal to the Conscience of the Civilized World* (New York: National Association for the Advancement of Colored People, 1920), 9–12. "Blood-Curdling Lynching Witnessed by 2,000 Persons," *Chattanooga Times,* February 13, 1918, and "Gruesome Details Given on Estill Springs Lynching," *Chattanooga Times,* February 14, 1918, quoted in Ginzburg, *100 Years of Lynchings,* 114–18.

88. Paul P. Reuben, "Chapter 9: Walter White," *PAL: Perspectives in American Literature—A Research and Reference Guide,* http://web.csustan.edu/english/reuben/pal/chap9/white.html.

89. Walter White, "The Lynching of Jim McIlherron: An Investigation," *Crisis,* May 1918, 19–21.

90. Litwack, *Trouble in Mind,* 286.

91. Anne P. Rice, *Witnessing Lynching: American Writers Respond* (New Brunswick, N.J.: Rutgers University Press, 2003), 5.

92. Wells-Barnett and Royster, *Southern Horrors and Other Writings,* 94–97, 202–3. Patterson also describes the lynching in Paris in *Rituals of Blood* (193–94).

5. Violent Masculinity

Epigraph from Claude McKay, "The Lynching," in *Black on White: Black Writers on What It Means to Be White,* ed. David Roediger (New York: Schocken, 1998), 335.

1. Patricia Bernstein, *The First Waco Horror: The Lynching of Jesse Washington and the Rise of the NAACP* (College Station: Texas A&M Press, 2005), 95.

2. Ibid., 103–11.

3. NAACP Collection, Group I, Series C, Box 370, Subject File: Lynching, Waco, Tex., 1916, Elizabeth Freeman report. Grace Hale's account of the lynching mentions Washington's castration (Hale, *Making Whiteness: The Culture of Segregation in the South, 1890–1940* [New York: Pantheon Books, 1998], 218). Afterward, the mob attached Washington's corpse to a car and dragged it to the local blacksmith shop to hang for public viewing. Other accounts include James M. SoRelle, "The Waco Horror: The Lynching of Jesse Washington," *Southwestern Historical Quarterly* 86 (April 1983): 517–36.

4. As social constructions, race and gender are mutually reinforcing, contextually variable, and inseparable (Joan Scott, "Gender: A Useful Category of Historical Analysis," *American Historical Review* 91, no. 5 [December 1986]: 1053–75).

5. This ritual united whites along class lines, allowing lower-class whites to commit acts of violence that would go unpunished, creating an illusion of their own power (William Fitzhugh Brundage, *Lynching in the New South: Georgia and Virginia, 1880–1930* [Urbana: University of Illinois Press, 1993], 15). Grace Hale argues that lynchings functioned for white adults to strengthen segregation by helping create "a collective, all-powerful whiteness." In addition, communal lynchings would not have been possible without the consent and often the participation of the social elite (Hale, *Making Whiteness*, 237).

6. See Mary Douglas, *Purity and Danger: An Analysis of Concepts of Pollution and Taboo* (London: Pelican, 1970), chap. 8. See also J. William Harris, "Etiquette, Lynching, and Racial Boundaries in Southern History: A Mississippi Example," *American Historical Review* 100, no. 2 (April 1995): 392.

7. Orlando Patterson, *Rituals of Blood: Consequences of Slavery in Two American Centuries* (Washington D.C.: Counterpoint, 1998), 182–83.

8. René Girard, *Violence and the Sacred* (Baltimore: Johns Hopkins University Press, 1977), 85–88.

9. Harris, "Etiquette, Lynching, and Racial Boundaries in Southern History," 392.

10. Brundage, *Lynching in the New South*, 82.

11. Stanley J. Tambiah, "A Performance Approach to Ritual," in *Readings in Ritual Studies*, ed. Ronald Grimes (Upper Saddle River, N.J.: Prentice Hall, 1996), 497; Catherine Bell, *Ritual Theory, Ritual Practice* (New York: Oxford University Press, 1992), 37–39.

12. Judith Butler, "Performative Acts and Gender Constitution: An Essay in Phenomenology and Feminist Theory," in *Performing Feminisms: Feminist Critical Theory and Theatre*, ed. Sue-Ellen Case (Baltimore: Johns Hopkins University Press, 1990), 278.

13. Erving Goffman, *The Presentation of Self in Everyday Life* (New York: Doubleday, 1959), 22–72.

14. David D. Gilmore, *Manhood in the Making: Cultural Concepts of Masculinity* (New Haven: Yale University Press, 1990), 222–23.

15. Judith Butler, *Bodies That Matter: On the Discursive Limits of "Sex"* (New York: Routledge, 1993), 2–3.

16. See chapter 4 of this volume.

17. Terence Finnegan, "Lynching and Political Power in Mississippi and South Carolina," in *Under Sentence of Death: Lynching in the South,* ed. William Fitzhugh Brundage (Chapel Hill: University of North Carolina Press, 1997), 201.

18. Mary Church Terrell, "Lynching from a Negro's Point of View," *North American Review* 178 (1904): 853.

19. United States, *Punishment for the Crime of Lynching: Hearings before a Subcommittee of the Committee on the Judiciary, United States Senate, Seventy-third Congress, Second Session on S. 1978: A Bill to Assure to Persons within the Jurisdiction of Every State the Equal Protection of the Laws and to Punish the Crime of Lynching, Part I, February 20 and 21, 1934* (Washington, D.C.: U.S. Government Printing Office, 1934), 174.

20. As Vincent Vinikas notes, if people of the time fail to see an event as noteworthy and record it as a meaningful event, it is difficult to recover its details (Vinikas, "Specters in the Past: The Saint Charles, Arkansas, Lynching of 1904 and the Limits of Historical Inquiry," *Journal of Southern History* 65, no. 3 [August 1999]: 536, 539; Stewart E. Tolnay and E. M. Beck, *A Festival of Violence: An Analysis of Southern Lynchings, 1882–1930* [Urbana: University of Illinois Press, 1995], ix).

21. Neil R. McMillen, *Dark Journey: Black Mississippians in the Age of Jim Crow* (Urbana: University of Illinois Press, 1989), 229.

22. Terrell, "Lynching from a Negro's Point of View," 853.

23. "A community of memory may include all those individuals who share a direct or indirect memory of a given event." Age, race, and gender influence how or if events are remembered. In addition, the size of the mob and the connections of the lynching to the community affect recollections of lynchings (Bruce E. Baker, "Lynching and Memory" in *Where These Memories Grow: History, Memory, and Southern Identity,* ed. William Fitzhugh Brundage [Chapel Hill: University of North Carolina Press, 2000], 325–32).

24. McMillen, *Dark Journey,* 225–27.

25. *New York World,* December 7, 1899, quoted in Ralph Ginzburg, *100 Years of Lynchings* (Baltimore: Black Classic Press, 1988), 24.

26. National Association for the Advancement of Colored People, *The Lynching of Claude Neal* (New York: National Association for the Advancement of Colored People, 1934), 2.

27. NAACP Collection, Group I, Series C, Box 363, Subject File: Lynching, Winston-Salem, N.C., 1918–1926; *Raleigh News & Observer,* November 18, 1919.

28. *Chicago Record-Herald,* June 24, 1903, quoted in Ginzburg, *100 Years of Lynchings,* 55.

29. Lawrence H. Larsen and Barbara J. Cottrell, *The Gate City: A History of Omaha* (Lincoln: University of Nebraska Press, 1997), 170.

30. For examples of active white women, see Crystal Nicole Feimster, "'Ladies and

Lynching': The Gendered Discourse of Mob Violence in the New South, 1880–1930" (Ph.D. diss., Princeton University, 2000).

31. *Atlanta Journal,* June 21, 1920, quoted in Ginzburg, *100 Years of Lynchings,* 133.

32. Scholars such as Gail Bederman link instruction in racial superiority to adult masculinity. She argues that white men lynched black men to reinforce their manliness. Doing so proved their masculinity against black men, cast as an inferior and unmanly race (Bederman, *Manliness & Civilization: A Cultural History of Gender and Race in the United States, 1880–1917* [Chicago: University of Chicago Press, 1995], 49–51). Joel Williamson, in a psychosexual interpretation of lynching, argues that whites projected their sexual fears onto African Americans (Williamson, *The Crucible of Race: Black/White Relations in the American South since Emancipation* [New York: Oxford University Press, 1984], 285–322). See also J. Douglas Smith, *Managing White Supremacy: Race, Politics, and Citizenship in Jim Crow Virginia* (Chapel Hill: University of North Carolina Press, 2002); and George M. Frederickson, *The Black Image in the White Mind: The Debate on Afro-American Character and Destiny, 1817–1914* (Middleport: Wesleyan University Press, 1971).

33. James Cameron, *A Time of Terror: A Survivor's Story* (Baltimore: Black Classic Press, 1994), 66.

34. Southern Commission on the Study of Lynching and George Fort Milton, *Lynchings and What They Mean: General Findings of the Southern Commission on the Study of Lynching* (Atlanta: Southern Commission, 1931), 39.

35. Arthur Franklin Raper, *The Tragedy of Lynching* (Baltimore: Black Classic Press, 1933), 323.

36. NAACP Collection, Group I, Series C, Box 370, Subject File: Lynching, Waco, Tex., 1916, Elizabeth Freeman report, 1.

37. Bertram Wyatt-Brown, *Hearts of Darkness: Wellsprings of a Southern Literary Tradition* (Baton Rouge: Louisiana State University Press, 2003), 154.

38. Leon F. Litwack, *Trouble in Mind: Black Southerners in the Age of Jim Crow* (New York: Knopf, 1998), 288.

39. United States, *Punishment for the Crime of Lynching: Hearings before a Subcommittee of the Committee on the Judiciary, United States Senate, Seventy-third Congress, Second Session on S. 1978: A Bill to Assure to Persons within the Jurisdiction of Every State the Equal Protection of the Laws and to Punish the Crime of Lynching, Part I, February 20 and 21, 1934* (Washington, D.C.: U.S. Government Printing Office, 1934), 231. See also Paul Ortiz, *Remembering Jim Crow: African Americans Tell about Life in the Segregated South* (New York: New Press, 2001).

40. Most inquiries into lynching have found them to occur at hands of "parties unknown" despite obvious evidence to the contrary (see Phillip Dray, *At the Hands of Persons Unknown: The Lynching of Black America* [New York: Random House, 2002]).

41. United States, *Punishment for the Crime of Lynching* (1934), 43.

42. An example of male teenaged leaders occurred in Omaha, Nebraska, in 1919,

when a group of teenagers, led by two students beating on drums, marched the crowd to the courthouse to "get the Nigger." The crowd assembled on the school grounds, further showing that this crowd was organized, motivated, and led by teenage boys (Lawrence and Cottrell, *The Gate City,* 169).

43. Ronald L. Grimes, *Deeply into the Bone: Re-Inventing Rites of Passage* (Berkeley and Los Angeles: University of California Press, 2000), 108.Whether this rite within the lynching ritual definitively transformed southern white boys attending the event into southern white men is unknown, as there were many ways to accustom southern whites to the racial order of Jim Crow, but this was an especially dramatic and public one. Generally, I delineate between boys and young men based on their level of activity in the lynch mob.

44. *New York Herald,* June 9, 1903, quoted in Ginzburg, *100 Years of Lynchings,* 51.

45. *Atlanta Constitution,* June 1, 1930, quoted in Ginzburg, *100 Years of Lynchings,* 185.

46. Larsen and Cottrell, *The Gate City,* 169, 171.

47. *New York Times,* October 19, 1933, quoted in Ginzburg, *100 Years of Lynchings,* 200–202.

48. Ida B. Wells-Barnett and Jacqueline Jones Royster, *Southern Horrors and Other Writings: The Anti-Lynching Campaign of Ida B. Wells, 1892–1900* (Boston: Bedford, 1997), 202.

49. Bertram Wyatt-Brown, *Southern Honor: Ethics and Behavior in the Old South* (New York: Oxford University Press, 1982), 168.

50. Peter Spierenburg, *Men and Violence: Gender, Honor, and Rituals in Modern Europe and America* (Columbus: Ohio State University Press, 1998), 2.

51. Raper, *The Tragedy of Lynching,* 324.

52. Ibid., 323.

53. Dora Apel, *Imagery of Lynching: Black Men, White Women, and the Mob* (New Brunswick, N.J.: Rutgers University Press, 2004), 139.

54. *Chattanooga Times,* February 13, 1918, quoted in Ginzburg, *100 Years of Lynchings,* 114.

55. *Birmingham Post,* October 27, 1934, quoted in Ginzburg, *100 Years of Lynchings,* 223.

56. Apel, *Imagery of Lynching,* 136.

57. National Association for the Advancement of Colored People, *The Lynching of Claude Neal* (New York: National Association for the Advancement of Colored People, 1934).

58. Trudier Harris, *Exorcising Blackness: Historical and Literary Lynching and Burning Rituals* (Bloomington: Indiana University Press, 1984), 22.

59. Wells-Barnett and Royster, *Southern Horrors and Other Writings,* 116.

60. Harvey Young, "The Black Body as Souvenir in American Lynching," *Theatre Journal* 57, no. 4 (December 2005): 641–46.

61. *Baltimore Afro-American,* March 6, 1935, quoted in Ginzburg, *100 Years of Lynchings,* 226.

62. *Springfield Weekly Republican,* April 28, 1899, quoted in Ginzburg, *100 Years of Lynchings,* 12; Young, "The Black Body as Souvenir in American Lynching," 671.

63. James Allen, *Without Sanctuary: Lynching Photography in America* (Santa Fe: Twin Palms, 2000), 8–9.

64. Patterson, *Rituals of Blood,* 182–83.

65. Eager customers in Pennsylvania bought some of Zachariah Walker's remains from resourceful boys (Dennis B. Downey and Raymond M. Hyser, *No Crooked Death: Coatesville, Pennsylvania, and the Lynching of Zachariah Walker* [Urbana: University of Illinois Press, 1991], 38–39).

66. *Chicago Record-Herald,* February 27, 1901, quoted in Ginzburg, *100 Years of Lynchings,* 37.

67. Orlando Patterson has argued that such actions were perhaps a form of communal rape upon African American men (Patterson, *Rituals of Blood,* 174).

68. NAACP Collection, Group I, Series C, Box 370, Subject File: Lynching, Gordonsville, Va., 1936–1937, *Virginia Journal and Guide,* May 23, 1936.

69. *Chicago Record-Herald,* June 29, 1903, quoted in Ralph Ginzburg, *100 Years of Lynchings,* 58.

70. NAACP Collection, Group I, Series C, Box 354, Subject File: Lynching, Fayette, Ga., 1919.

71. United States, *Crime of Lynching: Hearings before a Subcommittee on the Judiciary, United States Senate, Seventy-sixth Congress, Third Session on H.R. 80: An Act to Assure to Persons within the Jurisdiction of Every State Due Process of Law and Equal Protection of the Laws, and to Prevent the Crime of Lynching, February 6, 7, March 5, 12, and 13, 1940.* (Washington, D.C.: U.S. Government Printing Office, 1940), 42.

72. NAACP Collection, Group I, Series C, Box 360, Subject File: Lynching, Pelahatchee, Miss., 1934, S. D. Redmond, Attorney at Law, Jackson, Mississippi, to Mr. Walter White, August 14, 1934.

73. NAACP Collection, Group 1, Series C, Box 349, Subject File: Lynching, Little Rock, Arkansas, 1927, from "Special Investigation of the John Carter Lynching, Little Rock, Ark.," 10.

74. McMillen, *Dark Journey,* 225, 227.

75. NAACP Collection, Group I, Series C, Box 366, Subject File: Lynching, Laurens, S.C., 1920–1921, *New York Glove,* April 2, 1920.

76. Brundage, *Lynching in the New South,* 1–2.

77. NAACP Collection, Group 1, Series C, Box 350, Subject File: Lynching, Nodena, Ark., 1921, *Memphis (Tenn.) News Scimitar,* January 26, 1921.

6. "Is This the Man?"

Epigraph from NAACP Collection, Group I, Section C, Box 360, Subject File: Lynching, Ellisville, Miss., 1919, Newsclippings, *New Orleans States-Item,* June 26, 1919.

1. NAACP Collection, Group I, Series C, Box 361, Subject File: Lynching, Vicksburg, Miss., 1919, Newsclippings, *Vicksburg (Miss.) Evening Post,* May 14, 1919.

2. *Vicksburg (Miss.) Herald,* May 15, 1919, quoted in Ralph Ginzburg, *100 Years of Lynchings* (Baltimore: Black Classic Press, 1988), 120. This account refers to the victim as Miss Lulu Belle Bishop, while all others name the victim as Maddie Hudson. The lynching takes place at the same time and place and identifies Clay as the victim, so I include it in this analysis.

3. National Association for the Advancement of Colored People, *Burning at Stake in the United States: A Record of the Public Burning by Mobs of Six Men during the First Six Months of 1919 in the States of Arkansas, Florida, Georgia, Mississippi and Texas* (New York: National Association for the Advancement of Colored People, 1919), 6.

4. NAACP Collection, Group I, Series C, Box 361, Subject File: Lynching, Vicksburg, Miss., 1919, Newsclippings, *Baltimore Daily Herald,* June 17, 1919; J. William Harris, "Etiquette, Lynching, and Racial Boundaries in Southern History: A Mississippi Example," *American Historical Review* 100, no. 2 (April 1995): 407.

5. *New York Age,* June 14, 1919, quoted in Ginzburg, *100 Years of Lynchings,* 121. Additionally, Clay's brother spent the entire night of the supposed crime in his company (Harris, "Etiquette, Lynching, and Racial Boundaries in Southern History," 408).

6. William Fitzhugh Brundage, *Lynching in the New South: Georgia and Virginia, 1880–1930* (Urbana: University of Illinois Press, 1993), 60. While the plurality of African American lynch victims faced murder charges (40 percent), usually of a white person, rape charges, many leveled by young teenage girls, account for 25 percent and were the second-highest motivation for lynching black men. Although disproven as inaccurate, the numbers of the Tuskegee Archives are similar (Charles Chesnutt, "Causes Of Lynchings, 1882–1968," Archives at Tuskegee Institute, www.berea.edu/faculty/browners/chesnutt/classroom/lynching_table_causes.html).

7. See Angela Davis, "Rape, Racism and the Myth of the Black Rapist," in *Women, Race and Class,* ed. Davis (New York: Random House, 1981).

8. Gil Bailie, "Violence and the Sacred: René Girard's Insights into Christianity," *Aisling Magazine,* www.aislingmagazine.com/aislingmagazine/articles/TAM26/R.Girard.html.

9. Jane Turner Censor, *The Reconstruction of White Southern Womanhood, 1865–1895* (Baton Rouge: Louisiana State University Press, 2003), chap. 1. See also Laura Edwards, *Gendered Strife and Confusion: The Political Culture of Reconstruction* (Urbana: University of Illinois, 1997).

10. Peter W. Bardaglio's social and legal examination of prosecuting sexual violence in Old South argues that slaves received relatively fair trials, and that it was not until after emancipation that they lost due process (Bardaglio, "Rape and the Law in the Old South: 'Calculated to Excite Indignation in Every Heart,'" *Journal of Southern History* 60, no. 4 [November 1994]: 749–72). See also Peter W. Bardaglio, *Reconstructing the Household: Families, Sex, and the Law in the Nineteenth-Century South* (Chapel Hill: University of North Carolina Press, 1995).

11. Lisa Lindquist Dorr, *White Women, Rape, and the Power of Race in Virginia, 1900–1960* (Chapel Hill: University of North Carolina Press, 2004), 146, 9.

12. Diane Miller Sommerville, "The Rape Myth in the Old South Reconsidered," *Journal of Southern History* 61, no. 3 (August 1995): 481–518, esp. 483–85.

13. See Martha Hodes, *White Women Black Men: Illicit Sex in the Nineteenth-Century South* (New Haven: Yale University Press, 1997); and Peggy Pascoe, "Miscegenation, Court Cases, and Ideologies of 'Race' in Twentieth-Century America," *Journal of American History* 83 (June 1996): 44–69.

14. Dorr, *White Women, Rape, and the Power of Race in Virginia, 1900–1960,* 124–26.

15. *New York Post,* May 25, 1937, quoted in Ginzburg, *100 Years of Lynchings,* 231.

16. *New York Times,* June 11, 1900, quoted in Ginzburg, *100 Years of Lynchings,* 31–32.

17. *Chicago Record-Herald,* August 20 and 21, 1901, quoted in Ginzburg, *100 Years of Lynchings,* 41–43.

18. Crystal Feimster, "Ladies and Lynching: The Gendered Discourse of Mob Violence in the New South, 1880–1930" (Ph.D. diss., Princeton University, 2000), 85–86.

19. Other examples of girls who positively identified their alleged attackers occurred throughout the South. In 1922, a Georgia mob lynched a black man named Johnson on the farm where he had allegedly assaulted a prominent white farmer's daughter (NAACP Collection, Group I, Series C, Box 355, Subject File: Lynching, Sanderville, Ga., 1922, *New York World,* September 29, 1922). In 1925, a mob in Rocky Ford, Georgia, burned an "unidentified Negro" at a stake after being "identified by the girl" (NAACP Collection, Group I, Series C, Box 355, Subject File: Lynching, Rocky Ford, Ga., 1925, *World,* March 3, 1925). A *New York Times* headline for August 6, 1941, proclaimed "Negro Boy, 16, Is Lynched. He Is Shot 32 Times by Alabama Posse—Accused by Girl." His identifier was eleven years old (NAACP Collection, Group 1, Series C, Box 348, Subject File: Lynching, Haynesville, Ala., 1931, *New York Times,* August 6, 1941). In 1921, a Florida mob brought a girl from her home in a nearby town to identify Ben Campbell of Wauchula. After she identified him, the mob murdered Campbell (NAACP Collection, Group I, Series C, Box 353, Subject File: Lynching, Wauchula, Florida, *Jacksonville [Fla.] Times-Union,* February 12, 1921). In Houston, Texas, Joe Winters "was taken to Leonidas where the girl positively identified him." He was brought back to the courthouse square in town, where "thousands of persons, including women and children, witnessed" Winters being burned alive (NAACP Collection, Group I, Series C, Box 368, Subject File: Lynching, Conroe, Texas, 1922, *Houston [Tex.] Post,* May 20, 1922).

20. United States, *Punishment for the Crime of Lynching: Hearings before a Subcommittee of the Committee on the Judiciary, United States Senate, Seventy-third Congress, Second Session, on S. 1978, a Bill to Assure to Persons within the Jurisdiction of Every State the Equal Protection of the Laws and to Punish the Crime of Lynching, February 14, 1935* (Washington, D.C.: U.S. Government Printing Office, 1935), excerpted text from *New York World-Telegram,* August 25, 1934.

21. Donald G. Mathews, "The Southern Rite of Human Sacrifice," *Journal of Southern Religion* (August 2002), http://jsr.as.wvu.edu/mathews3.htm.

22. NAACP Collection, Group I, Series C, Box 369, Subject File: Lynching, Sour Lake, Tex., 1921, *Memphis Commercial Appeal,* November 27, 1921.

23. *Baltimore American,* July 24, 1900, quoted in Ginzburg, *100 Years of Lynchings,* 33–35.

24. NAACP Collection, Group I, Series C, Box 351, Subject File: Lynching, Fort Myers, Fla., 1924, *New York Journal,* May 26, 1924.

25. United States, *To Prevent and Punish the Crime of Lynching: Hearing before a Subcommittee of the Committee on the Judiciary, United States Senate, Sixty-ninth Congress, First Session on S. 121: A Bill to Assure to Persons within the Jurisdiction of Every State the Equal Protection of the Laws, and to Punish the Crime of Lynching, February 16, 1926* (Washington, D.C.: U.S. Government Printing Office, 1926), 27.

26. Other examples of lynchings based on nonidentifications include Len Hart of Jacksonville, Florida, who allegedly peeped into a white girl's window. A mob lynched him despite the fact that "the girl told two deputies that she could not remember what the intruder looked like" (*Memphis Commercial Appeal,* August 16, 1923, quoted in Ginzburg, *100 Years of Lynchings,* 172). In Rocky Ford, Georgia, a young girl who was hospitalized "was asked to identify the negro Sunday morning. She was not sure, but thought he looked like the one who had attacked her" (United States, *To Prevent and Punish the Crime of Lynching* [1926]), 26.

27. National Association for the Advancement of Colored People, *Can the States Stop Lynching?* (New York: National Association for the Advancement of Colored People, 1937), 8.

28. *Jackson (Miss.) Daily News,* June 26, 1919, quoted in Ginzburg, *100 Years of Lynchings,* 8.

29. NAACP Collection, Group I, Series C, Box 360, Subject File: Lynching, Foxworth, Miss., 1919, *New York Telegram,* November 20, 1919. In one case brought in a congressional hearing before a subcommittee of the Committee on the Judiciary, a young girl allegedly assaulted in a pea field "told her parents 'Jim Ivey did it.'" A mob captured Ivey and took him "before the girl at the hospital, she identified him after one glance, and then turned her head away." A crowd of six hundred people burned him alive (United States, *To Prevent and Punish the Crime of Lynching* [1926], 27).

30. United States, *To Prevent and Punish the Crime of Lynching* [1926], quoting *Memphis News Scimitar,* September 20, 1925.

31. *Omaha Bee,* October 5, 1919, quoted in Ginzburg, *100 Years of Lynchings,* 126–29.

32. NAACP Collection, Group 1, Series C, Box 349, Subject File: Lynching, Little Rock, Ark., 1927–1928, *Little Rock Daily News,* May 4, 1927.

33. *Birmingham Voice of the People,* April 1, 1916, quoted in Ginzburg, *100 Years of Lynchings,* 102. White communities became outraged against African Americans who

injured white children since that act seemed to whites to blithely ignore racial mores against the perceived most innocent and defenseless of victims. In Madisonville, Texas, a black man rode his horse over a little girl, injuring her. The town promptly lynched an African American male, only to discover the next day that "the wrong Negro had been gotten hold of by the mob. The guilty one made his escape" (*Chicago Tribune,* November 22, 1895, quoted in Ginzburg, *100 Years of Lynchings,* 9).

34. *New Orleans Tribune,* July 10, 1934 quoted in Ginzburg, *100 Years of Lynchings,* 219.

35. NAACP Collection, Group I, Series C, Box 369, Subject File: Lynching, Kirbyville, Tex., 1934, *Kansas City Call,* September 6, 1934. Another newspaper account noted that the girl with whom Griggs was arrested was jailed on a charge of vagrancy: "her name is given as Joan Rivers, age 19" (*Galveston [Tex.] Tribune,* June 23, 1934, quoted in Ginzburg, *100 Years of Lynchings,* 18).

36. *St. Louis Argus,* May 27, 1921, quoted in Ginzburg, *100 Years of Lynchings,* 150. The attempted roadside attack is a common tale. See also *Montgomery Advertiser,* August 12, 1913, 83–84; *Hickory (N.C.) Record,* April 28, 1936, 228; *New York Times,* June 11, 1900, 31–32; and *Houston Post,* June 11, 1900, all quoted in Ginzburg, *100 Years of Lynchings,* 32–33.

37. *Raleigh (N.C.) Independent,* July 17, 1920, quoted in Ginzburg, *100 Years of Lynchings,* 137–38.

38. *Chicago Record-Herald,* July 27, 1903, quoted in Ginzburg, *100 Years of Lynchings,* 60.

39. *New York Negro World,* October 4, 1930, quoted in Ginzburg, *100 Years of Lynchings,* 191–92.

40. NAACP Collection, Group I, Series C, Box 355, Subject File: Lynching, Thomasville, Ga., *World,* September 26, 1930, and *New York Evening Post,* September 25, 1930.

41. Brundage, *Lynching in the New South,* 61.

42. *Chicago Defender,* May 10, 1919, quoted in Ginzburg, *100 Years of Lynchings,* 119.

43. *Knoxville East Tennessee News,* December 2, 1920, quoted in Ginzburg, *100 Years of Lynchings,* 143.

44. Ibid., 142.

45. Mary Church Terrell, "Lynching from a Negro's Point of View," *North American Review* 178 (1904): 5.

46. White fears of African Americans' sexual advances often led to punishment in cases where no sexual contact had occurred. In 1912, the *Montgomery Advertiser* reported that Tom Miles, a twenty-nine-year-old African American, was "writing insulting notes to a white girl." Acquitted of this charge due to a lack of evidence, a mob hung Miles from a tree and riddled his body with bullets (*Montgomery Advertiser,* April 10, 1912, quoted in Ginzburg, *100 Years of Lynchings,* 76). In 1934, a similar incident occurred in Mississippi when twenty-five-year-old James Sanders was accused of writing an "insulting" letter to "a young Hinds County, white girl." The town citizens formed a

mob and shot him repeatedly (*Atlanta Constitution*, July 11, 1934, quoted in Ginzburg, *100 Years of Lynchings*, 220).

47. NAACP Collection, Group I, Series C, Box 353, Subject File: Lynching, Seminole, Fla., 1925, *Louisville (Ky.) News*, May 16, 1925.

48. NAACP Collection, Group 1, Series C, Box 348, Subject File: Lynching, Camp Hill, Ala., Newsclippings, *New York Evening Sun*, July 11, 1931.

49. Another example of hidden motives occurred in Johnson City, Tennessee, when Cooksey Dallas, a black man, was lynched allegedly because "he made improper advances to a white woman." Other sources claimed "he refused to sell moonshine whiskey to white soldiers" (*New York Mail*, October 29, 1920, quoted in Ginzburg, *100 Years of Lynchings*, 140–41).

50. NAACP Collection, Group I, Series C, Box 351, Subject File: Lynching, Florida, 1919–1922, deposition of H. A. Bryan, (Rev.) Sworn on July 31, 1919, notarized by Albertina T. Edmondson.

51. NAACP Collection, Group I, Series C, Box 355, Subject File: Lynching, Waycross, Ga., 1918–1919. This is an unsigned report, but a note was attached from H. H. Thweatt, president of the Waycross NAACP, that states, "I am enclosing more information about that liynching [*sic*]." The *Baltimore Daily Herald*, May 28, 1919, ran a report of the NAACP's investigation of a lynching at Blackshear, Georgia, which contains the same information as Thweatt's report, with a few minor grammar discrepancies.

52. NAACP Collection, Group I, Series C, Box 354, Subject File: Lynching, Dublin, Ga., 1919. The letter is unsigned and dated August 11, 1919.

53. Jacquelyn Dowd Hall argues that the threat of rape posed by African American men to white women allowed white men to maintain sexual control over women and, thus, racial supremacy. The fear of rape, she argues, "regulated white women's behavior" and required a chivalrous code of white male protection, which dictated the relationships between white men and women and African Americans. Yet, through examining women who opposed lynching, Hall found women activists exposing the rhetoric and the social mechanisms governing the rape-lynch complex (Hall, *Revolt against Chivalry: Jessie Daniel Ames and the Women's Campaign against Lynching* [New York: Columbia University Press, 1993], xxi). Crystal Feimster also argues that southern white women played powerful roles in shaping the discourse of the lynching ritual through demanding that white males punish African American bodies. In doing so, Feimster argues, white women utilized their newfound voice of authority to carve out a political space outside of the home (Feimster, "Ladies and Lynching," 45–48, 99, 139).

54. Thus, whether the affair was consensual or not, a young black man's showing romantic interest in a white girl was enough to merit his lynching. In this case, the lynching would have not have occurred if the girl had not partaken in planned retribution by reporting that she had been approached (*Memphis Commercial Appeal*, November 26, 1921, quoted in Ginzburg, *100 Years of Lynchings*, 156–57).

55. *Knoxville Journal*, July 23, 1933, quoted in Ginzburg, *100 Years of Lynchings*, 198.

56. NAACP Collection, Group I, Series C, Box 353, Subject File: Lynching, Athens, Ga., 1919, *New York Herald,* September 11, 1919. Such rewards were common. In April 1893, South Carolina governor Benjamin Tillman offered a $250 reward for the recapture of the alleged attacker of fourteen-year-old Mamie Baxter, who had escaped custody after his initial arrest (Kantrowitz, "White Supremacist Justice and the Rule of Law," 229).

57. Leon F. Litwack, *Trouble in Mind: Black Southerners in the Age of Jim Crow* (New York: Knopf, 1998), 304.

58. *Hickory (N.C.) Record,* April 28, 1936, quoted in Ginzburg, *100 Years of Lynchings,* 228.

59. *Montgomery Advertiser,* August 12, 1913, quoted in Ginzburg, *100 Years of Lynchings,* 83–84.

60. The ways in which female children engage in aggressive behavior are learned from their cultural environment. "Some of the differences in how parents socialize emotions in young girls and boys may also be due to parental stereotypes about gender. Simply being told that a particular infant is male or female changes how adults interpret infants' facial expressions" (Marion K. Underwood, *Social Aggression among Girls* [New York: Guilford Press, 2003], 61). Mothers and other adult women socialize girls in the appropriate ways in which to express emotion, influencing how children perceive and respond to those around them (ibid., 61–62). White girls' accounts of attempted rape show their awareness of the view that virile black men could not resist vulnerable white girls when they ventured away from white male protection.

61. Lynching reported in *St. Louis Argus,* June 6, 1926, quoted in Ginzburg, *100 Years of Lynchings,* 174; and NAACP Collection, Group 1, Series C, Box 350, Subject File: Lynching, Wilson, Ark., 1926, *Huntsville (Ala.) Times,* May 27, 1926. The St. Louis paper refers to the lynched man as "Blades," the Huntsville paper as "Blazer." Since St. Louis was his hometown, I use "Blades."

62. Underwood, *Social Aggression among Girls,* 4. Women committing violence is not a historical irregularity; in the antebellum South, on occasion, white women beat their slaves and even struck their children (Laura F. Edwards, "Law, Domestic Violence, and the Limits of Patriarchal Authority in the Antebellum South," *Journal of Southern History* 65, no. 4 [November 1999]: 743).

63. Nikki Crick also argues that girls were not typically seen as aggressive because researchers were looking at the wrong kind of aggression (Crick and J. K. Grotpeter, "Relational Aggression, Gender, and Social-Psychological Adjustment," *Child Development* 66 [1995]: 710–22). N. R. Crick, "The Role of Overt Aggression, Relational Aggression, and Prosocial Behavior in the Prediction of Children's Future Social Adjustment," *Child Development* 67 (1996): 2317–27; Underwood, *Social Aggression among Girls,* 136.

64. Underwood, *Social Aggression among Girls,* 40.

65. NAACP Collection, Group I, Section C, Box 360, Subject File: Lynching, Ellisville, Miss., 1919, Newsclippings, *Memphis Commercial Appeal,* June 27, 1919.

66. Lewis R. Gordon notes the contradictions in individual consciousness that allow

us to lie to ourselves. This cognitive dissonance, he argues, otherwise would make us uncomfortable. This understanding of humans as contradictory creatures also explains how white girls in the Jim Crow South could falsely accuse black men but still believe that they were either actually attacked or that the accusation was justified (Gordon, *Bad Faith and Antiblack Racism* [Atlantic Highlands, N.J.: Humanities Press, 1995]).

67. NAACP Collection, Group I, Series C, Box 356, Subject File: Lynching Millersburg, Ky., 1918–1922, *Maysville (Ky.) Public Ledger,* March 30, 1920.

68. In 2003, the journalist Barton Grover Howe traced out the events of the lynching of James Scott in 1923 (Howe, "Legacy of a Lynching," *Missourian,* May 6, 2003, www.digmo.org/news/story.php?ID=1854). Utilizing newspaper accounts, written and oral interviews, local archives, and regional histories, he explored the legacy of Scott's lynching (ibid, 2).

69. Ibid., May 6, 2003, 1.

70. Ibid., May 6, 2003, 2–4.

71. Ibid., May 7, 2003, 3.

72. Ibid., May 7, 2003. www.digmo.org/news/story.php?ID=1873.

73. Ibid., May 9, 2003, 1–3, http://digmo.com/news/story.php?ID=1916.

74. A separate account of this incident refers to the girl as Claude Foster (NAACP Collection, Group I, Series C, Box 355, Subject File: Lynching, Thomasville, Ga., *Birmingham Post,* February 27, 1927).

75. NAACP Collection, Group I, Series C, Box 355, Subject File: Lynching, Thomasville, Ga., *Columbia (S.C.) Record,* February 26, 1927.

76. *Chicago Record-Herald,* July 27, 1903, quoted in Ginzburg, *100 Years of Lynchings,* 53–57.

77. NAACP Collection, Group I, Series C, Box 343, Subject File: Lynching, General, Clippings, 1912–1914, *Greensboro (N.C.) News,* July 13, 1914.

78. Ibid., Group I, Series C, Box 359, Subject File: Lynching Mississippi General, 1929, Newsclippings: 1926–1929, *Baltimore Afro American,* December 31, 1927.

Conclusion

Epigraph from Leon F. Litwack, *Trouble in Mind: Black Southerners in the Age of Jim Crow* (New York: Knopf, 1998), 288.

1. Steven Hahn explores the relationships developed under slavery that allowed grassroots resistance to occur after emancipation (Hahn, *A Nation under Our Feet: Black Political Struggles in the Rural South from Slavery to the Great Migration* [Cambridge: Harvard University Press, 2004]). Grace Hale explores the cultural work of creating discourses of whiteness and blackness, which, she asserts, became the language of the new order of segregation. Hale argues that modernization broke down social categories, which whites responded to by commodifying race (Hale, *Making Whiteness: The Culture of Segregation in the South, 1890–1940* [New York: Pantheon, 1998]). For an

examination of the roles African Americans played in contesting white supremacy, see W. E. B. Du Bois, *Black Reconstruction in America: An Essay Toward a History of the Part Which Black Folk Played in the Attempt to Reconstruct Democracy in America, 1860–1880 (Cleveland: World, 1964).*

2. The early twentieth century also brought challenges to white supremacy, with World War I offering some black soldiers a glimpse of equality, which white southerners countered through increased brutality. The industrializing North, with a limit on European immigrants, created opportunities for work, as did some southern cities, mobilizing southern blacks. The economic depression, intensified in the South by the boll weevil infestations of cotton, furthered tensions between itinerant blacks in search of work and whites seeking laborers. After World War I, black mobility increasingly threatened segregation, and ironically, the lynchings whites employed to control African Americans exacerbated the labor shortage. Overall, African Americans between World War I and World War II became increasingly mobile. In 1900, approximately 90 percent of all African Americans lived in the South, with that number dropping by 11 percent in thirty years. Blacks also migrated within the South to cities as part of the larger urbanization movement, with 33 percent of southern blacks living in urban areas by 1930 (E. M. Beck and Stewart E. Tolnay, "Black Flight: Lethal Violence and the Great Migration, 1900 to 1930," *Social Science History* 14, no. 3 [1990]: 353, 356, 348).

3. See John Dollard, *Caste and Class in a Southern Town* (New York: Doubleday Anchor, 1937).

4. See Stewart E. Tolnay and E. M. Beck, *A Festival of Violence: An Analysis of Southern Lynchings, 1882–1930* (Urbana: University of Illinois Press, 1995), chap. 7; Mary Jane Brown, *Eradicating This Evil: Women in the American Anti-Lynching Movement, 1892–1940* (New York: Garland, 2000), chap. 9; and William Fitzhugh Brundage, *Lynching in the New South: Georgia and Virginia, 1880–1930* (Urbana: University of Illinois Press, 1993), 245–60.

5. Tolnay and Beck, *A Festival of Violence,* 204.

6. Leon Litwack, *How Free Is Free? The Long Death of Jim Crow* (New Haven: Harvard University Press, 2009), 56; Jacquelyn Dowd Hall, "The Long Civil Rights Movement and the Political Uses of the Past," *Journal of American History* 91, no. 4 (2005): 1233–63.

7. See Michael J. Klarman, *From Jim Crow to Civil Rights: The Supreme Court and the Struggle for Racial Equality* (New York: Oxford University Press, 2004).

8. David L. Chappell, *Inside Agitators: White Southerners in the Civil Rights Movement* (Baltimore: Johns Hopkins University Press, 1994), conclusion; James C. Cobb, *Away Down South: A History of Southern Identity* (New York: Oxford University Press, 2007).

9. Garth Williams, *The Rabbits' Wedding* (New York: Harper and Row, 1958).

10. Werner Sollors, *Neither Black nor White Yet Both: Thematic Explorations of Interracial Literature* (New York: Oxford University Press, 1997), 20–23. See also David R. Pichaske, "Dave Etter: Fishing for Our Lost American Souls," *Journal of Modern Literature* 23, no. 3/4 (Summer 2000): 393–427.

BIBLIOGRAPHY

Archives

Library of Congress, Washington, D.C.
Archive of Folk Culture
Daniel A. P. Murray Pamphlets Collection
National Association for the Advancement of Colored People Papers
Performing Arts Collection
Prints and Photographs Division
Rare Book and Special Collections

National Museum of American History, Smithsonian Institute
Ivory Project, Advertising Soap in America, 1838–1998
N. W. Ayer Advertising Agency Records, 1849–1996
Warshaw Collection of Business Americana

Southern Historical Collection, University of North Carolina at Chapel Hill
Southern Oral History Program Collection

Primary Sources

Allen, James. *Without Sanctuary: Lynching Photography in America.* Santa Fe: Twin Palms, 2000.

Allison, Mrs. John P. *A Confederate Catechism for Southern Children.* Concord: Kestler Brothers Printers, 1908.

Arkansas. *List of Approved Library Books for Classified Elementary Schools.* Little Rock: Arkansas State Board of Education, 1935.

An Art Commentary on Lynching. Exhibition catalog. New York: Arthur U. Newton Galleries, 1935.

Bannerman, Helen. *Little Black Sambo.* Racine: Whitman, n.d.

———. *The Story of Little Black Bobtail.* New York: Stokes, 1909.

———. *The Story of Little Black Mingo.* New York: Stokes, 1902.

———. *The Story of Little Black Quasha.* New York: Stokes, 1908.

———. *The Story of Little Black Sambo.* New York: Blue Ribbon Press, 1934.

———. *The Story of Sambo and the Twins.* New York: Stokes, 1936.

———. *The Story of the Teasing Monkey.* New York: Stokes, 1907.

Barbee, Lindsey. *The Thread of Destiny.* Chicago: Denison, 1914.

Bolton, Henry Carrington. *The Counting-Out Rhymes of Children: Their Antiquity, Origin, and Wide Distribution, A Study in Folk-lore.* Detroit: Singing Tree Press, 1969.

Boone, William Cooke. *What God Hath Joined Together: Sermons on Courtship, Marriage, and the Home.* Nashville: Broadman Press, 1935.

Boyle, Sarah-Patton. *The Desegregated Heart: A Virginian's Stand in Time of Transition.* New York: Morrow, 1962.

Braden, Anne. *The Wall Between.* New York: Monthly Review Press, 1958.

Caldwell, Erskine. Introduction to *An Art Commentary on Lynching.* Exhibition catalog. New York: Arthur U. Newton Galleries, 1935.

Cameron, James. *A Time of Terror: A Survivor's Story.* Baltimore: Black Classic Press, 1994.

Campbell, Will D. *Brother to a Dragonfly.* New York: Continuum, 2000.

Carpenter, Marie Elizabeth. *The Treatment of the Negro in American History School Textbooks: A Comparison of Changing Textbook Content, 1826 to 1939, with Developing Scholarship in the History of the Negro in the United States.* Menasha, Wis.: George Banta, 1941.

Chambliss, Rollin. "What Negro Newspapers of Georgia Say about Some Social Problems." Master's thesis, University of Georgia, 1934.

Chesnutt, Charles. Causes of Lynchings. www.berea.edu/faculty/browners/chesnutt/classroom/lynching_table_causes.html.

Children of the Confederacy. Home page. www.hqudc.org/CofC/.

Children of the Confederacy of the United Daughters of the Confederacy. *Minutes of the Fourteenth General Convention.* Augusta: United Daughters of the Confederacy, 1968.

Clemens, Mary. *Our Little Child Faces Life.* Nashville: Cokesbury Press, 1939.

Credel, Ellis. *Little Jeemes Henry.* New York: Thomas Nelson and Sons, 1936.

Cutler, James. *Lynch-Law: An Investigation into the History of Lynching in the United States.* New York: Negro Universities Press, 1969.

Eleazer, Robert Burns. *School Books and Racial Antagonism, A Study of Omissions and Inclusions That Make for Misunderstanding.* Atlanta: Executive Committee Conference on Education and Race Relations, 1937.

Faulkner, William. *Requiem for a Nun.* New York: Random House, 1951.

Florida. *A Suggested Library Book Lists for Florida Schools.* Tallahassee: State Department of Education, 1939.

Griffith, D. W., and Walter Huston. "Prelude" to *Birth of a Nation.* Ideal Pictures, 1930.

Hardin, E. O. *Phunology: A Collection of Tried and Proved Plans for Play, Fellowship and Profit.* New York: Abingdon-Cokesbury Press, 1923.

———. *Phunology: A Collection of Tried and Proved Plans for Play, Fellowship, and Profit, for the Use of Epworth Leagues, Sunday School Classes, and Other Young People's Societies.* Nashville: Dept. of Sunday School Supplies, 1920.

Harris, Joel Chandler. *Nights with Uncle Remus: Myths and Legends of the Old Plantation.* New York: Appleton, 1881.

Howe, Barton Grover. "Legacy of a Lynching." *Missourian,* May 6, 7, 9, 2003. www .columbiamissourian.com/media/multimedia/2010/09/11/media/legacyofalynching.

Johnson, Clifton. *Highways and Byways of the South.* New York: Macmillan, 1905.

Jones, Sam P. *Quit Your Meanness: Sermons and Sayings of Rev. Sam P. Jones.* Chicago: Cranston and Stowe, 1886.

King, Larry L. *Confession of a White Racist.* New York: Viking Press, 1971.

Knox, Rose B. *Gray Caps.* New York: Doubleday, Doran, 1932.

Koch, Frederick H. *Carolina Folk-Plays.* New York: Holt, 1924.

Ku Klux Klan and Junior Klan. *Constitution and By-laws.* N.p.: Junior Klan Publications, 1924.

———. *Kloran: Junior Order Ku Klux Klan.* N.p.: Junior Klan Publications, 1924.

Ladies' Home Journal. Philadelphia: Curtis, 1899.

Leetch, Dorothy. *Tommy Tucker on a Plantation.* Boston: Lothrop, Lee & Shepard, 1925.

Leonard, William Ellery. *The Lynching Bee and Other Poems.* New York: Huebsch, 1920.

Lindsay, Maud. *Little Missy.* Boston: Lothrop, Lee and Shepard, 1922.

Locke, John. *Some Thoughts Concerning Education.* Sioux Falls: NuVision, 2007.

Lofting, Hugh. *The Story of Doctor Dolittle.* New York: Stokes, 1920.

———. *The Voyages of Doctor Dolittle.* New York: Lippincott, 1950.

Louge, Helen J. "Angry Mob Rules in May 30, 1930." *Sherman Democrat Grayson County Sesquicentennial,* March 17, 1996.

Louisiana. *Library List for the Elementary Schools of Louisiana.* Baton Rouge: State Department of Education of Louisiana, 1934.

Lumpkin, Katharine Du Pre. *The Making of a Southerner.* Athens: University of Georgia Press, 1991.

Mabry, Woodford. *A Reply to Southern Slanderers In Re: The "Negro Question," "Lynch Law" etc.* Grove Hill, Ala.: n.p., 1934.

MacKenzie, Amy. "Walter White on Lynching." *Interracial Review* (1946).

Madigan, Tim. "Lynching on Northeast 12th." *Star Telegram,* October 9, 2002. www.dfw .com/mld/dfw/4244515.htm?template=contentModules/printsotry.jsp.

Mays, Benjamin. *Born to Rebel: An Autobiography.* New York: Scribner, 1971.

McKay, Claude. "The Lynching." In *Black on White: Black Writers on What It Means to Be White,* edited by David Roediger. New York: Schocken, 1998.

McLaurin, Melton. *Separate Pasts: Growing up White in the Segregated South.* Athens: University of Georgia Press, 1998.

Mitchell, H. L. *Mean Things Happening in This Land: The Life and Times of H. L. Mitchell, Co-Founder of the Southern Tenant Farmers Union.* Montclair, N.J.: Allanheld, Osmun, 1979.

Moody, Anne. *Coming of Age in Mississippi.* New York: Dial Press, 1968.

National Association for the Advancement of Colored People. *Anti-Negro Propaganda in School Textbooks.* New York: National Association for the Advancement of Colored People, 1939.

———. *An Appeal to the Conscience of the Civilized World*. New York: National Association for the Advancement of Colored People, 1920.

———. *Burning at Stake in the United States: A Record of the Public Burning by Mobs of Six Men during the First Six Months of 1919 in the States of Arkansas, Florida, Georgia, Mississippi and Texas*. New York: National Association for the Advancement of Colored People, 1919.

———. *Can the States Stop Lynching?* New York: National Association for the Advancement of Colored People, 1938.

———. *The Lynching of Claude Neal*. New York: National Association for the Advancement of Colored People, 1934.

———. *Rituals of Blood in the United States: A Record of the Public Burning by Mobs of Five Men, during the First Five Months of 1919, in the States of Arkansas, Florida, Georgia, Mississippi, and Texas*. Baltimore: Black Classic Press, 1986.

National Conference on the Christian Way of Life. *And Who Is My Neighbor?: An Outline for the Study of Race Relations in America*. New York: Association Press, 1924.

North Carolina. *Book List for the Elementary School Library*. Raleigh: State Textbook Commission, 1941.

North Carolina, James Yadkin Joyner, and Minnie Wells Leatherman. *Approved Lists of Books for Rural Libraries*. Raleigh: Superintendent of Public Instruction, 1907.

Owen, Marie Bankhead. *How Alabama Became a State: Third of a Series of Children's Plays in Commemoration of the Close of a Century of Statehood*. Montgomery: Paragon Press, 1919.

Page, Thomas Nelson. *Among the Camps, or Young People's Stories of the War*. New York: Scribner's Sons, 1891.

———. *Two Little Confederates*. New York: Scribner's Sons, 1932.

Parental Responsibility: A Sermon Preached before West Hanover Presbyterian, August 8, 1889. Richmond: Presbyterian Committee of Publication, 1889.

Peebles, Isaac Lockhart. *The Duty of Parents, or, The Training of Children*. Nashville: M. E. Church South, 1919.

Perkins, Sophie Huth. *Mirandy's Minstrels*. Chicago: Denison, 1906.

Poppenheim, Mary B., Maude Blake Merchant, and Ruth Jennings Lawton. *The History of the United Daughters of the Confederacy*. Richmond: Garrett and Massie, 1938.

Prynelle, Louise-Clarke. *Diddie, Dumps, and Tot*. New York: Grosset and Dunlap, 1882.

———. *Diddie, Dumps, and Tot*. Electronic Text Center, University of Virginia Library. http://wyllie.lib.virginia.edu:8086/perl/toccernew?id=PyrDidi .sgm&images=images/modeng&data=/texts/english/modeng/parsed&tag=publi c&part=16&division=div1.

Raper, Arthur Franklin. *The Tragedy of Lynching*. Baltimore: Black Classic Press, 1933.

Reddick, Lawrence D. "Racial Attitudes in American History Textbooks of the South." *Journal of Negro History* 19, no. 3 (July 1934): 225–65.

Rockwell, Ethel Theodora. *Children of Old Carolina: A Historical Pageant of North Carolina for Children.* Chapel Hill: University of North Carolina Extension Bulletin, 1925.

Rutherford, Mildred Lewis. *Monthly Programs for the Children of the Confederacy.* Athens: n.p., n.d. The programs are for the year 1915.

Scales, Junius Irving, and Richard Nickson. *Cause at Heart: A Former Communist Remembers.* Athens: University of Georgia Press, 1987.

Shannon, Thomas W., and Emory Adams Allen. *Personal Help for Parents: Vital Knowledge for Parents, Including a Talk to Fathers and a Talk to Mothers about the Responsibilities of Parenthood and a Specific and Comprehensive Guide for the Instruction of Children in the Delicate Matters of Sex.* Personal Help series, vol. 2. Marietta, Ga.: S. A. Mullikin, 1918.

Simon, S. Sylvan, ed. *Easily Staged Plays for Boys: Nine New Non-Royalty Plays.* New York: Samuel French, 1936.

Smith, Geo Gilman. *Childhood and Conversion.* Nashville: Publishing House of the Methodist Episcopal Church, 1891.

Smith, Lillian. *Killers of the Dream.* New York: Anchor Books, 1963.

South Carolina. *Elementary Library Catalog, 1938: Recommendations of Committee on Selection of Books for Elementary Schools, Including Delivered Prices When Purchased through Textbook Commission.* Columbia: State Department of Education, 1938.

Southern Commission on the Study of Lynching and George Fort Milton. *Lynchings and What They Mean: General Findings of the Southern Commission on the Study of Lynching.* Atlanta: Southern Commission, 1931.

Tennessee, and Pearl Williams Kelley. *Tennessee School Library List.* Nashville: State Department of Education, 1914.

Terrell, Mary Church. "Lynching from a Negro's Point of View." *North American Review* 178 (1904): 853–68.

Theobald, Ruth L. *Library Books for Elementary Schools.* Frankfort: Kentucky Department of Education, 1937.

Tri-K-Klub. *Influence: Trust, Races, INFLUENCE: Knowledge: Kindling, Leadership, Unity, Brains-Brawn-Breadth.* Tri-K-Klub series, no. 4. Little Rock: Tri-K-Klub, A Department of Women of the Ku Klux Klan, 1915.

———. *Races: Trust, RACES, Influence: Knowledge: Kindling, Leadership, Unity, Brains-Brawn-Breadth.* Tri-K-Klub series, no. 3. Little Rock: Tri-K-Klub, A Department of Women of the Ku Klux Klan, 1915.

Twain, Mark. *The Adventures of Huckleberry Finn.* New York: Harper and Brothers, 1912.

———. "The Adventures of Huckleberry Finn." University of Virginia Library. http://etext.lib.virginia.edu/images/modeng/public/Twa2Huc/twahuc11.jpg.

United Daughters of the Confederacy, Thomas K. Spencer Chapter #947. Children of the Confederacy: From Our Director. www.florida-scv.org/Camp556/augustajane/cofc.htm.

United States. *Crime of Lynching: Hearings before a Subcommittee on the Judiciary, United*

States Senate, Seventy-sixth Congress, Third Session on H.R. 80: An Act to Assure to Persons within the Jurisdiction of Every State Due Process of Law and Equal Protection of the Laws, and to Prevent the Crime of Lynching, February 6, 7, March 5, 12, and 13, 1940. Washington, D.C.: U.S. Government Printing Office, 1940.

———. *Punishment for the Crime of Lynching: Hearing before a Subcommittee of the Committee on the Judiciary, United States Senate, Seventy-fourth Congress, First Session on S. 24: A Bill to Assure to Persons within the Jurisdiction of Every State the Equal Protection of the Laws by Discouraging, Preventing, and Punishing the Crime of Lynching, February 14, 1935.* Washington, D.C.: U.S. Government Printing Office, 1935.

———. *Punishment for the Crime of Lynching: Hearings before a Subcommittee of the Committee on the Judiciary, United States Senate, Seventy-third Congress, Second Session on S. 1978: A Bill to Assure to Persons within the Jurisdiction of Every State the Equal Protection of the Laws and to Punish the Crime of Lynching, Part I, February 20 and 21, 1934.* Washington, D.C.: U.S. Government Printing Office, 1934.

———. *To Prevent and Punish the Crime of Lynching: Hearing before a Subcommittee of the Committee on the Judiciary, United States Senate, Sixty-ninth Congress, First Session on S. 121: A Bill to Assure to Persons within the Jurisdiction of Every State the Equal Protection of the Laws, and to Punish the Crime of Lynching, February 16, 1926.* Washington, D.C.: U.S. Government Printing Office, 1926.

United States, William L. Chenery, and Ella Arvilla Merritt. *Standards of Child Welfare: Children and Youth: Social Problems and Social Policy.* New York: Arno Press, 1974.

Virginia. *List of Books Suggested for First Purchase for Virginia Elementary Schools.* Richmond: Virginia State Board of Education, 1937.

White, Walter. "The Lynching of Jim McIlherron: An NAACP Investigation." *Crisis,* May 1918.

———. *A Man Called White: The Autobiography of Walter White.* Bloomington: Indiana University Press, 1948.

———. *Rope & Faggot: A Biography of Judge Lynch.* Notre Dame: University of Notre Dame Press, 2002.

Wilkes, Donald E., Jr. "The Last Lynching in Athens." *Flagpole,* September 1997.

Williams, Garth. *The Rabbits' Wedding.* New York: Harper Collins, 1958.

Wright, Alice Spearman. Interview by Jacquelyn Hall. February 28, 1976. Southern Oral History Program Collection, Southern Historical Collection, University of North Carolina at Chapel Hill.

Wright, Marion. Interview by Arnold Shankman. March 11, 1976. Southern Oral History Program Collection, Southern Historical Collection, University of North Carolina at Chapel Hill.

———. Interview by Jacquelyn Hall. March 8, 1978. Southern Oral History Program Collection, Southern Historical Collection, University of North Carolina at Chapel Hill.

Wright, Richard. *Black Boy.* New York: Harper and Row, 1946.

Wyeth, Adelaide H. *Hunkers' Corners: An Entertainment in Three Scenes.* Chicago: Dramatic Publishing, 1908.

Wynne, Frances Duke. *Preparing for Parenthood.* Miami: Hefty Press, 1935.

Books and Articles

Aboud, Frances E. *Children & Prejudice.* Oxford: Blackwell, 1998.

Aboud, Frances E., and Anna-Beth Doyle. "Parental and Peer Influences on Children's Racial Attitudes." *International Journal of Intercultural Religion* 20 (1996): 371–83.

Abrahams, Roger D., ed. *Jump Rope Rhymes: A Dictionary.* Austin: University of Texas Press, 1969.

Adams, Margaret, ed. *Collectible Dolls and Accessories of the Twenties and Thirties from Sears, Roebuck and Co. Catalogs.* New York: Dover, 1986.

American Civil War.com. "Confederate Civil War Song Lyrics: The Bonnie Blue Flag Confederate Civil War Song." http://americancivilwar.com/Civil_War_Music/song_lyrics/bonnie_blue_confederate_song.html.

Anderson, James. *The Education of Blacks in the South, 1860–1935.* Urbana: University of Illinois Press, 1988.

Anderson, Linda. *Autobiography.* New York: Routledge, 2001.

Apel, Dora. *Imagery of Lynching: Black Men, White Women, and the Mob.* New Brunswick, N.J.: Rutgers University Press, 2004.

Arac, Jonathan. *Huckleberry Finn as Idol or Target: The Functions of Criticism in Our Time.* Madison: University of Minnesota Press, 1997.

Aries, Philippe. *Centuries of Childhood: A Social History of Family Life.* London: Cape, 1962.

Arneil, Barbra. "Becoming versus Being: A Critical Analysis of the Child in Liberal Theory." In *The Moral and Political Status of Children,* edited by David Archard and Colin Murray MacLeod. Oxford: Oxford University Press, 2002.

Ayers, Edward. *Promise of the New South: Life after Reconstruction.* New York: Oxford University Press, 1993.

Bailie, Gil. "Violence and the Sacred: René Girard's Insights into Christianity." *Aisling Magazine.* www.aislingmagazine.com/aislingmagazine/articles/TAM26/R.Girard.html.

Baker, Augusta. "Guidelines for Black Books: An Open Letter to Juvenile Editors." In *The Black American in Books for Children,* edited by Donnarae MacCann and Gloria Woodard. Metuchen, N.J.: Scarecrow Press, 1972.

Baker, Bruce E. "Lynching and Memory." In *Where These Memories Grow: History, Memory, and Southern Identity,* edited by William Fitzhugh Brundage. Chapel Hill: University of North Carolina Press, 2000.

Bardaglio, Peter W. "Rape and the Law in the Old South: 'Calculated to Excite Indignation in Every Heart.'" *Journal of Southern History* 60, no. 4 (November 1994): 749–72.

———. *Reconstructing the Household: Families, Sex, and the Law in the Nineteenth-Century South*. Chapel Hill: University of North Carolina Press, 1995.

Beck, E. M., and Stewart Tolnay. "Black Flight: Lethal Violence and the Great Migration, 1900 to 1930." *Social Science History* 14, no. 3 (1990): 247–370.

———. "When Race Didn't Matter: Black and White Mob Violence against Their Own Color." In *Under Sentence of Death: Lynching in the South*, edited by William Fitzhugh Brundage. Chapel Hill: University of North Carolina Press, 1997.

Bederman, Gail. *Manliness & Civilization: A Cultural History of Gender and Race in the United States, 1880–1917*. Chicago: University of Chicago Press, 1995.

Bell, Catherine. *Ritual Theory, Ritual Practice*. New York: Oxford University Press, 1992.

Bernstein, Patricia. *The First Waco Horror: The Lynching of Jesse Washington and the Rise of the NAACP*. College Station: Texas A&M University Press, 2005.

Berry, Bill J., ed. *Located Lives: Place and Idea in Southern Autobiography*. Athens: University of Georgia Press, 1990.

Bigler, R. S., C. Spears Brown, and M. Markell. "When Groups Are Not Created Equal: Effects of Group Status on the Formation of Intergroup Attitudes in Children." *Child Development* 72, no. 4 (2001): 1151–62.

Blee, Kathleen M. *Women of the Klan: Racism and Gender in the 1920s*. Berkeley and Los Angeles: University of California Press, 1991.

Bloom, Lynn Z. "Coming of Age in the Segregated South: Autobiographies of Twentieth-Century Childhoods, Black and White." In *Home Ground: Southern Autobiography*, edited by Bill J. Berry. Columbia: University of Missouri Press, 1991.

Boskin, Joseph. *Sambo: The Rise & Demise of an American Jester*. New York: Oxford University Press, 1986.

Broderick, Dorothy. *Image of the Black in Children's Fiction*. New York: Bowker, 1973.

Brown, Marice C. *Amen, Brother Ben: A Mississippi Collection of Children's Rhymes*. Jackson: University Press of Mississippi, 1979.

Brown, Mary Jane. *Eradicating This Evil: Women in the American Anti-Lynching Movement, 1892–1940*. New York: Garland, 2000.

Brown, Nancy B. "The Ku Klux Klan and the Birth of a Nation." Tennessee Genealogy Web Project. www.tngenweb.org/giles/afro-amer/history/birth.html.

Brundage, William Fitzhugh. *Lynching in the New South: Georgia and Virginia, 1880–1930*. Urbana: University of Illinois Press, 1993.

———. *The Southern Past: A Clash of Race and Memory*. Cambridge: Belknap Press of Harvard University Press, 2005.

———, ed. *Under Sentence of Death: Lynching in the South*. Chapel Hill: University of North Carolina Press, 1997.

Burke, Timothy. *Lifebuoy Men, Lux Women: Commodification, Consumption, and Cleanliness in Modern Zimbabwe*. Durham, N.C.: Duke University Press, 1996.

Burton, Orville Vernon. *In My Father's House Are Many Mansions: Family and Community in Edgefield, South Carolina*. Chapel Hill: University of North Carolina Press, 1987.

———. "Race and Reconstruction: Edgefield County, South Carolina." *Journal of Social History* 12, no. 1 (1978): 31–56.

Butler, Judith. *Bodies That Matter: On the Discursive Limits of "Sex."* New York: Routledge, 1993.

———. "Performative Acts and Gender Constitution: An Essay in Phenomenology and Feminist Theory." In *Performing Feminisms: Feminist Critical Theory and Theatre*, edited by Sue-Ellen Case. Baltimore: Johns Hopkins University Press, 1990.

Cantwell, Robert. *When We Were Good: The Folk Revival.* Cambridge: Harvard University Press, 1996.

Cappon, Lester J. "The Provincial South." *Journal of Southern History* 16, no. 1 (February 1950): 5–24.

Carlton, David. *Mill and Town in South Carolina, 1880–1920.* Baton Rouge: Louisiana State University Press, 1982.

Cash, W. J. *The Mind of the South.* New York: Houghton Mifflin, 1941.

Cell, John W. *The Highest Stage of White Supremacy: The Origins of Segregation in South Africa and the American South.* Cambridge: Cambridge University Press, 1982.

Censor, Jane Turner. *The Reconstruction of White Southern Womanhood, 1865–1895.* Baton Rouge: Louisiana State University Press, 2003.

Chadwick-Joshua, Jocelyn. *The Jim Dilemma: Reading Race in Huckleberry Finn.* Jackson: University Press of Mississippi, 1998.

Chappell, David L. *Inside Agitators: White Southerners in the Civil Rights Movement.* Baltimore: Johns Hopkins University Press, 1994.

Chudacoff, Howard P. *Children at Play: An American History.* New York: New York University Press, 2007.

Church, Ellen Booth. "Performing Plays in Preschool." *Scholastic Parents.* www2 .scholastic.com/browse/article.jsp?id=983.

Clark, Kenneth B., and Mamie K. Clark. "Skin Color as a Factor in Racial Identification of Negro Preschool Children." *Journal of Social Psychology*, Bulletin 11 (1940): 159–69.

Cobb, James C. *Away Down South: A History of Southern Identity.* New York: Oxford University Press, 2007.

Cox, Karen L. *Dixie's Daughters: The United Daughters of the Confederacy and the Preservation of Confederate Culture.* Gainesville: University Press of Florida, 2003.

Cox, Mike. "Ghost of 1916 Lynching Still Haunts Texas City." *Austin American-Statesman*, July 3, 2005.

Crick, N. R. "The Role of Overt Aggression, Relational Aggression, and Prosocial Behavior in the Prediction of Children's Future Social Adjustment." *Child Development* 67 (1996): 2317–27.

Crick, N. R., and J. K. Grotpeter. "Relational Aggression, Gender, and Social-Psychological Adjustment." *Child Development* 66, no. 3 (1995): 710–22.

Cunningham, Hugh. *Children and Childhood in Western Society since 1500.* New York: Longman, 1995.

Davis, Allison, and John Dollard. *Children of Bondage: The Personality Development of Negro Youth in the Urban South.* Washington, D.C.: American Council on Education, 1940.

Davis, Allison, Burleigh B. Gardner, and Mary R. Gardner. *Deep South: A Social Anthropological Study of Caste and Class.* Chicago: University of Chicago Press, 1941.

Davis, Angela. "Rape, Racism and the Myth of the Black Rapist." In *Women, Race and Class,* edited by Davis. New York: Random House, 1981.

Dollard, John. *Caste and Class in a Southern Town.* New York: Doubleday Anchor, 1937.

Dorr, Lisa Lindquist. *White Women, Rape, and the Power of Race in Virginia, 1900–1960.* Chapel Hill: University of North Carolina Press, 2004.

Douglas, Mary. *Purity and Danger: An Analysis of Concepts of Pollution and Taboo.* London: Pelican Books, 1970.

Downey, Dennis B., and Raymond M. Hyser. *No Crooked Death: Coatesville, Pennsylvania, and the Lynching of Zachariah Walker.* Urbana: University of Illinois Press, 1991.

Dray, Phillip. *At the Hands of Persons Unknown: The Lynching of Black America.* New York: Random House, 2002.

Du Bois, W. E. B. *Black Reconstruction in America: An Essay toward a History of the Part which Black Folk Played in the Attempt to Reconstruct Democracy in America, 1860–1880.* Cleveland: World, 1964.

Dunbar, Anthony P. *Against the Grain: Southern Radicals and Prophets, 1929–1959.* Charlottesville: University Press of Virginia, 1981.

Eakin, Paul John. *How Our Lives Become Stories: Making Selves.* Ithaca, N.Y.: Cornell University Press, 2001.

Edgerton, John. *Speak Now Against the Day.* New York: Knopf, 1994.

Edwards, Laura. *Gendered Strife and Confusion: The Political Culture of Reconstruction.* Urbana: University of Illinois, 1997.

———. "Law, Domestic Violence, and the Limits of Patriarchal Authority in the Antebellum South." *Journal of Southern History* 65, no. 4 (November 1999): 733–70.

Elder, Glen H., Jr. *25th Anniversary Edition of Children of the Great Depression.* Boulder: Westview Press, 1999.

Emert, Barbara Jean. *The Georgia Division, Children of the Confederacy History, 1912–1987.* Georgia: Georgia Division, Children of the Confederacy, 1988.

Esteve, Mary. *The Aesthetics and Politics of the Crowd in American Literature.* Oxford: Cambridge University Press, 2003.

Ezell, John S. "A Southern Education for Southrons." *Journal of Southern History* 17, no. 3 (August 1951): 303–27.

Fanon, Frantz. *Black Skin, White Masks.* New York: Grove, 1967.

Faust, Drew Gilpin. *Mothers of Invention: Women of the Slaveholding South in the American Civil War.* Chapel Hill: University of North Carolina Press, 1996.

Feimster, Crystal Nicole. "Ladies and Lynching: The Gendered Discourse of Mob Violence in the New South, 1880–1930." Ph.D. diss., Princeton University, 2000.

———. *Southern Horrors: Women and the Politics of Rape and Lynching.* Cambridge: Harvard University Press, 2009.

Fields, Barbara. *Slavery and Freedom on the Middle Ground: Maryland during the Nineteenth Century.* New Haven: Yale University Press, 1985.

Finnegan, Terence. "Lynching and Political Power in Mississippi and South Carolina." In *Under Sentence of Death, Lynching in the South,* edited by William Fitzhugh Brundage. Chapel Hill: University of North Carolina Press, 1997.

Fishkin, Shelley Fisher. "Teaching Mark Twain's Adventures of Huckleberry Finn." PBS Online. www.pbs.org/wgbh/cultureshock/teachers/huck/essay.html.

Foner, Eric. *Reconstruction: America's Unfinished Revolution, 1863–1877.* New York: HarperCollins, 1988.

Fosl, Catherine. *Subversive Southerner: Anne Braden and the Struggle for Racial Justice in the Cold War South.* New York: Palgrave Macmillan, 2002.

Fox-Genovese, Elizabeth. "Between Individualism and Community: Autobiographies of Southern Women." In *Located Lives: Place and Idea in Southern Autobiography,* edited by Bill J. Berry. Athens: University of Georgia Press, 1990.

———. *Within the Plantation Household: Black and White Women of the Old South.* Chapel Hill: University of North Carolina Press, 1988.

Formanek-Brunell, Miriam. *Made to Play House: Dolls and the Commercialization of American Girlhood, 1830–1930.* New Haven: Yale University Press, 1993.

———. "Sugar and Spite: The Politics of Doll Play in Nineteenth-Century America." In *Small Worlds: Children and Adolescents in America, 1850–1950,* edited by Elliott West and Paula Petrik. Lawrence: University Press of Kansas, 1992.

Foucault, Michel. *Discipline and Punish: The Birth of the Prison.* 2nd ed. New York: Vintage, 1995.

Frankenberg, Ruth. *White Women/Race Matters: The Social Construction of Whiteness.* Minneapolis: University of Minnesota Press, 1993.

Frederickson, George M. *The Black Image in the White Mind: The Debate on Afro-American Character and Destiny, 1817–1914.* Middleport, Conn.: Wesleyan University Press, 1971.

Friedman, Jean E. *The Enclosed Garden: Women and Community in the Evangelical South, 1830–1900.* Chapel Hill: University of North Carolina Press, 1985.

Fulton, Joe. *Mark Twain's Ethical Realism: The Aesthetics of Race, Class, and Gender.* Columbia: University of Missouri Press, 1997.

Gast, David. "The Dawning of the Age of Aquarius for Multi-Ethnic Children's Literature." In *The Black American in Books for Children,* edited by Donnarae MacCann and Gloria Woodard. Metuchen, N.J.: Scarecrow Press, 1972.

Gilmore, David D. *Manhood in the Making: Cultural Concepts of Masculinity.* New Haven: Yale University Press, 1990.

Gilmore, Glenda. *Gender and Jim Crow: Women and the Politics of White Supremacy in North Carolina, 1896–1920.* Chapel Hill: University of North Carolina Press, 1996.

Ginzburg, Ralph. *100 Years of Lynchings*. Baltimore: Black Classic Press, 1988.

Girard, René. *Violence and the Sacred*. Baltimore: Johns Hopkins University Press, 1977.

Goffman, Erving. *The Presentation of Self in Everyday Life*. New York: Doubleday, 1959.

Gordon, Lewis R. *Bad Faith and Antiblack Racism*. Atlantic Highlands, N.J.: Humanities Press, 1995.

Gossett, Thomas F. *Race: The History of an Idea in America*. New York: Oxford University Press, 1997.

Grant, Donald Lee. *The Way It Was in the South: The Black Experience in Georgia*. Athens: University of Georgia Press, 2001.

Grimes, Ronald L. *Deeply into the Bone: Re-Inventing Rites of Passage*. Berkeley and Los Angeles: University of California Press, 2000.

Gross, Ariela J. "Beyond Black and White: Cultural Approaches to Race and Slavery." *Columbia Law Review* 101, no. 3 (2001): 640–81.

Hahn, Steven. *A Nation under Our Feet: Black Political Struggles in the Rural South from Slavery to the Great Migration*. Cambridge: Harvard University Press, 2004.

———. *Roots of Southern Populism: Yeoman Farmers and the Transformation of the Georgia Upcountry, 1850–90*. New York: Oxford University Press, 1983.

Hale, Grace. *Making Whiteness: The Culture of Segregation in the South, 1890–1940*. New York: Pantheon, 1998.

Hall, Jacquelyn Dowd. *Like a Family: The Making of a Southern Cotton Mill World*. Chapel Hill: University of North Carolina Press, 2000.

———. "The Long Civil Rights Movement and the Political Uses of the Past." *Journal of American History* 91, no. 4 (2005): 1233–63.

———. "'The Mind That Burns in Each Body': Women, Rape, and Racial Violence." In *Powers of Desire: The Politics of Sexuality*, edited by Ann Snitow, Christine Stansell, and Sharon Thompson. New York: Monthly Review Press, 1983.

———. *Revolt against Chivalry: Jessie Daniel Ames and the Women's Campaign against Lynching*. New York: Columbia University Press, 1993.

———. "'To Widen the Reach of Our Love': Autobiography, History, and Desire." *Feminist Studies* 26, no. 1 (Spring 2000): 231–47.

———. "'You Must Remember This': Autobiography as Social Critique." *Journal of American History* 85, no. 2 (September 1998): 439–65.

Harlan, Louis R. "The Southern Education Board and the Race Issue in Public Education." *Journal of Southern History* 23, no. 2 (May 1957): 189–202.

Harris, J. William. "Etiquette, Lynching, and Racial Boundaries in Southern History: A Mississippi Example." *American Historical Review* 100, no. 2 (April 1995): 387–410.

Harris, Trudier. *Exorcising Blackness: Historical and Literary Lynching and Burning Rituals*. Bloomington: Indiana University Press, 1984.

Hartman, Saidiya. *Scenes of Subjection: Terror, Slavery, and Self-Making in Nineteenth Century America*. New York: Oxford University Press, 1997.

Harvey, Paul. "Sweet Homes, Sacred Blues, Regional Identities: Studying Religion, Race, and Culture in the American South." *Religious Studies Review* 23 (July 1997): 231–38.

Hatt, Michael. "Race, Ritual, and Responsibility: Performativity and the Southern Lynching." In *Performing the Body/Performing the Text,* edited by Amelia Jones and Andrew Stephenson. New York: Routledge Press, 1999.

Herman, Ellen. "The Paradoxical Rationalization of Modern Adoption." *Journal of Social History* 36, no. 2 (Winter 2002): 339–85.

Heyse, Amy L. "Teachers of the Lost Cause: The United Daughters of the Confederacy and the Rhetoric of Their Catechisms." Ph.D. diss., University of Maryland, 2006.

Higginbotham, Evelyn Brooks. *Righteous Discontent: The Women's Movement in the Black Baptist Church, 1880–1920.* Cambridge: Harvard University Press, 1993.

Hill, Jackie. "Progressive Values in the Women's Ku Klux Klan." *Constructing the Past* 9, no. 1 (2008): 21–29.

Hobson, Fred. *But Now I See: The White Southern Racial Conversion Narrative.* Baton Rouge: Louisiana State University Press, 1999.

Hodes, Martha. *White Women Black Men: Illicit Sex in the Nineteenth-Century South.* New Haven: Yale University Press, 1997.

Holloway, Karla F. C. *Passed On: African American Mourning Stories: A Memorial.* Durham, N.C.: Duke University Press, 2003.

Howard, Walter T. *Lynchings: Extralegal Violence in Florida during the 1930s.* Selinsgrove, Pa.: Susquehanna University Press, 1995.

Hoy, Suellen. *Chasing Dirt: The American Pursuit of Cleanliness.* New York: Oxford University Press, 1996.

Hunter, Tera W. *To 'Joy My Freedom: Southern Black Women's Lives and Labors after the Civil War.* Cambridge: Harvard University Press, 1997.

Hutchinson, Stuart, ed. *Mark Twain: Tom Sawyer and Huckleberry Finn.* New York: Columbia University Press, 1998.

Jabour, Anya. "'Grown Girls, Highly Cultivated': Female Education in an Antebellum Southern Family." *Journal of Southern History* 64, no. 1 (February 1998): 23–64.

Johnson, Charles S. *Growing Up in the Black Belt: Negro Youth in the Rural South.* Washington, D.C.: American Council on Education, 1941.

Johnson, Clifton H., ed. *God Struck Me Dead: Religious Conversion Experiences and Autobiographies of Ex-Slaves.* Boston: Pilgrim Press, 1969.

Jones, Jacqueline. *Labor of Love, Labor of Sorrow: Black Women, Work, and the Family from Slavery to the Present.* New York: Vintage Books, 1985.

Kantrowitz, Stephen. "White Supremacist Justice and the Rule of Law: Lynching, Honor, and the State in Ben Tillman's South Carolina." In *Men and Violence: Gender, Honor, and Rituals in Modern Europe and America,* edited by Peter Spierenburg. Columbus: Ohio State University Press, 1998.

Kerbawy, Kelli R. "Knights in White Satin: Women of the Ku Klux Klan." Master's thesis, Marshall University, 2007.

Kern-Foxworth, Marilyn. *Aunt Jemima, Uncle Ben, and Rastus: Blacks in Advertising, Yesterday, Today, and Tomorrow.* Westport, Conn.: Praeger, 1994.

Kimmel, Michael. *Manhood in America: A Cultural History.* New York: Free Press, 1996.

Klarman, Michael J. *From Jim Crow to Civil Rights: The Supreme Court and the Struggle for Racial Equality.* New York: Oxford University Press, 2004.

Knight, Edgar W. "An Early Case of Opposition in the South to Northern Textbooks." *Journal of Southern History* 13, no. 2 (May 1947): 245–64.

Krentz, Arthur A. "Play and Education in Plato's *Republic.*" Paper presented at the Twentieth World Congress of Philosophy, Boston, 1998.

Larsen, Lawrence H., and Barbara J. Cottrell. *The Gate City: A History of Omaha.* Lincoln: University of Nebraska Press, 1997.

LeFalle-Collins, Lizzetta. "Memories of Mammy." In *Art and the Performance of Memory,* edited by Richard Cándida Smith. New York: Routledge, 2002.

Levine, Lawrence W. *Black Culture and Black Consciousness: Afro-American Folk Thought from Slavery to Freedom.* New York: Oxford University Press, 1978.

Lindon, Jennie. *Understanding Children's Play.* Cheltenham, UK: Nelson Thornes, 2001.

Link, William A. "Privies, Progressivism, and Public Schools: Health Reform and Education in the Rural South, 1909–1920." *Journal of Southern History* 54, no. 4 (November 1988): 623–42.

——. *The Social Context of Southern Progressivism, 1880–1930.* Chapel Hill: University of North Carolina Press, 1993.

Litwack, Leon F. *How Free Is Free?: The Long Death of Jim Crow.* Cambridge: Harvard University Press, 2009.

——. *Trouble in Mind: Black Southerners in the Age of Jim Crow.* New York: Knopf, 1998.

Lott, Eric. *Love and Theft: Blackface Minstrelsy and the American Working Class.* New York: Oxford University Press, 1993.

Loveland, Anne C. *Lillian Smith: A Southerner Confronting the South: A Biography.* Baton Rouge: Louisiana State University Press, 1986.

MacCann, Donnarae. *White Supremacy in Children's Literature: Characterizations of African Americans, 1830–1900.* New York: Routledge, 2001.

MacCann, Donnarae, and Gloria Woodard. *The Black American in Books for Children: Readings in Racism.* Metuchen, N.J.: Scarecrow Press, 1972.

MacLean, Nancy. *Behind the Mask of Chivalry: The Making of the Second Ku Klux Klan.* New York: Oxford University Press, 1994.

MacLeod, Anne Scott. *American Childhood: Essays on Children's Literature of the Nineteenth and Twentieth Centuries.* Athens: University of Georgia Press, 1994.

Manring, M. M. *Slave in a Box: The Strange Career of Aunt Jemima.* Charlottesville: University Press of Virginia, 1998.

Marchand, Roland. *Advertising the American Dream: Making Way for Modernity, 1920–1940.* Berkeley and Los Angeles: University of California Press, 1986.

Masteller, Richard N. "Caricatures in Crisis: The Satiric Vision of Reginald Marsh and John Dos Passos." *Smithsonian Studies in American Art* 3, no. 2 (Spring 1989): 23–45.

Mathews, Donald G. *Religion in the Old South.* Chicago: University of Chicago Press, 1977.

———. "The Southern Rite of Human Sacrifice." *Journal of Southern Religion.* http://jsr .as.wvu.edu/mathews.htm.

Matthews, Pamela R. "Between Ellen and Louise: Female Friendship, Glasgow's Letters to Louise Chandler Moulton, and *The Wheel of Life.*" In *Ellen Glasgow: New Perspectives,* edited by Dorothy M. Scura. Knoxville: University of Tennessee Press, 1995.

Maynes, Mary Jo. "Age as a Category of Historical Analysis: History, Agency, and Narratives of Childhood." *Journal of the History of Childhood and Youth* 1, no. 1 (Winter 2008): 114–24.

Mergen, Bernard. "Children's Play in American Autobiographies, 1820–1914." In *Hard at Play: Leisure in America, 1840–1940,* edited by Kathryn Grover. Amherst: University of Massachusetts Press, 1992.

———. "Made, Bought, and Stolen: Toys and the Culture of Childhood." In *Small Worlds: Children and Adolescents in America, 1850–1950,* edited by Elliott West and Paula Petrik. Lawrence: University Press of Kansas, 1992.

McClintock, Anne. *Imperial Leather: Race, Gender, and Sexuality in the Colonial Contest.* New York: Routledge, 1995.

McElya, Micki. *Clinging to Mammy: The Faithful Slave in Twentieth-Century America.* Cambridge: Harvard University Press, 2007.

McGaugh, James L. *Memory and Emotion: The Making of Lasting Memories.* New York: Columbia University Press, 2003.

McMillen, Neil R. *Dark Journey: Black Mississippians in the Age of Jim Crow.* Urbana: University of Illinois Press, 1989.

McPherson, James M. *This Mighty Scourge: Perspectives on the Civil War.* Oxford: Oxford University Press, 2007.

Mensh, Elaine, and Harry Mensh. *Black, White, & Huckleberry Finn: Re-Imagining the American Dream.* Tuscaloosa: University of Alabama Press, 2000.

Mercier, Denis. "From Hostility to Reverence: 100 years of African–American Imagery in Games." Ferris State University Jim Crow Museum of Racist Memorabilia. www .ferris.edu/news/jimcrow/links/games.

Mintz, Steven. *Huck's Raft: A History of American Childhood.* Cambridge: Harvard University Press, 2004.

Morrill, Alvin, Christine Yalda, Madelaine Adelman, Michael Musheno, and Cindy Bejarano. "Telling Tales in School: Youth Culture and Conflict Narratives." *Law & Society Review* 34, no. 3 (2000): 521–66.

Mrozek, Donald J. "The Natural Limits of Unstructured Play, 1880–1914." In *Hard at Play: Leisure in America, 1840–1940,* edited by Kathryn Grover. Amherst: University of Massachusetts Press, 1992.

Murray, Gail. *American Children's Literature and the Construction of Childhood.* London: Twayne, 1998.

Nasaw, David. *Schooled to Order: A Social History of Public Schooling in the United States.* New York: Harper and Row, 1988.

Nelson, Pamela. "Toys as History: Ethnic Images and Cultural Change." In Ethnic Images in Toys and Games, Balch Institute. www.balchinstitute.org/museum/toys/history.html.

The New Georgia Encyclopedia. "Erskine Caldwell." www.georgiaencyclopedia.org/nge/Article.jsp?id=h-497.

Newkirk, Pamela. "Ida B. Wells-Barnett: Journalism as a Weapon against Racial Bigotry." *Media Studies Journal* 14, no. 2 (Spring/Summer 2000): 26–31.

O'Dell, Darlene. *Sites of Southern Memory: The Autobiographies of Katharine Du Pre Lumpkin, Lillian Smith, and Pauli Murray.* Charlottesville: University Press of Virginia, 2001.

Olney, James. "Autobiographical Traditions Black and White." In *Located Lives: Place and Idea in Southern Autobiography,* edited by Bill J. Berry. Athens: University of Georgia Press, 1990.

———. *Memory and Narrative: The Weave of Life Writing.* Chicago: University of Chicago Press, 2001.

"Origin of the Pickaninny." Washington State University. http://salc.wsu.edu/Fair_S02/FS13/Entertainment/Pickaninny%200rigin.htm.

Ortiz, Paul. *Remembering Jim Crow: African Americans Tell about Life in the Segregated South.* New York: New Press, 2001.

Pascoe, Peggy. "Miscegenation, Court Cases, and Ideologies of 'Race' in Twentieth-Century America." *Journal of American History* 83, no. 1 (June 1996): 44–69.

Patterson, Orlando. *Rituals of Blood: Consequences of Slavery in Two American Centuries.* Washington D.C.: Counterpoint, 1998.

Pfeifer, Michael J. *Rough Justice: Lynching and American Society, 1874–1947.* Urbana: University of Illinois Press, 2004.

Pichaske, David R. "Dave Etter: Fishing for Our Lost American Souls." *Journal of Modern Literature* 23, no. 3/4 (Summer 2000): 393–427.

Pietrese, Jan Nederveen. *White on Black: Images of Africa and Blacks in Western Popular Culture.* New Haven: Yale University Press, 1992.

Pilgrim, David. "The Brute Caricature." Ferris State University Jim Crow Museum of Racist Memorabilia. www.ferris.edu/news/jimcrow/brute/.

———. "The Coon Caricature." Ferris State University Jim Crow Museum of Racist Memorabilia. www.ferris.edu/news/jimcrow/coon/.

———. "The Mammy Caricature." Ferris State University Jim Crow Museum of Racist Memorabilia. www.ferris.edu/news/jimcrow/mammies/.

———. "The Picaninny Caricature." Ferris State University Jim Crow Museum of Racist Memorabilia. www.ferris.edu/news/jimcrow/picaninny/.

———. "The Tom Caricature." Ferris State University Jim Crow Museum of Racist Memorabilia. www.ferris.edu/news/jimcrow/tom/.

Pollock, Linda A. *Forgotten Children: Parent-Child Relations from 1500 to 1900.* New York: Cambridge University Press, 1983.

Pope, Listen. *Millhands and Preachers: A Study of Gastonia.* New Haven: Yale University Press, 1946.

Porter, Judith D. R. *Black Child, White Child: The Development of Racial Attitudes.* Cambridge: Harvard University Press, 1971.

Pursell, Carroll W., Jr. "Toys, Technology, and Sex Roles in America, 1920–1940." In *Dynamos and Virgins Revisited: Women and Technological Change in History,* edited by Martha More Trescott. Metuchen, N.J.: Scarecrow Press, 1979.

Quirk, Tom. *Coming to Grips with Huckleberry Finn.* Columbia: University of Missouri Press, 1995.

Rabinowitz, Howard N. *Race Relations in the Urban South, 1865–1890.* New York: Oxford University Press, 1978.

Rable, George C. "The South and the Politics of Antilynching Legislation, 1920–1940." *Journal of Southern History* 51, no. 2 (May 1985): 201–20.

Reuben, Paul P. "Chapter 9: Walter White." *PAL: Perspectives in American Literature—A Research and Reference Guide.* http://web.csustan.edu/english/reuben/pal/chap9/white.html.

Rice, Anne P. *Witnessing Lynching: American Writers Respond.* New Brunswick, N.J.: Rutgers University Press, 2003.

Ritterhouse, Jennifer Lynn. *Growing up Jim Crow: How Black and White Southern Children Learned Race.* Chapel Hill: University of North Carolina Press, 2006.

———. "Reading, Intimacy, and the Role of Uncle Remus in White Southern Social Memory." *Journal of Southern History* 69, no. 3 (August 2003): 585–622.

Rivkin, Julie, and Michael Ryan, ed. *Literary Theory: An Anthology.* Oxford: Blackwell, 2004.

Roberts, Mary Louise. "Gender, Consumption, and Commodity Culture." *American Historical Review* 103, no. 3 (January 1998): 817–84.

Roediger, David R. *Wages of Whiteness: Race and the Making of the American Working Class.* New York: Verso, 1999.

Roper, John Herbert. *C. Vann Woodward: Southerner.* Athens: University of Georgia Press, 1987.

Rotundo, E. Anthony. Review of *Growing Pains: Children in the Industrial Age, 1850–1890,* by Priscilla Ferguson Clement. *Journal of Social History* 32, no. 3 (Spring 1999): 671–76.

Sallee, Shelley. *The Whiteness of Child Labor Reform in the New South.* Athens: University of Georgia Press, 2004.

Schechter, Patricia A. *Ida B. Wells-Barnett and American Reform, 1880–1930.* Chapel Hill: University of North Carolina Press, 2001.

Schroeder, Bill. *The Standard Antique Doll Identification and Value Guide, 1700–1935.* Paducah, Ky.: Collector Books, 1976.

Schwalm, Leslie A. *A Hard Fight for We: Women's Transition from Slavery to Freedom in South Carolina.* Urbana: University of Illinois Press, 1997.

Scott, Joan. "Gender: A Useful Category of Historical Analysis." *American Historical Review* 91, no. 5 (1986): 1053–75.

Shorter, Edward. *The Making of the Modern Family.* New York: Basic Books, 1975.

Simkins, Francis B. "Tolerating the South's Past." *Journal of Southern History* 21, no. 1 (February 1955): 3–16.

Sivulka, Juliann. *Stronger Than Dirt: A Cultural History of Advertising Personal Hygiene in America, 1875 to 1940.* Amherst, N.Y.: Humanity Books, 2001.

Slasinski-Griem, Carolyn. "State Control of Education." *American Journal of Comparative Law* 38 (1990): 473–90.

Smith, J. Douglas. *Managing White Supremacy: Race, Politics, and Citizenship in Jim Crow Virginia.* Chapel Hill: University of North Carolina Press, 2002.

Smith, Sidonie, and Julia Watson. *Reading Autobiography: A Guide for Interpreting Life Narratives.* Minneapolis: University of Minnesota Press, 2002.

Sollors, Werner. *Neither Black nor White Yet Both: Thematic Explorations of Interracial Literature.* New York: Oxford University Press, 1997.

Sommerville, Diane Miller. *Rape and Race in the Nineteenth-Century South.* Chapel Hill: University of North Carolina Press, 2004.

———. "The Rape Myth in the Old South Reconsidered." *Journal of Southern History* 61 (August 1995): 481–518.

SoRelle, James M. "The Waco Horror: The Lynching of Jesse Washington." *Southwestern Historical Quarterly* 86, no. 4 (April 1983): 517–36.

Spero, James, ed. *Collectible Toys and Games of the Twenties and Thirties from Sears, Roebuck and Co. Catalogs.* New York: Dover, 1988.

Spierenburg, Peter. *Men and Violence: Gender, Honor, and Rituals in Modern Europe and America.* Columbus: Ohio State University Press, 1998.

Stone, Lawrence. *The Family, Sex, and Marriage in England, 1500–1800.* New York: Harper and Row, 1977.

Strasser, Susan. *Satisfaction Guaranteed: The Making of the American Mass Market.* New York: Pantheon, 1989.

Sullivan, Patricia. *Days of Hope: Race and Democracy in the New Deal Era.* Chapel Hill: University of North Carolina Press, 1996.

Tambiah, Stanley J. "A Performance Approach to Ritual." In *Readings in Ritual Studies,* edited by Ronald Grimes. Upper Saddle River, N.J.: Prentice Hall, 1996.

Thompson, Holland. *From the Cotton Field to the Cotton Mill: A Study of the Industrial Transition in North Carolina.* New York: Macmillan, 1906.

Toll, Robert. *Blacking Up: The Minstrel Show in Nineteenth-Century America.* New York: Oxford University Press, 1974.

Tolnay, Stewart E., and E. M. Beck. *A Festival of Violence: An Analysis of Southern Lynchings, 1882–1930.* Urbana: University of Illinois Press, 1992.

Turner, Patricia A. *Ceramic Uncles & Celluloid Mammies: Black Images and Their Influence on Culture.* Charlottesville: University of Virginia Press, 1994.

Underwood, Marion K. *Social Aggression among Girls.* New York: Guilford Press, 2003.

United Daughters of the Confederacy. "Founder and Co-Founder." www.hqudc.org/about/founder.html.

Vendryes, Margaret Rose. "Hanging on Their Walls: An Art Commentary on Lynching, the Forgotten 1935 Art Exhibition." In *Race Consciousness: African-American Studies for the New Century,* edited by Judith Jackson Fossett and Jeffrey A. Tucker. New York: New York University Press, 1997.

Vinikas, Vincent. *Soft Soap, Hard Sell: American Hygiene in an Age of Advertisement.* Ames: Iowa State University Press, 1992.

———. "Specters in the Past: The Saint Charles, Arkansas, Lynching of 1904 and the Limits of Historical Inquiry." *Journal of Southern History* 65, no. 3 (August 1999): 535–64.

Wajda, Shirley. "A Room with a Viewer: The Parlor Stereoscope, Comic Stereographs, and the Psychic Role of Play in Victorian America." In *Hard at Play: Leisure in America, 1840–1940,* edited by Kathryn Grover. Amherst: University of Massachusetts Press, 1992.

Waldrep, Christopher. *The Many Faces of Judge Lynch: Extralegal Violence and Punishment in America.* New York: Palgrave Macmillan, 2002.

———. "War of Words: The Controversy over the Definition of Lynching, 1899–1940." *Journal of Southern History* 66, no. 1 (2000): 75–100.

Wallach, Jennifer Jensen. *"Closer to the Truth Than Any Fact": Memoir, Memory, and Jim Crow.* Athens: University of Georgia Press, 2008.

Watson, Jay. "Uncovering the Body, Discovering Ideology: Segregation and Sexual Anxiety in Lillian Smith's *Killers of the Dream.*" *American Quarterly* 49, no. 3 (September 1997): 470–503.

Wells-Barnett, Ida B., and Frederick Douglass. *The Red Record: Tabulated Statistics and Alleged Causes of Lynching in the United States.* Cirencester, U.K.: Echo Library, 2005.

Wells-Barnett, Ida B., and Jacqueline Jones Royster, eds. *Southern Horrors and Other Writings: The Anti-Lynching Campaign of Ida B. Wells, 1892–1900.* Boston: Bedford, 1997.

Whites, LeeAnn. *The Civil War as a Crisis in Gender: Augusta, Georgia, 1860–1890.* Athens: University of Georgia Press, 2000.

Williamson, Joel. *The Crucible of Race: Black/White Relations in the American South since Emancipation.* New York: Oxford University Press, 1984.

———. *Rage for Order: Black-White Relations in the American South since Emancipation.* New York: Oxford University Press, 1986.

Wilson, John Scott. "Race and Manners for Southern Girls and Boys: The 'Miss Minerva' Books and Race Relations in a Southern Children's Series." *Journal of American Culture* 17, no. 3 (Fall 1994): 69–74.

Wilson, Woodrow, and Donald Day. *Woodrow Wilson's Own Story.* Boston: Little, Brown, 1952.

Wood, Amy Louise. *Lynching and Spectacle: Witnessing Racial Violence in America, 1890-1940*. Chapel Hill: University of North Carolina Press, 2009.

Woodward, C. Vann. *Origins of the New South, 1877-1913*. Baton Rouge: Louisiana State University Press, 1951.

———. *The Strange Career of Jim Crow*. New York: Oxford University Press, 1955.

Wyatt-Brown, Bertram. *Hearts of Darkness: Wellsprings of a Southern Literary Tradition*. Baton Rouge: Louisiana State University Press, 2003.

———. *Southern Honor: Ethics and Behavior in the Old South*. New York: Oxford University Press, 1982.

Young, Harvey. "The Black Body as Souvenir in American Lynching." *Theatre Journal* 57, no. 4 (December 2005): 639-57.

Yuill, Phyllis J. *Little Black Sambo: A Closer Look*. New York: Racism and Sexism Resource Center for Educators, 1976.

Index

activism
African American, 39, 105–10, 157
social reformers, 5, 6, 14, 18–19,
22–25, 28–32, 97, 99–100, 105,
108–9, 111, 153, 155
white, 25, 32, 97, 155
See also antilynching
adolescents
adaptation to segregation, 8, 132
in the lynching ritual, 3, 63, 115
organizations for, 84–91
white female, 5, 84–86, 131–32, 134,
145–51, 156
white male, 4, 17, 24, 33, 86–87, 97,
121–29
See also children, white
Adventures of Huckleberry Finn, The
(Twain), 51–53
Adventures of Tom Sawyer, The
(Twain), 51–52
advertising, 15–16
campaigns, 61–62
as form of racial oppression, 63–67,
69–74
children in, 63–65, 67–70
See also caricatures; *individual
products*
African Americans
activist, 39, 105–9, 110, 157
civilization, perceived lack of, 44, 55,
59, 67, 74
general representations of, 20, 37,
46–47, 52, 55, 62–63, 154
humanization of, 29–32, 51–52
interactions with whites, 8, 13, 23
in literature, 38, 43–60, 154
men, 5, 38, 44, 46, 50, 52, 65, 69,
71–72, 123, 126
plays, representations of in, 79–82
positive images of, 51–52, 60, 97, 98
repression and control of, 3, 5, 9–10,
17, 21–25, 28, 32–33, 35, 49–50,
65, 75–77, 83–84, 92, 94, 97, 103,
132, 154
resistance to whites, 38, 116–17, 153,
156
rhymes, representations of in, 78–79
role in segregation, 6–7, 29, 129, 158
sexuality, 5, 17, 43, 44, 106, 114, 119,
122, 123–24, 134, 155–56
soldiers, 81, 106, 125–26
in textbooks, 39–43, 154
toys, representations of in, 75–78
white fears of, 7, 17, 26, 29–31, 81,
92, 101, 106, 114, 118–19, 123,
125, 132, 155–56
women, 21, 69–71, 150
See also children, African American;
dehumanization of African
Americans; education, white;
lynching(s)
aggression. *See* violence, racial
Alabama
historical play, 80
lynchings, 100, 109–10, 117, 136,
143
state book list, 45, 57
"Always Did 'Spise a Mule" toy, 76

America in the Making: From Wilderness to World Power (Chadsey, Weinberg, Miller), 41
American People and Nation, The (Tryon and Lingley), 41
American Civil Liberties Union, 121
America's March toward Democracy (Rugg), 41
Ames, Jessie Daniel, 107
antebellum South, 4, 7, 36, 38, 47, 49–54, 60–61, 69, 77–78, 80, 89, 114, 119, 122, 133, 149, 154
antilynching
  activists, 2, 110, 155
  bills and hearings, 120–21, 155
  movement, 105–9, 111, 116, 156
  See also NAACP (National Association for the Advancement of Colored People); Wells-Barnett, Ida B.; White, Walter
Arkansas
  lynchings, 102, 122, 126–27, 139, 145–46
  state reading list, 45, 57
  textbooks, 40
Arm & Hammer baking soda, 69, 70
Art Commentary on Lynching, An, 107
Association of Southern Women for the Prevention of Lynching (ASWPL), 107
  See also Ames, Jessie Daniel
audiences at lynchings. *See under* lynching(s)
Aunt Jemima
  advertising campaign, 61
  doll, 77
  representation of, 44, 69–70
  See also caricatures
autobiographies, 18–20, 94
  of African Americans, 18
  of white social activists, 5–6, 19–20,

23–24, 26–27, 29–30, 39, 47, 93, 95

Bannerman, Helen, 55–56
"Bean-em" game, 76
Bedford, Henry, 126
Bible, the, 83, 86–87
Bilbo, Theodore Gilmore, 106
Birth of a Nation, The (film), 62, 82, 86
Black Boy (Wright), 18
black-face. *See* minstrel, black-face
black sexuality. *See under* African Americans; sexuality
Blades, Albert, 146–47
Blue, Dick, 126
Boone, William Cooke, 17
Born to Rebel: An Autobiography, (Mays), 18
Boyle, Sarah Patton, 13, 20–21, 24, 30, 33
Braden, Anne McCarty, 20–21, 31, 91, 97–99
bravery. *See under* masculinity
British Empire, 66
Brooks, Allen, 104
Brooks, Thomas, 109
Brown, Jeff, 138–39
Brownies Book, The (magazine), 60
Brown v. Board of Education, 157
brutality, physical
  in advertisements, 63–66, 71
  childhood experiences with, 22, 94–96
  depictions of African American, 5, 134
  effects on children, 105, 107, 155
  See also castration; lynching(s); violence, racial
"brute" caricature, 44
Bryan, H. A., 143

Cade, Henry, 136
Caldwell, Erskine, 107–8
Cameron, James, 119
Campbell, Will D., 25
"Can You Tip the Bell Boy?" toy, 77
caricatures
    "brute," 44
    "Coon," 44, 59, 62, 75–76, 78
    "Jezebel," 44
    "Mammy," 43–44, 47–48, 55, 57–58,
        62, 66, 69–70, 76–77, 80, 82
    "Pickaninny," 44, 46, 62, 69–70
    "Sambo," 44, 52, 54–56, 62, 76–77
    "Uncle Tom," 44, 53, 55, 62–63, 65,
        71, 82
carpetbaggers, 42
Carter, Eugene, 135
Carter, John, 127
caste system, 21, 23, 114, 154
castration, 38, 110, 114, 123–25, 150,
    156
catechisms, 89–91
ceremony, lynching. *See under*
    lynching(s)
Chambliss, Rollin, 32–33
chants, jump rope, 78, 79, 91
"Charleston Trio" toy, 75–76
Chase, William, 108
chastity. *See under* sexuality
"Chicken Snatcher" toy, 76
childhood, 7, 14–15, 33, 106
recollections of, 6, 13, 22–23, 26–27,
    94–95
    studies of, 8, 18–19, 94
    See also under autobiographies;
    memory; socialization of white
    children
child labor, 7–8, 15, 75
child-rearing guidebooks, 15–19, 57,
    120
children, African American

in advertisements, 66–70
boys, 24, 69–71, 107, 123, 126–28
girls, 22, 66–68
in literature, 45, 47, 51, 54, 60
as playmates of whites, 23
studies of, 8
violence against, 126–28
See also African Americans;
    lynching(s)
children, white
boys in literature, 52–54
boys learning social code, 24–25, 33
boys' participation in violence,
    121–22, 125–28, 135
girls in literature, 49–50
girls learning social code, 17, 40, 86
girls' participation in violence, 10,
    133, 135–38
learning femininity, 5, 27, 77, 85, 133
learning masculinity, 38, 76, 120, 122
portrayal of boys in advertising, 63,
    65, 71
portrayal of girls in advertising,
    66–67
young children, 9, 14, 83, 115, 117
youth activities, 63
See also adolescents; femininity;
    masculinity; socialization of white
    children; *individual children's
    organizations*
Children of Old Carolina (play), 79
Children of the Confederacy, 62, 74,
    82, 88–91, 154
children's Ku Klux Klan. *See under* Ku
    Klux Klan
children's organizations. *See under*
    Confederacy; Ku Klux Klan, the
    (KKK); Tri-K-Klub
church, 81, 100, 103, 125, 135, 157
church pageants. *See* plays
civil rights movement, 6, 157

civilization, African Americans' lack
of. *See under* African Americans
Civil War, 4, 7, 36, 47–48, 50, 82–83,
89–91, 100, 133–34, 150
Clark, Elijah, 136
class, 4, 10, 75, 96, 114, 133–34, 150
distinctions, 9, 19, 20, 30, 40, 146
lower class, 9, 21, 101, 133
middle class, 14, 66, 73
unity, 102, 114
upper class, 21
Clause, Ed, 140–41
Clay, Lloyd, 131–32
cleanliness, 67
Clemens, Samuel (Mark Twain), 38,
51, 52, 53, 54
Code, Joe, 138
Colburn, George W., 120–21
"Colored Minstrel Boys, Oh, What
Music!" toy, 75
"Colorful Darky Dancer Does a
Lifelike Buck and Wing" toy, 75
comic relief. *See* humor
Coming of Age in Mississippi (Moody),
18
Commission on Interracial
Cooperation, 106
commodification of black bodies. *See
under* dehumanization of African
Americans
Communists, 143
community
African American, 25, 105–6,
115–17, 135, 157
role of white, in segregation, 1,
3–4, 10, 25, 33, 93, 97, 102–3,
114, 120, 122, 126, 128, 132–34,
137, 141–43, 145–46, 148, 150,
154–55
white male, 3, 19, 28, 119, 121, 124,
127–28

Confederacy, 88
Children of the Confederacy, 62, 74,
82, 88–91, 154
history, 89–91, 96
portrayal in southern texts, 48, 50,
82
United Daughters of the
Confederacy (UDC), 88–91
veterans, 19, 22, 35, 37, 88–89
See also "Lost Cause"
consumer culture. *See under*
advertising; mass culture
"Coon" caricature. *See under*
caricatures
"coon dip" game, 76
counternarratives in southern texts,
38, 43, 51–59
Cox, Obe, 145
Coy, Ed, 122
Cream of Wheat, 61, 63–65, 71
cultural productions. *See* plays
Czar baking powder, 61, 69

Daniels, Lige, 110
Datebook (magazine), 27
Davis, George, 136
dehumanization of African Americans
commodification of black bodies, 66,
76, 109, 124
justifying segregation, 94
in media accounts, 63, 111
rejection of, 97
in school texts, 38–39
Democrats, 62
*Desegregated Heart: A Virginian's Stand
in Time of Transition, The* (Boyle),
13
Diddie, Dumps, and Tot (Prynelle), 47,
49, 90
Dixie Holiday (Mosby), 108
doggerels. *See* chants, jump rope

dolls, 77–78
  See also toys
Du Bois, W. E. B., 39, 60
"Dump the Nigger" game, 76
Dunning school of thought, 41
  See also Reconstruction

Easily Staged Plays for Boys (Simon), 80
Eberhart, John Lee, 99–100
Edgerton, John, 18
education, African American, 37, 45
education, white
  antebellum, 36, 61
  expenditures, 37
  reform, 37, 91
  standardization of education, 7, 9,
    36–37, 60
  state book lists, 45–59
  textbooks, 39–43
  See also socialization of white
    children
Emancipation Proclamation, 85
emasculation of African American
  men. *See under* masculinity
encyclopedia articles, 39
Essential Facts in American History
  (Evans), 41
Evans, Augusta Jane, 28
executions, 25, 102
  See also vigilante

Fairy Soap, 67–68
false accusations of rape. *See* rape
"Famous Alabama Coon Jigger" toy, 75
femininity
  challenges to, 28
  defiance of, 28, 133
  expectations of, 14, 118
  feminization of black males, 46, 59,
    65, 123
  stereotypes of, 50, 57

fetishism, racial. *See under* sexuality
Florida
  lynchings in, 1, 137, 142–43
  state book list, 45–46, 53, 57
Foreman, Clark, 99–100
Foxworth, Amen Neville, 137
Freeman, Elizabeth, 104

Gathers, Philip, 118
Geary, Mary Alice, 91
Georgia
  lynchings in, 99, 118, 124, 134,
    140–42, 144–46
  state book list, 45
Gildersleeve, Fred, 109
Glasgow, Ellen, 28–29
Godley, Will, 135
Gold Medal baking powder, 71–72
Gone with the Wind (film), 39
Goodlett, Caroline Douglas
  Meriwether, 88
Gray Caps (Knox), 49
Griggs, John, 139
*Growth of the American People and
  Nation* (Kelty), 41

Harrington, Elizabeth S., 116
Harris, Joel Chandler, 51, 53–54
Hays, Arthur Garfield, 121
Hicks, Robert, 145
Hillman, Charles, 100
History of America (Fish), 41
History of the American People, A
  (Beard and Bagley), 40
History of the Ku-Klux Klan (Rose),
  35–36
*History of the People of the United
  States* (Thompson), 42
History of the United States (Beard and
  Beard), 40
honor, white male. *See under* masculinity

Hose, Sam, 124
Houston, Matthew, 128
How Alabama Became a State (play),
    80
H. Sears and Co. Fine Cutlery, 71, 73
Hudson, Mattie, 131–32, 148
Hughes, George, 104, 122–23
humanity of African Americans, 29,
    38, 51–52, 98
    See also counternarratives in
        southern texts; dehumanization of
        African Americans; racism
humor
    in depictions of African Americans,
        43, 47–48, 52–53, 57, 59, 80–81
    in images, 56, 71–73
    violence toward African Americans
        and, 52, 71–73, 76
Hunker's Corner (play), 81–82

idealization
    of race relations, 92, 94
    of white males, 50
    See also nostalgia
identification of lynching victims,
    131–32, 137, 140
    misidentification, 137–41, 149
    positive identification, 136, 138, 141,
        148
    See also lynching(s)
illustrations
    in children's texts, 41, 46–47, 52, 58,
        60
    of African Americans, 43–44, 54–55,
        57, 69
    of whites, 107–8
imperialism, 66
industrialization, 7, 15, 61, 74–75
inequality
    economic, 7
    perceptions of, 37

political, 7, 106
    racial, 27, 30, 94, 97–98, 106
    social, 7, 20, 31–32, 125
    See also activism
International Labor Defense, 143
interracial liaisons. *See under* sexuality
In This Our Life (Glasgow), 28
Invisible Empire. *See* Ku Klux Klan
Ivory soap, 67

Jackson, Stonewall, 20
"Jezebel" caricature. *See under*
    caricatures
Jim Crow. *See* segregation
Johnson, Bud, 143
Johnson, Jack, 61
Johnson, James Weldon, 104, 110
jump rope chants, 78–79, 91
Junior Ku Klux Klan. *See under* Ku
    Klux Klan

Kelly, Charles, 125–26
Kentucky
    lynchings, 117, 148
    state book list, 45, 57
Killers of the Dream (Smith), 27
King, Larry, 30, 39, 42
Kirkland, Willie, 141
Kloran, the, 86
Knox, Rose B., 47, 49
Ku Klux Klan, the (KKK), 22, 35–36,
    42, 79, 102
    children's KKK, 74, 83–84, 154
    Invisible Empire, 82–83
    Junior KKK, 84, 86–87, 89
    second incarnation, 83
    Women's Ku Klux Klan, 83–84

labor
    African American labor, 46, 58, 69,
        78, 92, 102, 144

child labor, 7, 8, 74
labor reform and reformers, 15, 23
See also sharecropping
Leetch, Dorothy, 47, 48
legal action, circumvention of, 97,
99–102, 106, 119–20, 124, 143,
157
Lindsay, Maud, 47, 49
Lingon, Scott, 99
Little Black Sambo series (Bannerman),
54
"Little Darky Shooting Gallery" game,
77
Little Jeemes Henry (Credle), 46
Little Missy (Lindsay), 49–50
Locke, Alain, 31
Locke, John, 74, 77
Lofting, Hugh, 57–59
"Lost Cause," 19, 91, 96
Louisiana
lynchings, 139, 150
state book list, 45, 48, 50, 52–53, 57
Love, Emanuel K., 105
Lumpkin, Katharine Du Pre, 19,
21–22, 29–32, 35, 37, 47, 62,
83–84, 92, 95–96
lynching(s), 100–101
accusation of crime, 101, 103, 107,
111, 132–33, 135–36, 138, 142–43,
145–48, 150
African American response to, 116
audiences at, 110, 115, 117–19, 123,
155
children's attendance at, 2, 99, 104–5,
107–8, 111, 113, 115–18
in culture, 79, 106, 116, 120
decline of, 106, 156
as entertainment, 103–4, 111
function for white community, 3,
101–2, 109, 111, 115, 117, 120,
124, 128, 132, 135, 149, 155

function for white females, 4, 10,
118, 132–36, 142, 145, 147, 150
function for white males, 4, 102,
117–19, 121–25, 128
instigation of, 121–22, 133, 142, 145,
156
justifications of, 5, 44, 101–2, 105–6,
118, 133
mass mob lynching, 3, 7, 99, 101–3,
109, 115, 121, 123
media representations of, 99, 109–
11, 128, 134–41, 146, 149, 155
motives for, 101, 132, 141–45, 150
photographs and postcards of, 1–2,
10, 101, 109–10, 116, 158
ritual of, 3–4, 7, 9, 100–103, 109,
111, 114–15, 136
role in upholding segregation, 3, 8,
101, 111, 114–15, 127, 155
souvenirs from, 3–4, 100, 103, 114,
118, 124–25, 129
torture during, 3, 102–3, 105,
109–11, 117, 124
victims, 3, 102, 114–15
witness accounts of, 99–100, 103–4,
110–11, 116–17, 123, 125, 143, 156
See also antilynching; castration;
identification of lynching victims;
rape; *individual states and lynching
victims*

MacKenzie, Amy, 108
Making of a Southerner, The
(Lumpkin), 19
"Mammy"
in children's literature, 47–48, 50, 55,
57–58
in southern culture, 36, 62, 69, 76
See also under caricatures
manhood. *See* masculinity
Marsh, Reginald, 108

masculinity
 African American, 73, 125, 150
 demonstrations of, 114–15, 117–19,
  121, 123–25, 127–29, 146
 emasculation of African Americans,
  28, 65, 69
 regional definitions of, 4, 114
 southern idealization of, 9, 14, 40,
  59, 86–87
 virility in white males, 119, 121
 white male honor, 86–87, 120, 122, 128
 See also African Americans;
  patriarchy
mass culture, 7, 9, 44, 61–63, 65–66,
  74–76, 154
mass media. *See* mass culture
mass mob lynching. *See under*
  lynching(s)
McCarty, Anita, 91
McCloud, Andrew, 139
McGee, R. D., 137
McGill, Ralph, 62
McIlherron, Jim, 110
McLaurin, Melton, 26
Mean Things Happening in This Land
  (Mitchell), 93
mechanical toys. *See* toys
memorial associations. *See under*
  Confederacy
memory
 autobiographical, 94
 historical, 62
migration, African American, 117, 153
minstrel, black-face, 56, 70, 81
Mirandy's Minstrels (play), 81–82
misidentification of lynching victims,
  137–41, 149
Mississippi
 lynchings, 116, 131, 137–38, 145,
  147, 150
 representations in literature, 47, 52

Missouri
 lynchings, 135, 146, 148
 representations in literature, 51–52
Mitchell, Harry Leland (H. L.), 23–24,
  31–32, 93, 95–96, 99
mob law, 105, 101, 143
 See also legal action, circumvention
  of; lynching(s); vigilante
morality
 African American, 15, 60
 white, 14, 16–17, 81, 108, 148, 155
motives for lynchings. *See under*
  lynching(s)
mutilation. *See* castration;
  lynching(s)

NAACP (National Association for the
  Advancement of Colored People),
  1–2, 42, 104–6, 108–10, 119, 126,
  143–44, 157
 See also activism; antilynching
National Association for Colored
  Women, 107
National Student Council, 116
Neal, Claude, 109, 117, 124
Nebraska lynchings, 138
"Negro" doll, 78
"Negro Enjoyment," 69
New Deal, 156
New South, 3, 6–8, 14, 19, 23, 36, 38,
  42, 60, 69, 82, 89, 101, 114–16,
  133–34, 138, 155
newspapers. *See under* lynching(s)
Nightriders, 102
*Nights with Uncle Remus: Myths and
  Legends of the Old Plantation*
  (Harris), 53
North Carolina
 lynchings, 105, 120, 140, 142
 plays, 79–80
 state book list, 45, 53, 57

nostalgia, 14
  in advertisements, 61
  in literature, 46–48, 51, 54, 60
  racial, 38, 62–63, 71, 75–76, 82,
    89–91, 154–55
Nuys, Frederick Van, 120–21

Old South. *See* antebellum South
Our Little Child Faces Life (Clemens),
  57

Page, Thomas Nelson, 47, 48, 50
parades, 83, 85, 87, 102, 106, 115, 137
parental guidebooks. *See* child-rearing
  guidebooks
paternalism, 14, 16, 38, 40, 42, 44, 46,
  55, 59
patriarchy, 4, 6, 8, 9, 10, 28, 29, 32, 44,
  46, 57, 96, 115, 118, 128–29, 133,
  145, 155
patriotism, 50, 83, 86, 88
Pears' Soap, 66
performances
  by children, 63, 73–79, 81–82,
    91–92, 154
  of race and gender roles 4, 6, 9, 96,
    102, 115, 121–23, 128
  See also minstrel, black-face; plays;
    socialization of white children
Personal Help for Parents (Shannon
  and Allen), 16–17
photographs of lynchings. *See under*
  lynching(s)
*Phunology: A Collection of Tried and
  Proved Plans for Play, Fellowship,
  and Profit* (Hardin), 81
"Pickaninny" caricature. *See under*
  caricatures
plantation, genre in literature, 46–54
Plato, 74
playing, 74–75, 93
  as a child, 14, 16, 24, 26, 57
  with toys, 75–79
  See also child-rearing guidebooks;
    playmates
playmates
  black, 23–26, 128
  white, 62, 120
plays, 63, 79–82, 154
Plessy v. Ferguson, 36
political power, 6, 7, 9–11, 28, 41, 53,
  62, 89, 102, 106, 114, 119, 132,
  141, 143, 153, 156
populism, 114
postbellum South. *See* New South
postcards of lynchings. *See under*
  lynching(s)
Preparing for Parenthood (Wynne), 16
Progressive Era, 14
propaganda, 107, 116
public schools. *See* education, white
publishers, southern, 15–16, 36, 48,
  60, 154
punishment. *See* brutality, physical;
  violence, racial
purity. *See* racial purity

Rabbits' Wedding, The (Williams), 157
racial awakening, 4, 19, 32, 94–95, 98
See also racism
racial brutality. *See* brutality, physical;
  violence, racial
racial etiquette, 8, 21, 31
racial identity, 3, 6, 21, 94, 115
racial purity, 5, 15, 19, 26–28, 65, 67,
  85–86, 119, 136, 148–49
racial stereotypes. *See under* African
  Americans; caricatures
racism, 6
  effects of, 8
  in literature, 51
  rejection of, 5, 29–32, 95–96, 116

Radical Republicans, 42
radio, 100, 101, 104
rape, 98
    accusations against African
        Americans in New South, 98, 101,
        113, 122, 127, 131–32, 134–40,
        142, 144, 147–48, 150
    accusations against African
        Americans in the Old South,
        133–34
    accusations by community, 142–45
    false accusations of, 132–33, 135,
        140–41, 144–45, 147–49, 156
    as justification for lynching, 101–3,
        123, 135–36, 139, 146, 149–50, 155
    rape-lynch complex, 5, 101, 105, 118,
        133, 135–36, 138, 141, 143–44,
        146, 150, 155
    rhetoric behind, 5, 105, 107, 134
    roadway rape stories, 145–47
    by white men, 141–42
    See also lynching(s); sexuality
Rastus, 65
    See also Cream of Wheat
Ray, Sandy, 144
Reconstruction, 6–7, 36, 40–42, 100,
    155
redemption. *See* salvation
religion, 83, 86
reputation. *See* masculinity
rhymes. *See* chants, jump-rope
rioting, 104, 149
Roach, Ed, 140
Robertson, George, 127
Rutherford, Mildred Lewis, 35, 37,
    89–90

salvation, 103, 136
"Sambo Five Pins" game, 77
"Sambo" stereotype. *See under*
    caricatures

Sams, Hugh, 126
scalawags. *See* carpetbaggers
Scales, Julius Irving, 24–25
Scary Ape, The (play), 80–81
schools. *See* education, African
    American; education, white
schoolyard games, 78–79
Scott, James, 148–49
Sears, Roebuck and Company catalog,
    75–77
segregation
    creation of, 7
    decline of, 11, 154, 156–57
    enforcement of, 6, 8, 13, 21, 23–24,
        33, 71, 79, 99, 114, 154–57
    justifications of, 5, 11, 38, 62, 94, 156
    opposition to segregation, 6, 17, 22
    rejection of segregation, 5, 29–32,
        95–96, 116
    shifts in, 6, 7, 10, 100
    violations of, 4, 13, 21, 29, 31, 93, 97,
        101, 126–27, 145, 153
    white attempt to maintain, 1, 3, 7,
        13, 27, 36, 42, 62, 105, 114–15,
        128–29, 150, 153, 155
    white youth's role in, 4–5, 7–10, 21,
        27, 33, 66, 81, 87, 91, 93, 95–96,
        98, 111, 119, 145, 153, 155–56, 158
    See also socialization of white
        children
*Separate Pasts: Growing up White in
    the Segregated South* (McLaurin),
    26
servants, 15, 44, 49, 63, 65, 67, 79, 82, 96
sexual assault. *See* rape
sexuality
    chastity of white women, 5, 136
    circumvention of ideal white female,
        10, 132–33, 145, 150, 156
    control of women's, 4–5, 17, 28, 107,
        114–15, 118–19, 123, 128

ideal of female, 4, 67, 86
interracial sexual liaisons, 5, 17, 26,
   85–86, 114–15, 118, 132, 148, 150
lesbian relationships, 29
masturbation, 17
racial fetishism, 65, 69–70, 74
social repercussions for women
   regarding, 4, 17, 26, 67, 106, 114,
   124, 132, 151
women's fear of their own sexuality,
   5, 26–29, 146
See also femininity; masculinity;
   rape
sexual mutilation. *See* castration
sharecropping, 46, 47–48, 81, 92, 144
Shaw, Lint, 146
slaveholders, 91, 96
slavery, 4–5, 7, 14, 38, 40–42, 47–48,
   50, 52, 69, 76, 81–82, 84, 89–91,
   109, 114, 133–34, 153
Smith, Bert, 123
Smith, Grant, 148
Smith, Henry, 102–3, 111
Smith, Leroy, 139–40
Smith, Lillian, 23, 26–27, 29
soap advertisements, 66–68, 73
social aggression, 147
socialization of white children
   gendered aspects, 4, 6, 16–17, 19, 32,
      43, 47, 50, 66, 76, 79, 87, 95, 115,
      127, 133, 147, 154
   at home, 6, 9, 10, 14–20, 23, 31, 33,
      45, 97, 154, 157
   parental socialization, 15, 18–26, 33
   in public performances, 79–82
   rejection of socialization, 14, 19, 29,
      31–32, 96, 99, 111, 153
   through community youth groups,
      82–91
   through mass media, 63–74
   through play, 74–79

   to preserve white supremacy, 7, 10,
      62, 128–29, 150, 153
   violence as socialization, 3, 93,
      95–100, 111, 114–15, 119–27,
      135–38, 145–50, 155
   See also childhood; education, white;
      racism
South Carolina
   Council of the Commission of
      Interracial Cooperation, 28
   educational test, 60
   lynchings, 127, 142, 150
   Southern Education Board, 36
   state book list, 45–46, 48, 51–53
Southern Organizing Committee for
   Economic and Social Justice, 36
souvenirs from lynchings. *See*
   castration; lynching(s)
spectacle lynching. *See* lynching(s)
Stacy, Rubin, 1–2, 10
stereotypes. *See* caricatures
Story of Dr. Dolittle, The (Lofting), 57
Story of Little Black Sambo, The
   (Bannerman), 55–57
suffrage, 14, 114

teenagers. *See* adolescents
Tennessee
   lynchings, 104, 109, 137
   state book list, 45
Terrell, Mary Church, 107, 116
terrorist mobs. *See under* vigilante
Texas
   lynchings, 102, 104–5, 109, 113, 119,
      122–23, 136, 139
   state book list, 45, 53
textbooks
   manufacturing, 36–38
   southern, 38–43
Thirteenth Amendment, 38
This Is Her First Lynching (Marsh), 108

Thread of Destiny, The (play), 81–82
Tommy Tucker on a Plantation
    (Leetch), 48
torture. *See under* lynching(s)
toys, 15, 63
    as a form of socialization, 74–78
    manufacturing, 75
Tri-K-Klub, 84–86
Twain, Mark (Samuel Clemens), 38,
    51–54
Two Little Confederates (Page), 48, 50

Uncle Remus: His Songs and Sayings
    (Harris), 53
"Uncle Tom" stereotype. *See under*
    caricatures
United Daughters of the Confederacy
    (UDC), 88–91
United States Children's Bureau, 14
urbanization, 7, 15, 156

veterans
    African American, 81, 106, 125–26, 143
    Confederate, 19, 22, 35, 37, 88–89
victims of lynching. *See under*
    lynching(s)
vigilante
    committees, 100
    terrorist mobs, 102
    violence, 101, 127
    See also Ku Klux Klan; Nightriders
violations of social code, 4, 13, 21, 24,
    29, 31, 93, 97, 101, 104, 126–27,
    145, 153
violence, racial
    in advertisements, 65, 71
    in children's texts, 49–50
    extralegal, 102, 157
    function of, 6, 9, 102, 111, 115, 117,
        128, 129, 132, 149, 155
    images of, 109–10

instigated by men, 122, 126–28
instigated by women, 133, 142, 145,
    151
justification of, 5, 93, 99, 101, 105,
    134, 155
in media, 111
in parental lessons, 22
rejection of, 95, 96, 111, 116, 155
as socialization, 3, 5, 9, 94, 103, 105,
    107
in toys, 76
See also brutality, physical;
    lynching(s)
Virginia, state book list of, 45–46, 48,
    50, 53, 57
virility. *See under* masculinity
virtue. *See under* sexuality
Voyages of Doctor Dolittle (Lofting), 59

Wade, Andrew, 98
Wale, William, 125
Walker, Lee, 104
Wall Between, The (Braden), 20
Walters, Jim, 144
"War Between the States." *See* Civil
    War
Ward, George, 125
Washington, George, 41
Washington, Jesse, 104, 109, 113–14,
    119, 124
Well, Noon, 25
Wells-Barnett, Ida B., 105, 107, 110
West, Jack, 142
West Virginia, state book list of, 45,
    53, 57
White, George, 118
White, Walter, 2, 108, 110
    See also activism; antilynching;
        NAACP (National Association
        for the Advancement of Colored
        People)

white children. *See* children, white
white community. *See under*
    community
White House Conference on Standards
    of Child Welfare, 14
white man's burden, 55, 59
white supremacy. *See* segregation
Williams, Milton, 137
Wilson, "Bubber," 137
Wilson, Woodrow, 14
womanhood. *See* femininity
Women's Ku Klux Klan (WKKK). *See*
    under Ku Klux Klan
women's suffrage. *See* suffrage

Woodward, C. Vann, 100
working-class whites. *See* class
World War I, 82, 94, 106, 125, 143,
    148, 153
    See also veterans
World War II, 11, 156–57
Wright, Alice Spearman, 28, 29, 31
Wright, Marion, 24, 97, 99

Yarbrough, Jeff, 99
Young Women's Christian Association,
    1, 29
youth groups. *See under* Confederacy;
    Klux Klan; Tri-K-Klub